GREAT CYCLE TOURS

of Britain

GREAT CYCLE TOURS

of Britain

TIM HUGHES

NEW
ORCHARD

Reprinted 1994

© Text & photographs W. T. Hughes 1988
© Illustrations & maps Ward Lock Limited 1988

First published in Great Britain in 1988 by Ward Lock,
Villiers House, 41-47 Strand, London,
WC2N, 5JE, a Cassell imprint.
Special edition for Bookmart Ltd
Desford Road, Enderby, Leicester LE9 5AD
by New Orchard Editions, A Cassell plc Imprint

Map artwork by Elly King
Line illustrations by Simon Roulstone
Text filmset in Linotron 202 Rockwell Light
by Fakenham Photosetting Limited,
Fakenham, Norfolk
Printed and bound in Hong Kong by Wing King Tong Co. Ltd.

British Library Cataloguing in Publication Data

Hughes, Tim
    Great cycle routes
    1. Great Britain. Cycling, Practical
    information
    I. Title
    796.6'0941

ISBN 1-85079-255-0

CONTENTS

ACKNOWLEDGEMENTS   6

INTRODUCTION   7
The cyclist's Britain   8
The routes   9
Maps for cycling   11
The cyclist and the countryside   12

THE 'WEEKEND' ROUTES   15
Bedfordshire and Cambridgeshire   16
Berkshire and Wiltshire Downs   24
Cotswolds   32
Dorset   41
Eden Valley   53
Herefordshire and Shropshire   64
Lincolnshire Wolds   73
Peak District   82
Rutland, Leicestershire and Northamptonshire   93
Weald of Kent and Sussex, and Romney Marsh   104

THE FIVE LONGER TOURS   115
East Anglia   116
South Downs and New Forest   124
Mid Wales   133
Roman Wall, Northumberland and the Borders   142
North-west coast of Scotland   150

SOME PRACTICAL CYCLING ADVICE   161
Bicycles and cycling   161
    Bicycles for easy cycling   161
    Riding position and size of bicycle   161
    Gearing   163
    Lightweight bicycles   164
    Comfort   165
    Taking it steady   165
    Clothing and the weather   165
    Safety   168
Bicycles by rail, road and air   169
Bicycle Hire   172

BIBLIOGRAPHY AND USEFUL ADDRESSES   173
Further reading—books and magazines   173
Useful addresses   175

INDEX   176

ACKNOWLEDGEMENTS

I would like to record my thanks to my cycle-touring colleagues, nearly all of them members of the CTC's Chiltern Hills section, who knowingly or much more often inadvertently 'modelled' for the cycling pictures. But the greatest debt of gratitude I owe to Jennie Reason; without her support and very practical help in following the routes and unearthing much of the information provided, this book would still be a pile of disordered notes. I hope all those 'lost weekends' of spring, summer and autumn 1987 were worth it in the end!

INTRODUCTION

The bicycle is a quite remarkable invention. It is entirely human-powered, yet rapid by the standards of walking. But its pace remains essentially on a human scale. Most of the sounds, sights, smells and sensations that greet a walker in the countryside equally greet an unhurried cyclist. The bicycle is almost silent—provided it is reasonably looked-after—and often quieter even than walking in the countryside. And it is relatively cheap to buy and to run. Apart from the very modest waste from the small amount of metal, plastic and rubber used in its manufacture it is utterly non-polluting. By and large a bicycle doesn't disturb the countryside it travels through. As near as can be, the bicycle is environmentally impeccable.

But that isn't all: riding a bicycle is actually *enjoyable*. Of course it is still more enjoyable if the bicycle is one that runs well and is suited to the job and the rider, but basically any bicycle will do for at least the gentler routes in this book. Having one with all the trimmings, especially low

gears, will make things easier—but don't delay your first trip just because you aren't perfectly kitted out to the last detail. I remember once on our travels abroad meeting three young cyclists whose rudimentary baggage, carried in nothing grander than plastic carrier bags, was held onto elderly rattling bicycles with string, hope and elastic straps—but there was nothing to suggest that their enjoyment of the sheer thrill of discovering France by bicycle had been any less than ours, for all our sophisticated machinery. There's a moral there somewhere.

The routes in this book are really intended to nudge newcomers to cycling in the right direction, although I hope that the more experienced will find at least some corners of Britain that they don't know well, or perhaps hadn't even considered. Even in travelling the roads to research the book—and I'd picked places I thought I knew quite well—I met many new lanes and undiscovered villages. I was also reminded time and again of the delightful minutiae that make up cycle-touring. It is these miniature chance observations, utterly incapable of classification or real description, perhaps forgotten in detail but still there as faint brush-strokes on the canvas of experience, which are for me the delight of travel by bicycle. Who, in compiling a questionnaire on the delights of bicycling, would ask if you had noticed the way that the sun glistened on those little mineral facets on the rock by the side of the road? Or whether you had marvelled at the utter blackness of that peaty pool, set off by the pale emerald of the few blades of grass rising from the surface? Or if you had shivered at swooping through the sudden cold patch at the foot of the hill on a calm autumn evening?

I am not a lover of towns and cities, nor an architectural historian. Although I can be moved by a great cathedral or a fine street, it is likely to be the first glimpse of that cathedral dominating the skyline, or the glint of light on the cobblestones of the street that I shall remember.

All this means that the routes have an unashamed rural bias. But there is a further reason for their avoiding the urban. Apart from lurid tales of saddle-soreness, would-be cyclists usually have a few well-defined cycling fears: rain, punctures, traffic and hills. I can't really do much about rain and punctures, although the practical hints and one or two of the books in the bibliography will tell you how to tackle them. All I need to say here is that neither rain nor a puncture nor even both together quite make up one of life's major tragedies.

But I can, though, steer you away from traffic. It is obviously much more pleasant to cycle where there isn't the constant noise, smell and hazard of passing cars and lorries. Although Britain is a crowded little island, with nearly sixty million of us wedged into a space the third of France, fortunately most of those sixty million, and at least the ones who drive cars, cram themselves into only a small fraction of that. Even in congested Britain there are fine, well-surfaced roads where you can literally ride for an afternoon in the height of summer and meet not a single car.

Wherever possible the routes follow very minor roads, where you will encounter little if any traffic, together with a few bridleways where you will encounter none at all. Again wherever possible, major routes are avoided or crossed at

relatively easy places. And, of course, some of the areas, such as Rutland, Lincolnshire and the Eden valley, are intrinsically quiet.

All that you really need to tackle the final bogey, hills, is patience, to remember that you are riding for pleasure, and that cycling for pleasure is not a race. A bicycle with low or very low gears will allow you to ride gently up hills that you might otherwise feel like walking, but you still won't be hurrying. (Hurrying can make even the flattest road hard: the Tour of Holland is rated one of the toughest of amateur races because of its sheer speed!) You need the sort of fatalistic confidence that tells you that you will reach the top eventually but that in any case it doesn't *really* matter how long it takes. Don't let yourself be caught in the trap of having to ride to a schedule that hustles you along: take time to browse in the villages, enjoy a look at the view, explore the inviting detour, become a thoroughgoing romantic. You'll find the injunction to loiter repeated at appropriate points in the route descriptions.

As it happens, there are one or two areas on the routes which actually *are* dead flat. Although, as at sea, there's a tremendous feeling of openness under the giant sky, I feel sure that you'll agree after a little experience that the utterly flat is fine in moderate doses but that wide horizons take a depressingly long time to change. Roland Barthes may have been tilting at romanticism when he wrote disparagingly that the 'picturesque appears to begin as soon as the ground becomes uneven', but the exploring cyclist may well have more than passing sympathy with the notion.

• THE CYCLIST'S BRITAIN •

Britain has a variety of scenery unrivalled in Europe. There are lush lowlands, rolling hills, quite appreciable forests, open moorland and mountain, and a splendidly changing kaleidoscope of coastline. The only features missing are true deserts (and there aren't many of those in Europe) and really high mountains—and even here Britain's northerly latitude can make our little mountains quite alpine in season. Britain's highest mountain may be only 1344 metres high, but those 1300-odd metres rear straight up from the sea. Scotland's highest roads may go only half as high as that, but to tackle at least one of them—

the Bealach na Bà on the north-west coast—as it clings to the flank of the mountain and reaches up to the scudding clouds is quite as thrilling as the great climbs of the Alps.

Quite often, in setting the scene for a route, the question of the geology of a region crops up. The nature of the underlying rocks is fundamental to the pattern of scenery, and to the factors which make life agreeable, hard or impossible in a particular place. Basically, Britain is like a plank of wood which has been gently tilted towards the south-east and then planed off on the slant, so that different aspects of the grain show up as you cross the surface. The grain is made up of the successive layers of rock that have been deposited and hardened over geological time. In general and drastically simplified, the newer and softer of the deposited rocks ('new' in geological terms, that is—the geological time-scale stretches out to hundreds of millions of years) show up to the south and east, while the older and harder ones become progressively more prominent as you move north and west.

The softer rocks (and to a geologist clays and sands are rocks, too) are less resistant to the weathering processes that over a long time shape a landscape. This means that the lower, rounded hills lie in the south-eastern parts and the higher and more jagged mountains to the north-west. It is in the north and west, too, that most of Britain's hard and rugged 'igneous' rocks occur—those which began as molten magma. To take a journey from Kent to Sutherland is to pass through country of ever-increasing grandeur—and of increasing wildness, to say nothing of rainfall.

Population and agriculture, or at least the arable branch of it, are mainly concentrated in the lower and usually more fertile regions. In turn, this means that the easier routes through softer and more domestic landscapes lie in the south and east, with the wilder and more spectacular ones further north and west—where three of our longer tours are based. But don't expect effete southern hills necessarily to be less steep, even if they may be shorter. I once wrote—and it wasn't entirely tongue-in-cheek—that I felt that more cycling romances had foundered because newcomers to the bicycle had chosen an unfamiliar tandem, well-filled panniers, and Devon and Cornwall as ingredients for the first holiday

together, than from any other single cause. I suspect one could still write the same today, though perhaps you'd have to add Brittany and the Dordogne to the list. As compensation for the concentration of population in the lower-lying areas, there are far more minor roads, giving plenty of scope for quiet and enjoyable cycle routes.

• THE ROUTES •

There are fifteen routes altogether, covering a wide cross–section of what Britain has to offer. Ten of them are what I like to think of as weekend routes, each of them with optional detours and possible short-cuts, so that the total mileage runs from about 45 as a minimum up to perhaps 120 (say 70 to 190km). There is of course no compulsion to complete them in two days—nor, come to that, any reason why you shouldn't belt round in a day, except that you would certainly enjoy them more at a gentler pace. These routes are described in some detail and are keyed to the appropriate Ordnance Survey maps—more on these later. These ten routes follow circuits (in alphabetical order, to avoid any accusation of favouritism) in Bedfordshire and Cambridgeshire, the Berkshire and Hampshire Downs, the Cotswolds, southern Dorset, the Eden valley of Cumbria, Herefordshire and Shropshire, the Lincolnshire Wolds, the Peak District, Rutland and adjoining counties, and the Weald of Kent and Sussex.

The remaining five routes are longer tours: four of them are around 200 miles (300 km or a little more), perhaps a week's gentle riding, although the more strenuous ones would repay spending a longer time; all would amply repay the efforts of exploring a few detours. These tours sample East Anglia, southern England and Sussex to the New Forest by way of the Isle of Wight, mid-Wales, and Northumbria with the Borders and the Roman Wall. The final tour is longer, some 475 miles (about 750km) altogether, with suggestions for dividing it into sectors, and follows the north and west coasts of Scotland. These tours are described in less detail than the shorter ones: in some places, particularly where there are several choices, a definite route isn't prescribed, merely a general direction.

There are many splendid and spectacular areas of our country which are not covered by any route, for two reasons. First, a mere fifteen tours obviously cannot cover the whole country: the ten 'weekends' aim to show beginners, particularly, a sample of the variety there is and how to enjoy it, and the longer trips how to build on that start. The second reason, and the one that explains why there is no tour in, for example, the Lake District or Snowdonia, arises from the sheer popularity of these places. At most seasons of the year the relatively few roads in the Lake District are busy with visiting traffic; there is quite serious concern as to whether the region can support all the tourists it receives. It is a superb area for some admittedly pretty strenuous cycling—provided you can make it in, say, November to catch the last and often brightest autumn colours, or in February or early March, when it is still deep mid-winter on the tops but where signs of incipient spring are beginning to appear in the valleys. At other times the roads can be far too full of cars for enjoyable cycling.

Some of the weekend routes and the tours do visit quite popular areas, though. In most cases the potentially crowded places are avoided, though it is worth remembering that in most of Britain the peak holiday and travel season is relatively short. It's well worth considering cycle-touring outside the busy summer season: I've already hinted at possible times to visit the Lakes, but many other quieter places will well repay an out-of-season trip, and some of the areas are particularly suited to certain seasons. Almost everywhere is delightful in early spring—those too few weeks from the beginning of May when leaves appear—but the routes with forests, the Weald, the New Forest and part of the Berkshire Downs, Dorset, Cotswold and Shropshire ones, are superb then. From about the third week of October until surprisingly late in November the same places will be brilliantly golden as the leaves prepare to fall.

Several of the routes have a charm of their own even in the colder and generally more barren winter months, too, when the absence of leaves opens up wide new vistas, or the crispness of a bright, frosty day brings a whole new gamut of

Opposite: *Camping at Plockton*

colour. I hope that some of the 'out-of-season' pictures in this book will entice you out at these different times of the year. The short practical hints after the route descriptions, and some of the books in the bibliography, tell you how to keep warm and comfortable.

• MAPS FOR CYCLING •

Since the routes are for the most part intimate and on small roads they are best followed on a quite detailed map. The sketch maps with each route are intended to allow you to place the route on the appropriate larger-scale map. The best for detail is undoubtedly the Ordnance Survey's Landranger series at a scale of 1:50 000—which works out at 2cm on the map representing 1km or about 1¼ inches to the mile. At this generous scale virtually every path, track and road is shown, as well as most buildings and other features, particularly in remote or very open, wide-ranging areas where they are useful landmarks.

Relating the map to the landscape is an art which becomes quite easy with only a little practice, once you have learnt the relatively simple 'language' of the symbols and learnt, too, how far a mile or kilometre feels on the road. Despite the fact that in their standard folded form these maps are a bit cumbersome to carry, handle and consult on or from a bicycle (and they are quite expensive, too, if you have to buy several) all the

Below: *Map reading* en route

routes are keyed to them. The one exception is the Cotswold route which is designed to be followed on the os Cotswold Tourist Map, which is at the time-honoured old scale of one inch to the mile (or the fine round figure of 1: 63 360). To make the load and the cost as light as possible, all but one of the ten short routes are designed to use no more than two maps, and as often as possible only one.

Paradoxically, in some of the most remote areas where you might expect a very detailed map to be essential, it is quite possible to get away with the smaller-scale 1:250 000 os Routemaster series. Provided you don't expect to do any detailed off-road exploring, the west coast of Scotland route, for example, can be quite adequately followed at this scale. There will necessarily be a lack of detailed information and, if you've been used to the 1:50 000, you may feel that you're progressing painfully slowly across the map at times.

One feature all Ordnance Survey maps share, and one that I make quite considerable use of in the route descriptions, is the position-defining system known as the National Grid. This Grid comprises a network of metric coordinates which can define a relatively small area in which a place or feature lies. For convenience these coordinates are marked at intervals across the map—in the case of the 1:50 000 series the markings are in blue every kilometre, dividing the map into a series of numbered kilometre squares. It is thus possible to specify the kilometre square in which the required feature lies by quoting the 'Grid Reference' coordinates of its bottom left-hand (or south-west) corner. This gives a four-figure number. At the 1:50 000 scale it is quite easy to estimate the position of a small feature, such as a road junction, in terms of a tenth of the side of one of these kilometre squares, that is, to the nearest 100 metres. This is quite close enough for practical purposes and yields a six-figure number. This is the form of Grid Reference (labelled GR) that I use where it is necessary to define road junctions or other features closely: for clarity I give the number in two groups, west-to-east (or x-coordinate, 'eastings' to the os) first, then south-to-north (y-coordinate, or os 'northings'). There is a short explanation, with a worked example, of this six-figure Grid number and how it is estimated in the

information panel down the right-hand side of every 1:50 000 map. The four-figure and six-figure numbers will be unique as far as that sheet of the map and the ones either side are concerned, although they repeat every 100km. (The os are one step ahead and have a further system of letters to define 100km squares, and hence to define a point uniquely, but that need not concern us here, because it will always be obvious which sheet we're referring to. There are full explanations in the book *Ordnance Survey Maps: A Descriptive Manual*, published by the os, and in *Follow the Map*. The os also produce an explanatory leaflet.)

Although the Ordnance Survey have gone determinedly metric, nearly all roadside signposts and suchlike give distances in miles. In the route descriptions I use a pragmatic, if in theory quite indefensible, mixture. *Distances* are quoted first in Imperial measure, then to the appropriate degree of precision in metric units. The metric equivalents are often useful even to confirmed Imperialists because of the Grid's kilometre markings on the map. *Heights*, however, are all quoted in metres, usually without translation, because that's how they appear on the map. If you wish to convert, taking 30m as 100ft, 300m as 1000ft, and so on, is accurate enough for most things except the *Guinness Book of Records*.

• THE CYCLIST AND THE COUNTRYSIDE •

The bicycle is officially a vehicle (legally a 'carriage') and so the cyclist has to conform, when on a road, with normal traffic regulations. This includes observing traffic signals, mandatory and prohibitory road signs and so on. However, the law reasonably enough recognizes that there is an essential difference between the gentle human-powered bicycle and the motor vehicle—you could say that most of the regulations to which the bicycle is subject place it between the unfettered state of the pedestrian and the much more detailed legislation which governs the motor-car.

This is further recognized, in England and Wales at least, by the right of way accorded to bicycles on bridleways. For over twenty years now cyclists have had under the Countryside Act of 1968 the general right to use paths defined as bridleways, together with foot and horse traffic: the only restriction is that cyclists have to give way to walkers or riders if conditions demand. Bridleways are distinctively marked, with a red dashed line, on the English and Welsh sheets of the os 1:50 000 map. An explanatory booklet *Cycling off-road and the law*, detailed in the bibliography, gives fuller information on the cyclist's legal position on tracks and paths, including those in Scotland.

Several of the routes suggest using sections of bridleway, either to avoid busy roads or because they offer a route through a choice bit of countryside, or both. I have avoided putting in any with surfaces which are not intrinsically easily ridable, and as far as possible they are all well-drained. Where they may be muddy in wet weather I give a warning and an alternative. In the cases of the Dorset Coast Path, the Tissington Trail and the Three Shire Heads path in the Peak District, and the track over from Pooley Bridge on the western fringe of the Eden valley route, the new vistas these tracks open up are such that they shouldn't be missed. In the route descriptions detailed instructions are given for these sections so that there should be no difficulty in following them.

One form of traffic that you may meet on minor country roads or bridleways is the horse. On bridleways you are legally bound to defer to horses; on other roads take care. Although horses obviously *can* be trained not to be frightened of bicycles (I think you could probably ride under a Metropolitan Police horse without upsetting it) most show a greater degree of at the least restiveness. The fear has a long pedigree. 'Horses, it must be admitted, do not like bicycles,' wrote *The Times* in 1878, and there was at least one proposal for a bicycle regiment to halt opposing cavalry by spinning their wheels to put off the horses. Towards the end of the twentieth century my advice is to slow down and pass as widely as possible, both to keep out of trouble and to let the horse see you properly as early as possible. Take particular care in overtaking or if the rider is a child; if possible ensure, by a gently spoken remark, that horse and rider are aware of your approach. Silent approach and surprise seem to cause the most upset. No animal likes to leave its flank ex-posed and will naturally tend to turn to protect it.

The minor roads used for the shorter 'weekend' routes have been chosen to be as free as possible of traffic. In several parts of the country one of the features that makes a road bicycle-friendly and motor-car-hostile is the presence of gates. Gated roads are particularly common where grazing animals are kept in fields beside unfenced roads, to prevent their straying too far, or into adjacent crops. To the motorist they represent an unwelcome stop-get out-open gate-get back in again-drive through gate-stop-get out-close gate-get back in again sequence; to the cyclist a gate is a mere interlude. The golden rule is to leave all gates exactly as you find them—unless somebody has obviously just left one open for you, having seen you approaching.

In many places cattle-grids replace or complement gates. These are a succession of rails or scaffolding-style tubes ranged at about 10in (25cm) intervals across the road above a recess. Cattle and sheep are supposed to be unwilling or unable to cross them because they offer no secure footing for little hooves (although there are stories of sheep evolving a rolling technique to get to the inevitably greener grass on the other side). These grids can look alarming but are in practice quite easily cycled across, and best at a quite fast normal speed, *unless* they have obvious damage or have subsided to leave a sharp kerb or edge on the far side. If you have to walk you'll sympathize with the cattle; it may be possible to find a slightly less precarious path by walking across a reinforcing strip.

One last feature you will meet, particularly in Scotland, is the road marked as 'single-track with passing places'. The wider passing places are marked with white diamond signs; they are primarily intended to allow meeting cars to get by each other, but it is a reasonable courtesy, if a car is coming up behind you, to ease into one of these places to let it pass. Similar but for the most part unmarked passing places often occur on narrow roads in England and Wales.

Finally and most importantly, always remember that the balance of our British countryside can be quite fragile. Don't threaten the very things you come to see by litter, damage, fire or noise. If the bicycle can be environmentally impeccable, then so can its rider.

THE 'WEEKEND' ROUTES

The descriptions of the ten 'weekend' routes which follow are largely self-explanatory. They are quite detailed and are intended to be followed on the 1:50 000 maps listed in the information box accompanying each route. In each case the information box also lists alternative starting points, rail and road access, accommodation possibilities, tourist information offices, cycle shops and cycle hire centres. Total route distances range from about 40 miles (65km) to 100 miles (150km); these too are indicated in the information box. In some cases there are suggested extra detours as well.

BEDFORDSHIRE AND CAMBRIDGESHIRE

• WEEKEND ROUTE •

It is probable that, apart from the city of Cambridge and a few great houses, Bedfordshire and Cambridgeshire do not figure very highly on most people's lists of tourist areas—and neither does the north-east corner of Hertfordshire which adjoins them. But even here, in the gentlest of the routes, the subtle changes in the underlying geology give quite a range of lowland scenery in a very small compass. Narrow bands of sands and clays cross Bedfordshire from south-west to north-east, with here and there a small outcrop of limestone. The south-eastern part is dominated by the chalk, with the low Hertfordshire hills the gentler north-eastern extension of the Chilterns.

The country is mainly cultivated, largely for cereals in the south-east with more of a mixture, including vegetables and whatever constitutes the year's favoured eurocrop, in the north-west. Long before farming mechanization swept away many of the hedgerows of eastern England, the rolling fields of Cambridgeshire and north Hertfordshire were some of the largest in the country. With the absence not only of hedgerows but of the hedgerow trees that go with them there are stretches where the rounded swelling and rolling of the soft spurs and hollows gives a particular pure landscape of interlocking curves, dominated by the sky. Because of the dominance of cultivation, the countryside of this route probably shows more marked change with the seasons than most of the others, as the great fields progress from the white and brown of winter through the soft green haze of early spring, the deeper green of maturity and the gold of the harvest back to the brown of ploughland once more.

Perhaps the main attractions of the country through which the route winds, though, apart from the network of surprisingly quiet little lanes, are the villages with their wide variety of styles and colours—from the plaster and timber of Ashwell and the weatherboarding of Barkway to the golden stone of Potton. It is an unspectacular landscape but an essentially human one—the sort of countryside you would associate with returning to a log fire and buttered toast as the November dusk fades, or of crossing between high walls of wheat with larks in the summer sky. It's a friendly place which you will find grows on you after a while.

The most convenient starting point is probably Baldock, the largest town on the route, although Cambridge is less than 10 miles (some 15km) away at the route's nearest point. Alternatively, Audley End—the station for Saffron Walden and actually in the village of Wendens Ambo—or Ashwell would allow you to start off straightaway in open country.

• THE ROUTE •

Baldock is an old coaching town—indeed it was a modern coaching town, too, with several large cafes dedicated to servicing the thirsty occupants of coaches on the run up the Great North Road from London, until the building of the A1(M) Baldock bypass relieved the town's traffic problem but took away some of its business and bustle. However, the town is still easy to reach by road or rail. The origin of Baldock's name is quite curious: it comes from the Old French name for Bagdad—*Baldac*—and was conferred on the town by the Knights Templar who held the manor here before the twelfth century.

The route leaves Baldock to the south-east by the A507—straight on at the traffic lights if you are coming from the railway station—and promptly goes off the Bedford map at GR 247 340. Just over a ¼ mile (about 500m) further on, turn left off the A507 at a small roundabout on a road signposted 'Wallington and Sandon'; after another ¼ mile (400m) or so, by a growing estate of new houses, turn right off this road, again following the signpost 'Wallington'.

You are at once launched into an open landscape of cornfields; on the spring morning when we set off they were soft and rounded green carpets, while above larks sang in the hazy sky. Although the road is neither hedged nor fenced, there are curious remnants of hedges, now trimmed into blocks with mechanical precision. By GR 256 340 you are back on the map for a spell, only to leave it at 285 340 as the road climbs between steep banks up to the zigzag village of Wallington, with its prominently-towered church. After Wallington and two or three more right-angle bends the road drops to join the valley road at a T-junction. Go left and right to climb up to Roe Green, rejoining the map eventually at GR 318 340.

Sandon, the next village, has a fine open green where we were brought to a halt as a posse of ducks waddled across the road on their way from the pond. From here the route follows the narrow road past Partridge Hall Farm through to Kelshall and Therfield, through a lush landscape of coppices and small fields. I don't know whether it's innate modesty or a fine regard for absolute accuracy, but Therfield's village board describes it as no more than 'one of Hertfordshire's best-kept small villages'. Just out of Therfield a turning to the left directs you towards Reed End and—after a dog-leg crossing of the busy A10—Reed. This is a complex little village with roads patterned in a couple of squares: you can take almost any combination. It also has a pub curiously named 'The Cabinet'. From the open road as you approach Barkway there is a broad view out over Royston towards Cambridge.

Barkway has a fine main street which is almost an encyclopaedia of Hertfordshire vernacular architecture. Here you will find warm red brick, pargeted plaster, white-painted weatherboard-

ing, and tile, slate and thatch. This village and the next one, Barley, lay on the old coaching route from Cambridge to London, now the B1368. The route leaves Barkway northwards on this road, dropping through a magnificent avenue of horse chestnuts, nearly all of which fortunately survived the devastating storm of October 1987. The entrance to Barley is marked by the inn sign straddling the side road, across the top of which hounds permanently pursue a fleeing fox. The route passes under the sign to join the B1039 to Great Chishill.

This rolling, open road leads up to the first of several windmills on the route, this one a well-preserved, white-painted and weatherboarded post mill—the style of mill in which the whole body of the mill used to turn to bring the sails facing the wind. This particular one was rebuilt in 1819 using materials from a 1726 mill. In Great Chishill the route turns left off the climbing high street by the church, to pass through orchards to Heydon. A right turn leads down and up to the attractive village of Elmdon and so back to the B1039. Collectors of such things may note that you will have been in three counties—Hertfordshire, Cambridgeshire and Essex—in as many miles. From here there's a splendid gently downhill run to Wendens Ambo, particularly exhilarating with the prevailing westerly wind at your back. Wendens Ambo has a fine rank of colour-washed plastered cottages leading up to the needle-spired church. The rather curious 'Ambo' part of the name (the Latin *ambo* means 'the two') is merely a classical amalgamation of the former parishes of Great and Little Wenden, in the same spirit that peppered the countryside with Parvas and Magnas.

From here there is a choice of route. By making a dogleg crossing of the B1383 (possibly still marked A11 on some maps) you can reach the pleasant town of Saffron Walden, with its timber-framed buildings and superb pargeted decorative plasterwork. The town also has plenty of shops and eating places. Alternatively you can continue on the B1383 for about 2 miles (3km) to Littlebury, passing en route the magnificent frontage of the seventeenth-century Audley End House, set in its park landscaped by Capability Brown. The house is open to visitors from spring to early autumn. Later in autumn geese and ducks

• INFORMATION •

Starting point
As described the route starts and finishes at Baldock; other convenient points would be Audley End or Ashwell. It would be possible to start from Royston, Cambridge or Biggleswade, joining the route at Barley, Little Eversden and Potton respectively.

Access
Rail routes are to Baldock, Ashwell and Royston from London (Kings Cross) and to Audley End and Cambridge from London (Liverpool Street), King's Lynn and Norwich. Some bicycle restrictions. Main access roads are the A1 and A505 to Baldock, the A10 and A14 to Royston and the A11 and M11 to Audley End.

Accommodation
There are B&B or hotel possibilities on or near the route in Baldock, Caxton, Great Shelford, Little Eversden, Old Wimpole, Saffron Walden, Whittlesford. There are campsites at Ashwell, Comberton, Great Gransden, Longstowe and Shepreth, and youth hostels at Cambridge and Saffron Walden. If you need to consult directories or listings, check under Bedfordshire, Cambridgeshire, Hertfordshire and Essex.

Tourist information offices
Cambridge and Saffron Walden.

Cycle shops and hire
There are cycle shops in Cambridge, Saffron Walden and Royston. There is also cycle hire in Cambridge and at the Shepreth campsite.

Maps
The route is on OS 1:50 000 sheets 153 and 154. The total distance is about 75 miles (120km).

Wendens Ambo

crowd onto the small lake—actually an artificially dammed arm of the River Cam—in front of the house.

Littlebury is an attractive village, too, with colour-washed plastered houses, and several back alleys that will repay exploration. It is one of several villages and small towns on this route which have a new access of civilization now that most of the heavy traffic takes to the M11. The way out of Littlebury is by a small road which goes straight on where the B-road bears right in the middle of the village. There's an unexpectedly steep little climb up over the railway to the motorway bridge—one of the few steep pitches on this route. The narrow road flanks a wood and then emerges onto a fine rolling stretch alternating between unfenced fields and avenues of trees. At one point, near Lodge Farm, there is a quite remarkable stretch—some 200yd (200m) or more—of dense lilac hedge, laden with flower in the spring.

For about ¾ mile (1km) or so near Chrishall Grange the route follows the line of the Icknield Way, the ancient trackway along the edge of the chalk hills. Turn right where the Icknield Way crosses the Elmdon road at GR 444 424; it is possible to cut the route short by coming direct to this junction from Great Chishill. It was here that we came unexpectedly across a domesticated herd of grazing deer. The next junction, at GR 445 430 just after Chrishall Grange, where you turn left for Fowlmere is far less prominent than the map would suggest: take care not to miss it, since this route is the only one which avoids an appreciable distance along the very busy A505.

Fowlmere seems a very settled kind of village, as though the houses, individually unremarkable, had been planted there as seeds and had taken root, growing up as part of the landscape. The name Fowlmere means, literally, 'the mere [or lake] where birds live' so it is fitting that the remains of the mere, to the west of the village, should now be a nature reserve administered by the Royal Society for the Protection of Birds. It can be visited on foot and there is a nature trail.

From Fowlmere to Little Eversden there is a choice of route. The direct one goes straight to Shepreth and then to the outskirts of Barrington, where you turn left to the corner at GR 383 506. From here a dry-weather bridleway carries

BEDFORDSHIRE AND CAMBRIDGESHIRE ROUTE

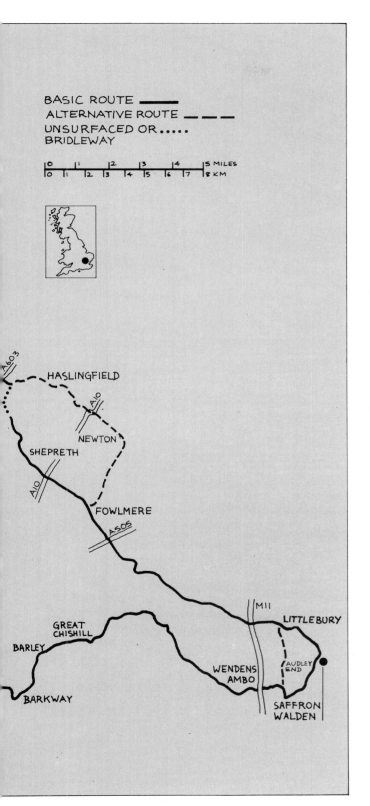

BASIC ROUTE ————
ALTERNATIVE ROUTE — — —
UNSURFACED OR . . . . .
BRIDLEWAY

straight on up the hill between broad hedges. At the top of the rise, just beyond a small band of woodland, a view over the great cornfields opens up, while to the right the radio-telescope dishes of Cambridge University's Mullard Laboratory stretch out in a long array. This is peewit country; the air is full of their thin cries, competing with the larks higher in the broad sky. The track rejoins the surfaced road at GR 380 523 opposite Drift Cottage, a name which suggests, as do the widely spaced hedges, that this was once a section of drove road.

The alternative road route from Fowlmere follows the B1368 to Newton, forking left at the Queen's Head and then through Harston, Haslingfield and Harlton. Once across the A603 at the Wheatsheaf, the route meanders through the Eversdens and Kingston to Bourn, where a left fork at Caxton End leads to a shallow ford and then up to another post mill, Bourn Mill—although it's virtually in Caxton. The next pair of villages on the far side of the old Roman Ermine Street, now more prosaically the A14, also boast a post mill. This one, at GR 277 555, has the date 1614 carved on a beam; it was a working mill up to 1911.

From Great Gransden a fine little road leads up to the estate village of Waresley, where you join the B1040 Potton road. Now that they are recolonizing Britain's roadsides, cowslips are prominent in spring along many of the roads hereabouts. The route turns off the B-road at the next junction, marked '65' (m above sea level). In the angle of the junction lies Gamlingay Vineyard, one of the larger English vineyards. It is open to visitors and prospective buyers.

After Gamlingay Cinques (a name whose origin I have been unable to find) a sudden change in the soil colour to a quite vivid red shows that the local geology has changed, and the next village, Potton, is a warm stone and brick place, with a remarkable range of building styles bordering its winding high street. It is a thriving little place, with the facilities of a small town, set around a pleasing square. Potton and its neighbours, Sandy and Biggleswade, are centres of vegetable production and market gardening.

Leave Potton by the B1040 Biggleswade road up Galley Hill, turning left at the top to Sutton, another warm stone village with a ford which bypasses the handsome packhorse bridge, now

a footbridge only. On the afternoon that we passed, water rats were crossing and recrossing the
little stream above the bridge in an obscure
bustle of ratrace activity, the water scarcely wet-
ting their fur.

From Sutton the route follows a narrow road
through increasingly large fields as we approach
cereal country again to Eyeworth, with its rather
bizarre little church, apparently a collection of
architectural afterthoughts. From here there are
two possible routes to Ashwell—right-and-left by
way of Mobbs Hole, or left-and-right through
Guilden Morden, with a possible further detour
via Steeple Morden if you wish to collect another
windmill.

Ashwell is one of the most delightful villages
anywhere on the route. It is a maze of little back
roads, centred on a fine church whose spire
makes it a landmark for miles around. Many of the
houses are timber-framed and there is a great
deal of simple plaster decoration. A cool hollow in
the centre of the village houses a gravelly pool
where the springs rise which feed the western
arm of the River Cam. Ashwell also has surprisingly a miniature one-way road system, and to
leave it you have to find the minute road signposted 'Bygrave' that leaves the main street
almost opposite the Three Tuns.

The road climbs steadily over Claybush Hill
and then opens out to one of the finest vistas on the
whole route, across to the rolling chalk hills over
which the route began. From here the open little
road sweeps down past a sadly long-unfrocked
pub and rolls its way over the open fields by the
hamlet of Bygrave down to Baldock once more.

Audley End House

BERKSHIRE AND WILTSHIRE DOWNS

• WEEKEND ROUTE •

The Downs of Berkshire, Wiltshire and Hampshire, for all their nearness to London, really mark the north-eastern boundary of Wessex. Indeed, Wessex's most famous king was born here. To travel, even today, over the rolling green openness of the downs, perhaps along one of the ancient trackways, is to experience the landscape across which Thomas Hardy's failed heroes, exiled from their native Dorset, tramped their desperate way to their doomed academic appointments in 'Christminster'. Even today, too, considering the homely domesticity of much of the landscape, parts are incredibly remote; on this route there are several stretches of some miles without habitation.

The word 'down' derives from the old British word *dun* meaning 'hill'; the word 'dune' has the same origin. These Downs thus involve a fair amount of up: the highest point in south-east England—Walbury Hill, 297m or a shade under the magic 1000ft mark—lies only just off the route at the top of Inkpen Hill.

These chalk downlands are where the east-to-west ridges of the North and South Downs meet the north-east to south-west chain of the Chiltern Hills. Between them, these chalk hills form a great semi-circular arc, one of the most marked topographical features of south and east England (and a feature which has its parallel in northern France). Chalk is a distinctive soft, pure, white limestone, made up largely of the fossilized shells of minute marine organisms.

Because chalk is porous, the uplands are relatively well-drained. In early Stone Age times, with the Strait of Dover yet unbreached and much of the clay lowland waterlogged forest, these barer and drier hills offered the easiest routes west and north from the continent. As a result these downlands have an unparalleled richness of Stone and Bronze Age remains. By Bronze Age times—some 3000 BC—these routes along the crests of the hills had become to a degree formalized roads, and Berkshire and Wiltshire have many of them. The route gives a chance of sampling the best-known of these tracks, the Ridgeway, and of making short detours to Neolithic and Bronze Age sites.

The two distinct downland massifs, Berkshire and Wiltshire to the north and mainly Hampshire to the south, are divided by the wide valley of the River Kennet, a major tributary of the Thames. The main Bath road, the picturesque and ambitious Kennet and Avon Canal—intended to link London and Bristol—and the later railway which killed the canal's chances of commercial success all follow the same valley.

The route may conveniently be started at Wantage, its northernmost point. Other possible starting points are Marlborough and Hungerford, while Newbury is no more than 5 miles (8km) away from the route at Boxford.

• THE ROUTE •

Wantage is now in Oxfordshire, moved in that same boundary revision that swallowed up Rutland and Westmorland. The county boundary now follows an extremely tortuous path south of the ridge of the downs, but everybody still thinks of the hills as the Berkshire Downs. Wantage was indeed the birthplace of Wessex's best-known king, Alfred. A stern statue of Alfred dominates

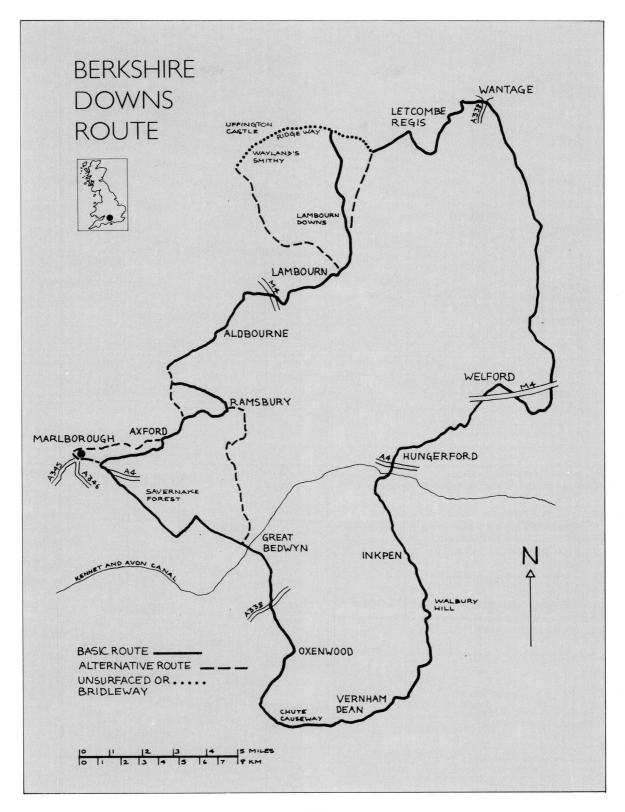

BERKSHIRE
DOWNS
ROUTE

UFFINGTON CASTLE
RIDGE WAY
WAYLAND'S SMITHY
LAMBOURN DOWNS
LAMBOURN
M4
ALDBOURNE
RAMSBURY
AXFORD
MARLBOROUGH
A345
A346
A4
SAVERNAKE FOREST
GREAT BEDWYN
KENNET AND AVON CANAL
A338
OXENWOOD
CHUTE CAUSEWAY
VERNHAM DEAN
INKPEN
WALBURY HILL
HUNGERFORD
A4
WELFORD
M4
LETCOMBE REGIS
WANTAGE
A338

N

BASIC ROUTE ——————
ALTERNATIVE ROUTE ‑ ‑ ‑ ‑
UNSURFACED OR . . . . .
BRIDLEWAY

0   1   2   3   4   5 MILES
0 1 2 3 4 5 6 7 8 KM

• INFORMATION •

Starting point
As described the route starts and finishes in Wantage; other convenient points would be Marlborough and Hungerford. It would be possible to start from Newbury or Andover, joining the route at Boxford or Chute Causeway respectively.

Access
Rail routes are to Didcot (about 8 miles (13km) E of Wantage) from London (Paddington), Oxford, Swindon, Bristol and Birmingham; to Newbury, Hungerford and Great Bedwyn from Reading (infrequent and not on Sundays); and to Andover from London (Waterloo) and Salisbury. Main access roads are the A34 then A417, or M4 then A338 to Wantage; M4/A4 to Hungerford and Marlborough; or M3 then A303 to Andover.

Accommodation
There are B&B or hotel possibilities on or near the route in Aldbourne, Ashbury, Grove (nr Wantage), Lambourn, Letcombe Regis, Newbury, Uffington and Westcot (nr Kingston Lisle). There are campsites at Marlborough (Savernake Forest), Newbury, Vernham Dean and Wantage. There is a youth hostel at Courthill above Letcombe Regis. If you need to consult directories or listings, check under Oxfordshire, Berkshire, Wiltshire and Hampshire.

Tourist information offices
The nearest are in Marlborough, Newbury and Didcot.

Cycle shops
There is one in Marlborough, otherwise the nearest appears to be in Thatcham, just E of Newbury.

Maps
The whole route is on OS 1:50 000 sheet 174. Basic route distance is about 80 miles (130km).

River Kennet at Axford

the little open market square in the town centre—a square now, like so many, a car park for most of the week.

You leave Wantage by the B4507, a road which winds westwards along the foot of the Downs; it leaves the A338 Hungerford road at traffic lights at the south end of the town. The road is quite narrow at first, sunk between high banks, and after about ¾ mile (1km) you take the left turn towards Letcombe Regis and Letcombe Bassett. As you reach the outskirts of Letcombe Regis you see the first 'Racehorses crossing' warning, a reminder that the Berkshire Downs are a major breeding and training centre. Letcombe Regis is a complex little village but the route through is fairly straightforward and the road to Letcombe Bassett drops into the unexpected little ravine of the Letcombe Brook past the old watercress beds. The road climbs briskly out of the village to join the B4001 at GR 362 862. Here you turn left on the rather daunting climb of Hackpen Hill—daunting mainly because it's straight and open, so that you can see the whole task laid out before you.

At the top of the climb there is a choice: you can continue, gently downhill now, on the B-road, sweeping past the characteristic beech copses fringing the hills, past the racehorse training gallops straight down into Lambourn—or you can sample the Ridgeway.

The Ridgeway is now part of the long-distance Ridgeway Path, and the whole of the western part—the 45 miles (some 72km) from Overton Hill to Streatley—is legally cyclable and, to varying degrees, physically ridable. For beginners, at least, it's best attempted in dry weather: wet chalk can be very slippery.

It's not only the ridability but the whole mood of the Ridgeway that changes with the weather. The larks singing in the haze above the ripe cornfields seem to inhabit a different world from the pheasants scurrying for cover as torn clouds and icy March showers whip across the track. But to be there on the right day with towering white cumulus is to experience a solitude, an openness, rare in southern England.

This particular section of the ancient track—for 2 miles (about 3km) westwards from the B4001 at GR 343 851—is both one of the more spectacular and one of the more rideable. After the first ¼ mile

(400m) or so of hard base where it doubles as the drive to Hill Barn Farm it becomes the characteristic chalky track, on this section rising and plunging across the far from even contours of the ridge. There are extensive views north across the Vale of the White Horse far below, and unexpectedly from time to time to the south. For thirsty travellers there's a water tap just after Hill Barn (GR 338 854) with a poignant plaque dedicating it to the memory of a young countrylover.

If this taste of the Ridgeway is enough, you can leave it at the top of Blowingstone Hill (GR 323 863), turning left down to Lambourn. (The Blowing Stone, at the foot of the hill in the opposite direction, is a hollow sarsen which can, with the right technique, be blown to yield a mournful foghorn wail. It is in the front garden of a cottage; you are expected to make a donation to a village charity for the privilege.)

If you're still game for more Ridgeway you can follow the track for another 4 miles (6km) past the Neolithic landmarks of Uffington Castle—a large earthwork—and the White Horse, and the burial mound of Wayland's Smithy. This stretch is rougher, if flatter, and not so well drained, so it can be *very* sticky in or after wet weather. There is no escape Lambourn-wards until you meet the B4000 above Ashbury at GR 273 843, although there are a couple of chances of following roads down the scarp to the north—which means climbing back later from Ashbury. Either way don't expect to move fast on this part of the Ridgeway.

If you have followed the Ridgeway right through to the B4000, the road passes Ashdown Park on the right with a field full of the sarsen stones which were the raw material for so many of the stone circles and barrows on the Downs. This road offers a superb downhill run into Lambourn, a comfortable-looking and lived-in village—and the area's best-known racehorse centre. If you declined the Ridgeway, or turned off it before the Ashbury road, then the alternative routes also will have brought you to Lambourn. The route leaves Lambourn by the shallow valley of Farn Combe, to climb to the old Roman road, the Ermin Way, that runs along the ridge and which you follow to Baydon. Here you turn left for the fine descent into the pleasant largely brick-and-flint village of Aldbourne.

Leave Aldbourne by the left of the two roads which leave the centre of the village at the rather complex junction at GR 264 756; the road climbs quite a steep little pitch and swings round to the right on a road which opens out to give fine views back over the dry Aldbourne valley. The long road climbs steadily between cereal fields to Stock Lane, where you turn left. After about ½ mile (800m), as the road begins to fall, turn left on the small road signposted 'Ramsbury 2', which has a superb avenue of oaks and skirts the southern side of a wood before dropping quite steeply to Ramsbury. Ramsbury is a delightful little village with some very handsome runs of brick-and-flint cottages. The village lies in the valley of the River Kennet and there are several possible routes from here; all of them eventually meet in Great Bedwyn.

The first choice—the forest route—takes a westward loop, following the Kennet valley to Axford, after an initial climb up White's Hill which you could avoid by coming straight down from Stock Lane, rather than going into Ramsbury. A series of right-angle bends brings you to Stitchcombe and then a fine climb up from the valley with tremendous views down to the river. At the right season there are fine displays of wild yellow iris along the Kennet. Savernake Forest, although largely managed by the Forestry Commission, has been privately owned since before the Norman conquest and is now the only English forest in private hands. Cycle-tourists are welcome to use the tracks which cross it but are naturally expected to respect the trees, the wildlife and the essential peace and quiet. Some of the rides are stony but easily ridable, one or two are rougher and demand some care, while the main northwest to south-east route—the Grand Avenue—is now surfaced. The forest is mainly beech, but with quite a lot of oak and areas of conifers. We also noted some fine stretches of hornbeam.

There are two possible routes to Savernake Forest from the fork at GR 227 693, just after Stitchcombe: you can climb over the ridge to reach the Bath Road, the A4, at GR 224 680. From here a right turn along the A4 for about ¾ mile (1km) brings you to the entrance to the Grand Avenue through the forest at GR 210 683. Alternatively you can follow the little road which contours above the river to join the A4 at GR 203 687, turning left on the main road to enter the Grand Avenue at the top of the hill. (From this junction, or by the direct route from Axford by way of Mildenhall, it is possible to drop into the handsome town of Marlborough, one of several to claim to have Britain's widest high street. It also has several eating places and a full complement of shops. You leave Marlborough by the A4 eastwards to the start of the Grand Avenue.) From the T-junction at the southeastern end of the Avenue a left turn, followed by first right, brings you to Great Bedwyn.

The alternative route from Ramsbury follows the Kennet and Avon Canal and involves crossing the Kennet at the east end of the village and then climbing the steep hill to the ridge. At the junction marked '177' (m above sea level), a left turn takes you to Froxfield and the A4, with a handsome run of almshouses at the old Somerset Hospital fronting the main road. About ¼ mile (400m) east of the village you turn right off the main road by a pub called 'The Pelican', to follow the Kennet and Avon Canal down to Great Bedwyn. This ambitious canal, completed in 1810 as the last link in a waterway from London to Bristol, was destined within a few years to be overtaken by the railway age. The considerable rise, and the consequent enormous number of locks it involved in rather dry country, meant that water had to be pumped to the highest parts of the canal. The pumping engine at Crofton, about 2 miles (3km) south-west of Great Bedwyn, is preserved and may be visited. A great deal of restoration work is now in progress on the canal, with the aim of returning it to navigability for pleasure craft. Great Bedwyn can also be reached from the junction at GR 275 700 by the direct route through Chisbury.

The route leaves Great Bedwyn by crossing the railway and canal past a fine run of thatched cottages. After about ¾ mile (1km) take the right fork towards Vernham Dean, which climbs steadily to cross the A338. After a series of roadside copses the road begins to climb quite sharply and a superb view left along the edge of Rivar Down opens up, with the firm rounded shape of the down crowned by trees. On the spring afternoon that we climbed up, lines of brown cattle grazed between clumps of hawthorn, white with blossom. Just over the top of the hill is the hamlet of Oxenwood, which boasts a minute shop. Turn right here, and left at the next junction, to begin a

steady tree-lined climb to Silver Down. This old Roman road, known as Chute Causeway, then contours round the down, opening up superb views leftwards across to the earthwork of Fosbury Camp, and later to the right over Andover and down to the hills of Salisbury Plain. Although this is essentially a domestic landscape, there is a stretch of some miles with no human habitation.

At the fork at GR 326 553, you can either follow the road down Conholt Hill with views of an almost hidden and exquisite little valley to the left to Vernham Dean, or fork right along a fine avenue of small oaks down to Ankers Farm and up to the striking farmhouse of Vernham Manor. From here a series of pleasant, hedged, narrow lanes lead you to the valley road that leads up to Combe. There's quite a steep pitch up to the sharp right-hand bend by Combe church and then a long climb of ¾ mile (1km) or so up Walbury Hill. The road clings to the flank of the slope beneath the earthwork with all the panache of an alpine pass to reach the summit at a junction of roads and tracks. About 300yd (300m) up the left-hand track is a grim reminder of harsher times, Inkpen Gibbet; today's gibbet is a modern reconstruction. From here there are views to the north over the wooded valley of the Kennet.

What goes up must come down—so there is a tremendous downhill stretch to Inkpen village, followed by pleasant hedged and wood-fringed lanes through to the open space of Hungerford Common. Turn right in the middle of the common along the chestnut avenue and at the end of the open space, turn sharp left. The road almost doubles back to cross the railway, the canal, the River Kennet and the A4 in rapid succession. On the far side of the Bath Road a succession of delightful winding and wooded little lanes lead gently up to Wickham and down to Welford. Here you are in the valley of the clear Lambourn Brook, at the time when we passed dotted with the white flowers of the trailing water crowsfoot. Turn right on the B1000 for about 1½ miles (2km) to Boxford, then left and second left beside the river. From here there's a whole range of lanes to take you through to the B4494. Once on the B-road it's a gentle climb to cross the Ridgeway for the last time and then a final plunge back to Wantage'.

In Savernake Forest

COTSWOLDS

• WEEKEND ROUTE •

The Cotswold Hills are the quintessential rural England of the tourist brochure and picture postcard: golden cottages in picturesque villages, rolling open country with artistically placed woodlands, gently-flowing streams in broad valleys, and bustling market towns. This means that the Cotswolds are also very popular, and in summer the best-known of the towns and villages—such as Chipping Camden, Broadway, Bourton-on-the-Water, Upper and Lower Slaughter, Bibury, Stow-on-the-Wold and Burford—become very crowded with visitors. These places *are* very attractive, nevertheless, so if you have the chance of visiting them mid-week in early spring, late autumn or even winter, take it. The route, though, is designed to take you to less well-known places along roads which are quiet at any time. As on several of the other routes, using these minor lanes means that you will be taking a rather hillier course—as always take the climbs steadily, walk up a few steep ones if you like, look at the views, pause by the streams, browse in the villages. Of all the routes, the Cotswolds are perhaps least to be hurried.

The Cotswolds are the middle part of a broad limestone ridge that sweeps across England from Dorset in the south-west to the margins of the Fens in the east. The soft limestone is known geologically as 'oolite' ('egg-stone'), from its structure of minute nodules like fish roes. This stone *is* the Cotswolds: it is used for buildings of all kinds and for the characteristic dry-stone mortar-less walls that divide the fields in many places. The colour mellows as the stone weathers and varies from place to place as its iron content changes—from a soft grey, through honey-coloured and golden to a deep brown. At one time the richest in iron, the darkest, was quarried on a massive scale for smelting. On the route you will find villages with a whole range of colours, giving each a quite different character. The route shows as well two different aspects of the Cotswolds: the western part, hillier but the more conventionally picturesque, the eastern gentler and more domestic.

• THE ROUTE •

Burford, our starting point, is a typically Cotswold small town. The broad high street drops steeply to the River Windrush and is dominated by a cathedral-like church, witness of the Cotswolds' prosperity as wool exporters in the fifteenth century. Nowadays Burford is an essential tourist stop and in the season the accents of Minneapolis and Kyoto seem as frequent as those of Swinbrook and Barrington. And, a sentimental point, the town was the first night's stop on my first-ever bicycle tour.

The first part of the route follows the Windrush and its tributary, the Sherborne Brook. Leave Burford by the B4425, Sheep Street, but soon look out for the start of the very narrow Windrush valley road (GR 243 123). It's not signposted but you come to it after about ½ mile (800m), on the right, soon after the end of a long stone wall; there's a bright red post box prominently fixed to an old tree trunk. For the next 8 miles (13km) or so there follows a succession of small streamside villages—Little Barrington, Windrush, Sherborne and Farmington—some no more than a few stone cottages huddled round the church and the big house.

The quite rolling and plunging little road has in fact been climbing steadily and by the time you reach the A429, 1½ miles (2½km) past Farmington, you are past the headwaters of the brook and on the edge of the high dry uplands of the Cotswolds. Here (GR 118 158) you go straight over the main road and turn right after ¼ mile (400m) on the Turkdean road. After a false start with a short

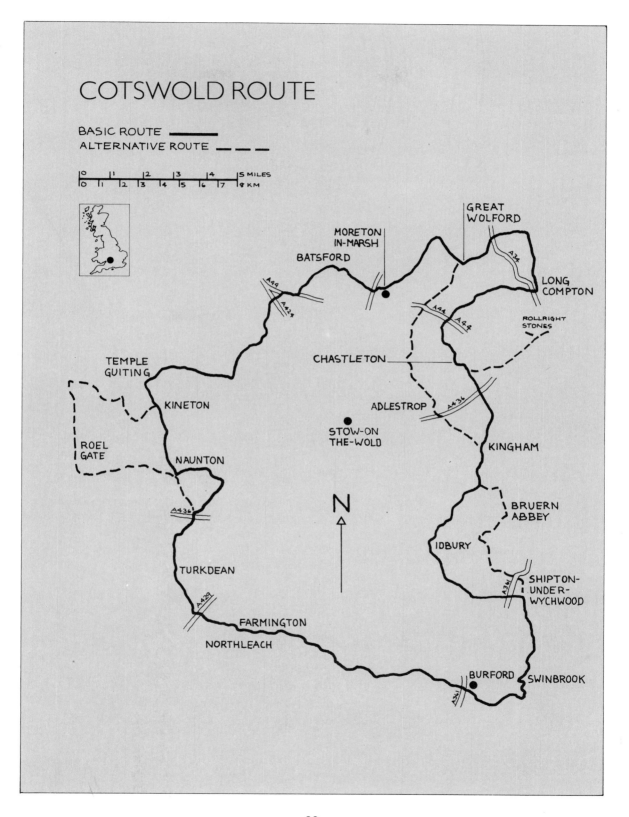

COTSWOLD ROUTE

BASIC ROUTE ———————
ALTERNATIVE ROUTE — — — —

• INFORMATION •

Starting point
As described the route starts and finishes at Burford; another convenient point would be Moreton-in-Marsh. It would also be possible to start from Banbury, from Chipping Norton or from Cheltenham, joining the route at Long Compton, Kingham and Roel Gate respectively.

Access
Rail routes are to Moreton-in-Marsh or Kingham from London (Paddington), Oxford and Worcester; or to Banbury from London (Marylebone), Oxford or Birmingham (plus an amazing list of other places from which perhaps one train a day passes through Banbury). Main access roads are the A40 to Burford and the A44 and A429 to Moreton-in-Marsh.

Accommodation
There are B&B or hotel possibilities on or near the route in Bledington, Blockley, Burford, Great Wolford, Idbury, Kingham, Moreton-in-Marsh, Naunton, Northleach, Stow-on-the-Wold, Temple Guiting, Todenham and the Wychwood villages, Churchill, Minster Lovell and Chipping Norton. There are campsites at Kingham and Long Compton, and youth hostels at Stow-on-the-Wold and Charlbury. If you need to consult directories or listings, check under Gloucestershire, Oxfordshire and Warwickshire.

Tourist information offices
Burford, Moreton-in-Marsh and Stow-on-the-Wold.

Cycle shops
There is a small bike-cum-toy shop in Moreton-in-Marsh which also hires out bikes. Otherwise the nearest are in Banbury, Carterton, Witney or Cheltenham.

Maps
The whole route is on OS Tourist Map 'Cotswold' or on 1:50 000 sheets 150 (for a very short distance), 151 and 163. Total route distance is about 50 to 70 miles (80 to 115km).

Looking down to Naunton village

downhill past the superbly-sited Leygore Manor, you swoop sharply down into a narrow valley, followed by a climb between high banks and beneath towering arches of beech trees to reach the tightly clustered hamlet of Turkdean.

The name Turkdean has nothing to do with Turks or Turkey—it means 'the valley of the River Turce'. *Turce* is a Celtic word, related to the Welsh for a mole or badger: it was used, presumably by the obvious association, for streams in limestone country which burrow underground, only to reappear further down the valley. Sure enough, the os map shows just such a stream in the valley north and west of the village. (Interestingly the River Mole in Surrey behaves in the same way.)

If it is a majestic avenue of mature beeches that leads you to Turkdean, then several superb lines of younger ones edge the road to Notgrove, a twisting switchback of a village that you can pass through or skirt to the west. Notgrove's Saxon name means 'the damp or wet wood'.

Beyond Notgrove, at the main A436 crossing (GR 113 210), you can go straight on, following the signpost via Aylworth, which holds on to a little of your hard-won height. Alternatively (and prettier but a couple of miles (some 3km) longer) turn right immediately after the main road, to go down the unsignposted open road. The sign at the junction warns 'ford' and after 1½ miles (2½km) the lane plunges literally to the River Windrush. The ford can be quite deep at some seasons and has a trickily-cobbled bottom; luckily there's a low stone footbridge that you can walk across. Beyond the ford, an almost direct crossing of the B4068 brings you to the long streamside village of Naunton, in summer almost hidden by the hedges from the main road above. Towards the west end of the village an apparent left turn takes you past the manor and to the steady climb back to the B4068. At the junction (GR 104 232) you rejoin the direct route—but there's still more choice.

The gentler of these, although it's by no means flat, is to turn right and follow the Windrush for about 4 miles (6km) through Kineton to Temple Guiting. A possible visit from here is to the Cotswold Farm Park at Bemborough Farm, about 1 mile (1½km) east of (and uphill from) Kineton.

The 8-mile (13km) longer and more strenuous but thoroughly worthwhile detour (particularly on

a clear day) begins by following the B4068 west for just over ¼ mile (400m) and then forking right at the Fox Hill Inn. The road drops at first and then climbs earnestly through the stolidly-set hamlet of Hawling to join the ridge road, the Salt Way. This is one of several 'salt' roads, radiating from Droitwich, the source of much of Roman—and later—England's salt. As you follow it northwards, this superb road lingers just below the 300-metre (1000ft) contour and gives tremendous views westwards over the Severn valley, as far as the Malvern Hills.

There are several ways back from the ridge to Temple Guiting; my favourite is to turn right at Sudeley Hill (GR 051 279), then right again just over ½ mile (800m) later at Lines Barn Farm to follow an insignificant-looking little road with grass down the middle, a road you could easily miss unless you're looking for it. The first part runs beside the infant stream through Guiting Wood. 'Guiting' is the old name for the Windrush but the modern map is ambiguous as to which of the upper branches is the river proper. The right turn in the wood that continues to follow the rapidly-growing stream is well worth taking, turning left after the gated lodge at GR 083 259 to Kineton and Temple Guiting.

Temple Guiting gets its name from the Knights Templar who owned it in the twelfth century; it seems a dour little village with high walls and heavy yews. A short climb from the village brings you to the B4077 and another ¼ mile (400m) of climb through the wood to the summit. From here it's a splendid 2 mile (3km) spin down the broad road, between dense beechwoods, until you burst out again into open country just before the junction at GR 134 283. The little road to the left climbs at first and then plunges into a veritable tunnel between close-ranked hazels, before climbing away from the marshy pools into open country again. When we last passed this way we were brought to a halt for a few minutes by the leisurely progress of a swaying herd of brown cows, filling the lane from bank to bank on their way to the evening milking. But then, as I said, the Cotswolds are no place to hurry.

At the A424 a signpost improbably proclaims the narrow lane opposite to be the A44 to Moreton-in-Marsh. It isn't: that road is about ¼ mile (400m) further on, close under the almost black squat bulk of Bourton Woods. After ½ mile (800m) of the A44, a left turn on the B4479, still flanking the dark wood, soon brings you to the turn for Batsford. The road skirts the impressive stone wall of Batsford Park; the little village itself is a few estate cottages grouped round the simple golden church. Batsford Park has an arboretum—claimed to have 900 varieties of trees and shrubs—and that modern addition, a garden centre. From Batsford it's a gentle 1½ miles (2½km) into Moreton-in-Marsh.

Moreton, the largest settlement on the route, is a more business-like town than Burford—less self-consciously pretty with an intriguing mix of styles and ages of building lining the broad high street and spanning at least five centuries. There's quite a selection of shops, overnight accommodation and eating places among them.

The route out is along a broad flat road which leaves the A429 just after the railway bridge at the north of the town. Todenham, the next straggling village, announces itself by its tall church spire long before you reach it, but the route turns right on the southern outskirts of the village, towards Great Wolford.

In Great Wolford there is a new choice of route. Turning right opposite the lane to the church leads after a couple of miles (some 3km) to the Four Shire Stone, at the staggered crossing of the main A44 (GR231 321). Nowadays only Gloucestershire, Warwickshire and Oxfordshire meet here but before a boundary revision in the 1930s removed such anomalies, the edge of a detached portion of Worcestershire also met at this point. Four-county meeting points were always rare; three-county ones are inevitable.

This route is the easier of the two, and beyond the A44 the road meanders gently through Evenlode and skirts Adlestrop Park. It was the station here that inspired Edward Thomas' poem 'Yes, I remember Adlestrop ...' when his train unexpectedly stopped here on a languid summer afternoon before the First World War. The railway remains but trains no longer stop at Adlestrop, even by mistake; the nearest station is now Kingham, 3 miles (5km) down the line. A shelter by the western end of the loop road through the village itself (at GR 242 272) preserves the station nameboard, while a plaque bearing the poem decorates one of the railway platform's old seats

with its clever Great Western Railway motif in cast iron, reading 'GWR' either way round. From here a left-and-right crossing of the A436 takes you through Daylesford with its squat pyramid-like spire and on to Kingham.

A hillier and about 6 miles (10km) longer alternative from Great Wolford heads north-east through Little Wolford to the A34. A left-and-right crossing at a bizarrely turreted ornamental gate-house then leads towards Cherington. About 1½ miles (2½km) after the main road, and just under a mile (1½km) short of Cherington, at a mute and armless signpost, a gate on the right gives access to a superb unfenced and gated road which climbs amidst grazing sheep through Weston Park, leading eventually down to the village of Long Compton.

This village boasts a church gate of unusual design, with a little thatched room built over it. Long Compton is one of those unfortunate villages which would be very pleasant if it didn't have a trunk road scything through the middle of it; this is the bane of many lovely country villages. You can leave the A34 behind by taking the Barton-on-the-Heath road on the right about 100yd (100m) after you reach the main road.

Barton-on-the-Heath could also have been reached by a direct 1½ mile (2½km) route from Great Wolford. Here the building stone is noticeably darker brown. The short main street leads to a shaded green with a memorial fountain, and opposite, a decorative wrought-iron gateway. The route to Kingham from here lies by Kitebrook (fairly flat) or Little Compton (decidedly hilly) to Chastleton with its four-gabled Jacobean house and Civil War legends. Then it's over the hill to Kingham or, if you've time for a detour, and one that involves some climbing, a visit to the Bronze Age Rollright Stones (GR 296 308). This 3500-year-old circle of unshaped stones lies beside a small pine copse in the ridge road.

Kingham was an important local railway centre when it was the major junction on the Oxford–Worcester and Gloucester–Banbury lines. The station is still there, but with one of the lines gone the village now straggles quietly down from a wide green. At the bottom of the green is a feature that will appeal to thirsty cyclists on a hot day:

Overleaf: *Near Kineton*

a working village pump that delivers clear cool drinking water.

From Kingham there's yet another choice of route. The high road to the west climbs to the village of Idbury, through Foscot and Bould, then winds round by Fifield and Upper Milton to the junction at GR 282 170, along roads in some places so narrow that you can almost touch the snowy banks of cow parsley on both sides. The lower eastern road—a fine choice at daffodil time— goes by Bruern Abbey and Milton- and Shipton-under-Wychwood to the same T-junction.

The final leg of the journey, from the valley of the River Evenlode back to the familiar Windrush, begins by climbing resolutely over a high open wold to the B4437. From here there's a glorious 2-mile (3km) run down to the winding village of Swinbrook, the last part of it beside a miniature stream, no more than a foot wide where you first meet it. On the afternoon that we passed, fat pheasants looked up from the banks of the stream as we went by, and then returned to more serious affairs.

The minor road through the centre of Swinbrook—the left fork in the village—has an easily ridable ford. Then, right at the bottom of the street, comes the Swan Inn, perfectly poised, to the eye or for a drink, beside the bridge over the Windrush.

The last hamlet upstream is Widford, which boasts fourteenth-century wall paintings in its minute and isolated church on the far side of the river. You reach it by way of a track and field path from the mill. The final 1½ miles (2½km) back to the towering spire of Burford—which you first glimpse peeping over the hill—follows a fine road above the willows and water-meadows of the Windrush.

DORSET

• WEEKEND ROUTE •

As the great chalk whaleback ridge of Southern England reaches its westernmost point it makes a splendid surge to meet the sea in a range of striking cliffs. Further inland more ridges stretch from the knuckle escarpment of north Dorset like the fingers of a giant hand pointing towards the sea. Between them and the cliffs lies a belt of sandy heath with mixed forests and quiet valleys where the quaintly-named River Piddle and the glass-clear River Frome work their way down to Wareham and the sea.

This heath is the centre of Thomas Hardy's Wessex; Hardy connotations crop up at every turn. (It comes as something of a surprise to learn that the rather lumpen tower of the Hardy Monument high on the down above Abbotsbury commemorates not the novelist but Admiral Hardy—to whom, as a young lieutenant, Nelson's dying 'Kiss me, Hardy' (or 'Kismet, Hardy', according to interpretation) was addressed at Trafalgar.) Even in today's relative affluence it's possible to feel—at the sudden sight of an isolated thatched cottage at the end of a rutted and muddy track, or of a rolling patch of rough heath—something of the sheer unremitting starkness of life and toil in Hardy's largely melancholy tales. This, then, is the setting for the Dorset route.

Unlike many other countries—and unlike Scotland, Ireland and parts of Wales—England in general lacks coast roads. Dorset is no exception, and so, to bring you at least within sight and sound of the sea, the route uses some stretches of ridable upland bridleway, most of it the inland branch of the Dorset Coast Path. But to see the coast properly you'll have to make one or two out-and-home detours, and perhaps even walk a little.

Dorset is a very popular holiday county. It lies just to the west of another popular area, the New Forest, and on the way to a third, south Devon and Cornwall. Consequently the main roads are often very busy and the well-known showpieces, such as Abbotsbury and Lulworth Cove, crowded at holiday times and summer weekends. The increasingly busy port of Weymouth, too, attracts its own traffic along the A353 and A354. The A35, which should at least bypass the town of Dorchester by the time this book is published, leads to the West Country and feeds the port roads, so it, too, is best avoided.

There's no denying that there are some steep climbs in the country north of Dorchester, particularly in crossing from one south-pointing chalk finger to the next. As always the advice is to be patient, linger when you wish, don't hurry. Take the magnificent views from some of the ridges and the superb swoops down from others as your reward.

• THE ROUTE •

The obvious starting-point, and really the focus for the whole route, is the city of Dorchester. Founded by the Romans, who knew it as *Durnovaria*, succeeding generations have added and subtracted bits, so that today it presents a mixture of styles and a number of rather unsympathetic recent 'improvements'. The greatest real improvement is likely to be the completion of the bypass, which should leave the city in some peace from the pounding traffic of the A35. Hardy is in Dorchester, too, of course. His monument—a seated statue—overlooks the centre of his 'Casterbridge', his birthplace at Upper Bockhampton is only some 3 miles (5km) to the east, while Stinsford church, where his heart is buried, is halfway between the two.

If the Romans founded the city, though, there was a settlement here much earlier at Maiden

Above: *On the Dorset Coast Path*

Opposite: *The Cerne Giant*

Castle, about 2 miles (3km) to the south-west, reached by a turning off the main Weymouth road, A354. Maiden Castle is basically an Iron Age hill fort, although archaeological evidence suggests that it was first settled in Neolithic times, around 3000 BC. It reached its final form between 100 and 75 BC, only to be conquered by the Romans and abandoned in AD 43, when the new city of *Durnovaria* was established. You can't keep a good fort down, though, and after some 350 years of disuse it became a religious precinct. Today its grass-grown ramparts, though quiet except for the song of larks, still dominate the surroundings.

The most pleasant way out of Dorchester, and a very convenient one if you have come by rail, is due south to Winterborne Herringston. The road is a turning left off the A354 Weymouth road, just after the railway bridge. Herringston has a fine wooded park through which the road passes on its way by the golf course to Came Wood. As you climb fine views open back over Dorchester and then, further up, in the other direction over Weymouth and its bay towards Portland. The 'Winterbo[u]rne' element of a place name is one that is very common in Dorset. *Bo[u]rnes* are brooks, and particularly in chalk country the flow of a stream is markedly affected by the seasons and rainfall: so, streams which flowed only or much more strongly in winter became *winterbo[u]rnes.*

The route goes east beside Came Wood and then, at GR 702 852, where the road bears left, follows the firm-surfaced track straight ahead to White Horse Hill. After passing under the electricity power line and reaching a ruined farm, the track climbs steadily for perhaps 200yd (200m). You then fork right off the main track (which is signposted 'Broadmayne') and follow the section through a field gate labelled 'Inland route to Osmington'—it's part of the inland section of the Dorset Coast Path. The top is a little disappointing—at least it was when we passed: it was just a field of kale. There's a second field gate, by a small tumulus from the top of which there are is a far better view out to sea. Just after this gate as you follow the edge of the field, there is a little grave under a hawthorn bush dedicated to 'Gentle Ben—a faithful friend 1975–1982'.

From here you can see the next field gate, a much more up-to-date tubular affair. Just on the

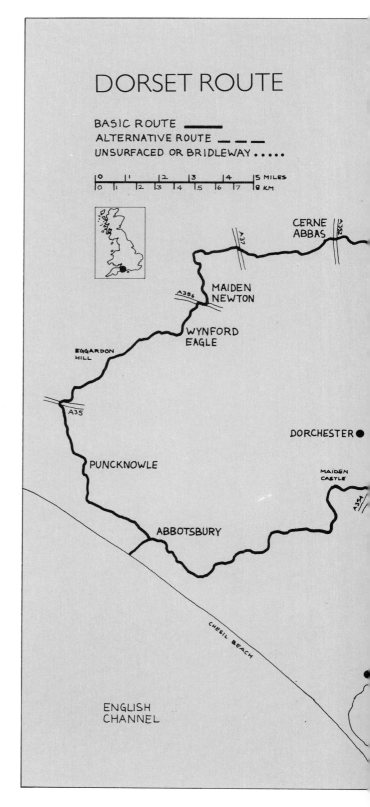

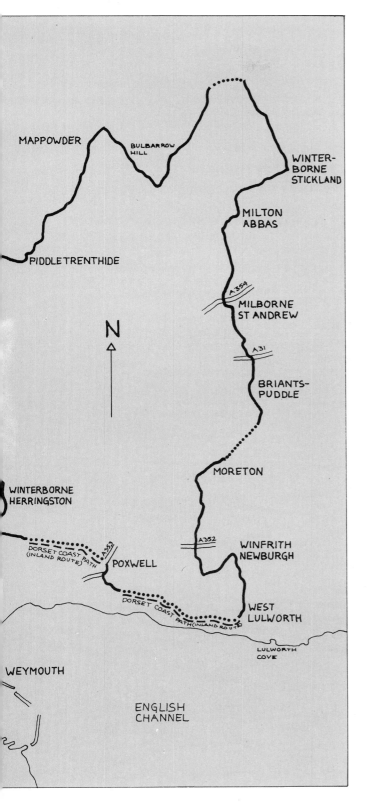

far side of it there's a path signpost on the left, in the bushes. Follow the track signposted 'Poxwell', straight on along the ridge. It comes down off the ridge as a pleasant grassy track to a waymarked gate by some dilapidated barns. From here you can see the hamlet of Poxwell to your left and you reach it by going through the gate and following the track beside the hedge. It *is* possible to go straight on at the gate, and slightly shorter, but it involves a rather unpleasant exit onto the main road. From Poxwell you turn right on the A353 for some ½ mile (800m).

At the end of a low wall on a curving right-hand bend, turn left down a steep little lane signposted 'Ringstead 1½'. The road drops and then climbs very determinedly until you reach a junction at GR 747 827. Here you go straight on at the wooden signpost labelled 'NT car park', which brings you onto a fine open stretch of downland with views down over Ringstead Bay; to the left is indeed the National Trust car park. Continue straight along the track and through another field gate. The track is still firm, between a fine array of gorse bushes, then downhill to a junction of stony tracks. From here you can make a detour down to Burning Cliff and the sea by a little path that turns right by the post box; the little chapel that should be a landmark turns out to be a tarred wooden shed.

The main route, however, follows the sign, 'West Lulworth 5—no cars please'. The first part of the track is quite a pull up, ridable with low enough gears, and the surface is firm and well-drained, with grass up the middle. At the top it becomes a grassier track, following a fence at first, until over the top you are within sight of the hills round Lulworth. Here you come out onto a superb open grassy down with magnificent views right along the coast from Portland and Weymouth to Worbarrow, one of the most exhilarating stretches of the whole route. Beside the path, to the left, is an intriguing series of oversize sculptures of shells, followed by a set of cunningly contrived wooden mussels; I have been unable to find out anything about them. At the end of the grassy stretch (keep over to the left) a firm-based chalk farm track brings you quite unexpectedly down to the Lulworth road.

Although it gets *very* crowded at popular times, the almost perfectly circular bay of Lulworth Cove is well worth a visit: this involves

• INFORMATION •

Starting point
As described the route starts and finishes in Dorchester; another convenient point would be Weymouth. It would also be possible to start from Wareham, joining the route at Milborne St Andrew.

Access
Rail routes are to Dorchester West Stn from Yeovil, Bristol and Swindon, and to Dorchester South Stn, Weymouth and Wareham from London (Waterloo), Bournemouth and Southampton. Ferries from Cherbourg and the Channel Islands travel to Weymouth. Main access road is the A35 to Dorchester.

Accommodation
B&B and hotel accommodation is relatively plentiful. Possibilities include Cerne Abbas, Dorchester, Lulworth, Milborne St Andrew, Milton Abbas, Osmington, Portesham, Sydling St Nicholas, Weymouth and Winfrith Newburgh. There are campsites at Ansty, Cerne Abbas, Chickerell (nr Rodden), Crossways (nr Moreton), Langton Herring (nr Rodden), Osmington Mills and Puncknowle. There are youth hostels at Litton Cheney (near Puncknowle) and Lulworth Cove. If you need to consult directories or listings, check under Dorset.

Tourist information offices
Dorchester and Weymouth.

Cycle shops and hire
There are cycle shops in Dorchester and Weymouth, and cycle hire from Weymouth Cycles.

Maps
The whole route is on OS 1:50 000 sheet 194. Basic route distance is about 85 miles (140km).

On the Dorset Coast Path

turning right to make an out-and-home detour of some 1½ miles (2km) each way. The cove was scooped out by the action of the sea which, having breached the relatively tough Purbeck Stone at the entrance, then hollowed out the circular bay in the softer clays behind it. There are other striking features and fine bays westwards from here—including the natural arch of Durdle Door—which can only really be reached on foot.

From the point where the coast track reaches the road it is a very pleasant run down a narrow valley to Winfrith Newburgh; on the morning that we passed, the chalky fields had lines of fine green down as the new crop began its cycle. Turn left at Winfrith church, up the valley between the two ridges beside the stream to East Chaldon, where you keep bearing round to the right, past the Sailor's Return. There's quite a sharp little pitch up to the ridge with the Five Marys, a line of tumuli, at the top.

The road crosses the busy A352 and plunges between high hedges, which seem all the higher because the route so far has been open. There are attractive thickets of willows and birches by the stream at Tadnall, from which the road rises to Red Bridge. Here it's right over the railway to Moreton. At the right-angle bend in Moreton, turn left down a gravelly track to the River Frome, here a wide clear stream with many water birds, crossed by a long footbridge: you will have to wheel your bicycle. There's an intriguing glimpse of Moreton House from the far end of the bridge. From here a fine gravel track, for the most part firmly based, leads through birch, pine and rhododendron up to the road junction at GR 819 911. Lawrence of Arabia's cottage, Clouds Hill, is to the right, but the route goes straight ahead, bearing left in the forest after rather over ¼ mile (some 600m) to Briantspuddle.

The River Piddle (or Trent) marks the boundary between the heath and the foothills of the downs, and from here through to the thatched village of Milborne St Andrew the country becomes increasing open. But the winding road does not: it is something of a characteristic of West Country lanes that they are often 'hollow roads' between banks surmounted by hedges, so that views occur only at gateways or on hills.

From Milborne a gentle valley road leads up to Milton Abbas, with views over the abbey lake at the foot of the village. When we passed great flocks of wild geese were combing the banks of the lake. Milton Abbas is a striking planned village, with neat symmetrical ranks of white thatched cottages set well back either side of the road behind a wide grassy green. Behind today's neatness—said to owe something to the skills of 'Capability' Brown—lies a dastardly tale of the systematic destruction of the original small town in the 1770s and 80s, when Lord Milton decided that it interfered with his enjoyment of the newly remodelled abbey, his manor.

From Milton Abbas, or even from Milborne St Andrew, the map shows any number of possible ways of shortening the route to Cerne Abbas. The route as described makes a feature of the northern escarpment above the Blackmoor Vale, before making for Cerne Abbas.

From the top of Milton Abbas's steep street, the ridge road leads to Winterborne Stickland, past Park Farm Museum with old farm implements and so on. Winterborne Stickland sports many brick-and-flint cottages in distinctive Dorset style, with the flints in broad bands, rather than as a continuous infill.

For the first part, the valley up to the ridge is broad and park-like but beyond Turnworth it closes in and the road, which had been climbing gently, becomes a little more earnestly uphill. At the top, at GR 813 093, there is a junction of tracks. Ahead there's a fine view out over the vale, and by following the quite ridable track to the left you can follow the ridge along. There are great sweeping views to the north-west and down into the Winterborne valley to the left. It's obviously a very breezy and windswept spot: the hawthorns beside the track are bent and bowed, leaning away from the prevailing westerlies. There is a short rutted 200-yd (200m) stretch at the top which you may prefer to walk, marked by the oak and elder copse of Turnworth Clump. As we passed kestrels and buzzards hovered and at one point rabbits scurried away at our approach, while pigeons flapped their noisy way out of the foliage. Within a short space, rather before the first of the two radio masts, the track has become gravelly again and remains firm and dry down to the road. For the last few yards the views over the vale open up again.

The road climbs steadily from the junction with

views down over the villages of Ibberton and Woolland to Bulbarrow Hill. A plaque at the top suggests that you should be able to see as far as the Blackdown Hills, Glastonbury Tor, the Quantocks and Shaftesbury—given a very clear day. From the 274-metre summit there's nowhere to go but down and it's a fine fast run past windswept beeches to Ansty Cross. The route goes right, out into the vale and the almost Cotswold-coloured village of Mappowder, along roads with notable hedgerow trees. The road rolls up through Folly, with the impressive slope of Ball Hill, crowned with a clump of trees on the right, and then drops into the pleasing grouping of thatched buildings that makes up Plush. Unusually, 'The Brace of Pheasants' proclaims its opening hours on a notice, and proclaims its name with a sign, a lamp, appliqué pheasants on the walls and two straw ones on the thatched roof. Also improbably, in the very narrow lane another notice forbids the turning of heavy goods vehicles. There follows a splendid, tree-lined drop into Piddletrenthide, a long straggle of a village beside the infant River Piddle, and an initially sharp climb over to Cerne Abbas. This is a tightly-clustered village—almost a small town—round a church built, like many of the houses, of a rather unusual mixture of limestone and flint.

Cerne Abbas' main claim to fame, though, is its priapic giant, an enormous chalk figure carved in the turf on Giant Hill above the village—a *graffito* on the grand scale. The 55-metre high giant appears to be brandishing a club and opinions differ as to whether he is of Roman origin—a representation of Hercules—or Romano-British, since there are suggestions that his traditional name was Helis. The figure is probably best seen from a footpath on the opposite hill at GR 657 016.

The next part of the route is quite up and down. As a reward for the climb from Cerne Abbas there's a fast, broad descent—with a shallow ford (and alternative footbridge) at the bottom. At the top of the next climb there's a choice between bearing left direct to Maiden Newton, or going straight on to Cattistock first. The crossroads at Stagg's Folly has one of the few remaining Dorset signposts with its Grid Reference marked on it—613 007.

Like Cerne Abbas, Maiden Newton is a virtual small town—with even a working railway station—whereas the next village, Wynford Eagle, barely exists. It has, though, one or two attractive cottages; smoke rose lazily from the chimneys to make a soft blue haze in the autumn evening as we passed. There's quite a steep pitch up past the church there, but then you come out onto the open grazing down, for another exhilarating stretch. A plaque at the entrance to Woolcombe Farm proclaims it unexpectedly to be a *source*—the spring from which Eggardon Natural Spring Water flows. Once over the top the road drops along a spur of the hill, while round to the right the rugged ramparts of the Iron Age hill fort on Eggardon Hill dominate the other side of the combe. Ahead the view stretches out to Bridport and Lyme Regis in a magnificent sweep, made all the more dramatic on one of our visits by the golden fire of an October evening.

The road drops sharply to Askerswell, with a quite remarkable junction in the middle at which traffic on every road has apparently to give way to all the others. A short climb brings you to the A35, which you cross in a right-and-left dogleg to enter a fine stretch of unfenced sheep-grazing to bypass the elusive village of Chilcombe, once more with fine views down to the sea.

The next village, Puncknowle (pronounced 'Pun'l') derives its name from 'the plum-tree knoll'. It is a fine grey stone village with two unusual tiled bay windows on one house. Yet another short climb, past the very knoll where the plum trees used to grow, leads to the main ridge route, the B3157. This road climbs in the main gently, although there are one or two steeper pitches, with tremendous views westwards along the coast opening up all the way. On that October evening we spent half an hour here watching the sun set and then the pinks and purples take over the sky as the sea faded to a deep indigo.

Then, as the road reaches the summit, you get your first breathtaking view ahead of one of the wonders of the Dorset coast—Chesil Beach. This immense pebble beach stretches in a smooth curve for some 10 miles (about 15km) as far as the 'Isle' of Portland, impounding behind it a brackish lagoon known as the Fleet. The pebbles are quite closely graded in size, getting larger as you progress eastwards; it is said that experienced local boatmen making a landfall on the Beach in fog can tell their position from the size of the stones.

Above: *Thatch at Wynford Eagle*

Opposite: *Abbotsbury*

From the vantage point on the B3157 at GR 560 860, the ruined fifteenth–century chapel of St Catherine on its knoll above Abbotsbury forms a perfect foreground frame for the blue backdrop of the Beach and Portland.

At the foot of the hill where the B-road turns sharply left, a small dead-end road leads down to the Beach, and you can scramble over its pebbly ridge to the seaward side. Down the same road are the Abbotsbury Sub-tropical Gardens, open from mid-March to mid-October, with a collection of sub-tropical shrubs and plants originating in the late eighteenth century and now covering 20 acres (8ha).

Abbotsbury is an almost too-perfect and homogenous village of warm stone and thatch along a long and straggling main street; we noticed one thatch covered in ferns almost like a Scandinavian turf roof. There are also the ruins of an abbey of similar date to the chapel, with an impressive stone barn. Abbotsbury is famous for its Swannery; in addition to swans many other birds flock to the Fleet lagoon and most of it is a bird sanctuary, with access restricted in the breeding season.

The route follows the narrow road past the abbey barn and the Swannery turning and, as it climbs, views open up over the Fleet and Chesil Beach. Then, almost as though it were deliberately turning its back on the sea, the landscape abruptly changes into rolling and very green grazing country. After Rodden a right-and-left crossing of the B3157 brings you into quaintly-named Cheese Lane to Shilvinghampton and Friar Waddon. There is a sudden unexpected patch with almost white stone walls here, and a glowingly-red brick Victorian water pumping station.

At the junction with the B3159 the most pleasant way back into Dorchester is to turn left over the hill and then right under the southern ramparts of Maiden Castle by Winterborne Monkton to the main Weymouth road, A354. If you want to avoid the 1½ miles (2km) or so of main road, or if you want to avoid Dorchester altogether, a right turn after a short distance brings you rapidly back to the picturesque village of Winterborne Herringston.

EDEN VALLEY

• WEEKEND ROUTE •

The valley of the River Eden lies wedged between the blue peaks of the Lake District to the west and the high grim line of the Pennine fells to the east. Yet, and despite its wild surroundings and its being the setting for the northernmost of the 'weekend' routes, the valley itself is a delightful fertile enclave of green fields and quite soft rolling hills. Neither is this the hilliest of the routes: for the most part I would judge it to be in easier country than the southernmost, Dorset.

Like Rutland, Westmorland—which used to encompass most of the Eden valley—was one of the small counties which theoretically disappeared in the revision of boundaries in the 1970s. Memories die hard here, too, and the old county town stubbornly remains Appleby-in-Westmorland, even though officialdom believes it to be in Cumbria.

The character of the countryside is quite definitely northern. The solid, handsome, stone, farm buildings are obviously designed to withstand storms and hard winters. The small towns and villages huddle together tightly and nestle in the shelter of little valleys or low hills. The luminous green mossiness of the stone walls where they are shaded bears witness to the higher rainfall; those who live here, though, are at pains to point out that this means, not more rainy days, but heavier rain when it falls. To the north and east of the Eden, close under the Pennines, are the lush grazing meadows of the cattle which have made the Eden valley famous for its dairy products. The cattle markets in the small towns are some of the busiest in the country, each with its traditional day of the week. The rather higher and more open limestone country to the west is very much sheep country: it was in the nearby village of Crosby Garrett that we saw a car sticker exhorting us to 'wear British wool—34 million sheep can't be wrong'.

There are only two towns of any size on the route, Penrith and Appleby, and either could serve as a starting point—as could Kirkby Stephen, which is only some 5 miles (8km) to the east of the route. Interestingly the names of these three towns give clues to some of the history of the area. The original language was a Celtic one, related to Welsh, Breton and Cornish: Penrith is a Celtic name meaning 'the head [or main] ford'. However, as in Lincolnshire, there was a great deal of Scandinavian activity hereabouts—this time Norse—and the Scandinavian '-by' endings of Appleby, Kirkby Stephen and a couple of dozen smaller villages remain as evidence.

Although the introduction of the book explains why none of the routes is wholly within the Lake District, it would be a pity to miss the lakes altogether and so a western loop takes in the fringe of Ullswater, with a fine moorland crossing as a bonus. To the east, there is the possibility of an out-and-home and very strenuous detour up the highest surfaced road in Britain, up to the 847-metre summit of Great Dun Fell.

• THE ROUTE •

Appleby-in-Westmorland lies strategically placed in a bend of the River Eden, with its twelfth–century castle high on a ridge dominating the western half of the town. The high street, flanked by the pink sandstone houses and shops which are characteristic of the district, slopes down quite steeply to the narrow bridge over the dark river, here flowing quite slowly and opening out below the bridge to reflect a fine avenue of

Overleaf: On Barton Fell Common, looking towards the head of Ullswater

sycamores. Appleby has quite a sprinkling of shops, accommodation and eating places; make the most of them because facilities are quite sparse in some of the small villages to come. To the east of the river lies the main residential part of the town and the railway station, on the periodically-threatened Settle to Carlisle line.

Fortunately the main A66, the trans-Pennine trunk road that links eastern England with Glasgow, now bypasses Appleby, following the natural boundary of the town. The way out of the town passes under first the railway and then the bypass in a series of left-and-right manoeuvres, following the signposts for Hilton. The winding road climbs beside the Hilton Beck and its small oakwood, and within 3 miles (5km)—on the outskirts of Hilton—you are already in hill country, with the great mass of the Pennines straight ahead. The route turns left to wind along the foot of the fells between often quite high sandstone walls through a succession of small villages, Murton, Keisley, Dufton and Knock. The villages seem to have a pattern: rather square-set, the pinkish sandstone or sometimes whitewashed houses often surround a small green—or indeed quite a large one in the case of Dufton.

It is from the green at Dufton that you get the first glimpse of the radio station on the Pennine ridge that marks the summit of the highest surfaced road in the British Isles. If you want to follow this extremely strenuous detour to the top of Great Dun Fell, you leave the valley road by turning right just short of Silverband at GR 676 274. It must be emphasized that this is a *very* hard climb: the pleasure of this detour lies largely in the achievement, although it also shows splendidly the stern and austere grandeur of the high Pennines. The thrill is one of the sheer scale. The road climbs some 645m, over 2100ft, in rather under 5 miles (8km): this means that the gradient *averages* nearly 9%, 1 in 11. In fact it rises in a series of steps, so that the steepest pitches are appreciably steeper. The weather at the top can be much harsher than that in the valley; on the October day that we first climbed it, the top 200m or so were snow-covered with swirling cloud while it was a fine, if brisk, sunlit afternoon in the valley. The official status of most of the road is that of a bridleway, while the last ¾ mile (1km) and 90m of climb is on the Civil Aviation Authority's private road.

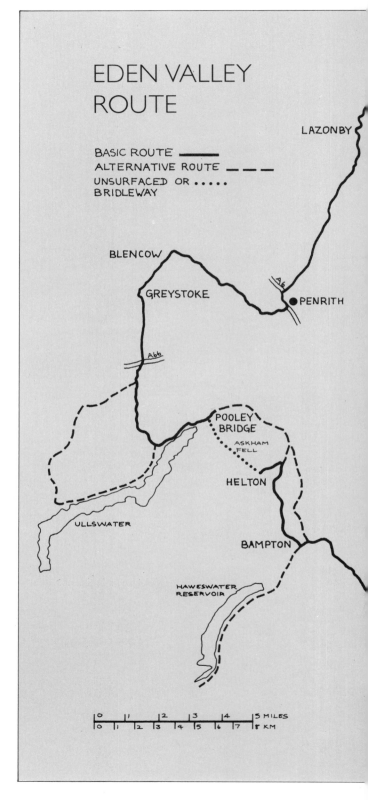

EDEN VALLEY ROUTE

BASIC ROUTE ⎯⎯⎯
ALTERNATIVE ROUTE ⎯ ⎯ ⎯
UNSURFACED OR • • • • •
BRIDLEWAY

LAZONBY

BLENCOW

GREYSTOKE

PENRITH

A66

POOLEY BRIDGE

ASKHAM FELL

HELTON

ULLSWATER

BAMPTON

HAWESWATER RESERVOIR

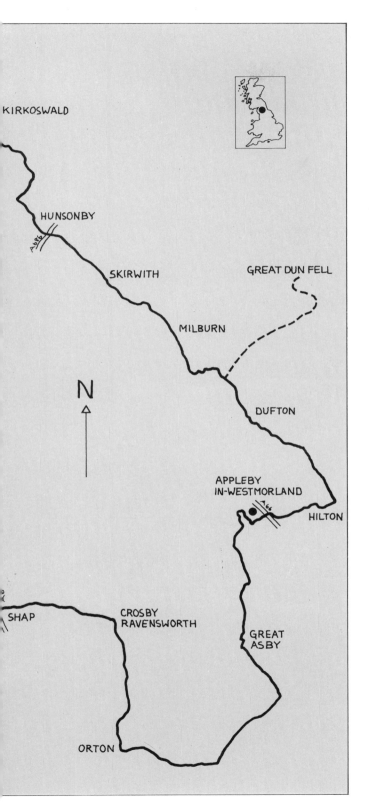

There is a nature reserve over the middle part of the climb; the best views across the Eden valley towards the Lakeland hills are from here or perhaps from a little higher up. The actual summit is rather far back on the plateau for a good view of the nearer parts of the valley. Allow plenty of time: it took us around an hour to get to the top— and about ten minutes to come down.

The main route continues, in more open country, between hedges rather than walls for the most part, through Milburn, Blencarn and Skirwith to Winskill and Hunsonby. The 'Hanging Walls of Mark Anthony' marked on the map about a mile (1½km) north-east of Blencarn, are said to owe their bizarre name to the inventiveness of a villager who was tiring of the persistent questioning of an early mapmaker. They are in fact old cultivation terraces. Along the road between Skirwith and Winskill we briefly chased a pheasant as it pattered along the road, until, still apparently unaware of the possibilities of flight, it scrambled through the hedge to safety. Equally inconsequentially, we noted with surprise that there is an ice-cream manufacturer in Hunsonby.

Beyond Hunsonby a short detour leads to the Bronze Age stone circle of Long Meg and her Daughters. At the crossroads at GR 573 367 you go straight ahead on the white road, then right after some 200yd (200m), past the entrance to Marian Lodge. Long Meg is a tall angular monolith, while the circle of the Daughters, 110yd (100m) or so across and made up of larger stones, lies a short distance away. In the centre of the circle a melancholy weeping tree sets off the sombre grey of the stones.

The next village, Glassonby, is an attractive grouping of houses, round the usual small green, a tranquil place where an elderly inhabitant was unhurriedly clearing the autumn leaves from the vividly lush grass. For a very brief spell, from GR 562 400 to 552 400, you leave the confines of the Penrith map to drop into Kirkoswald, with the unusual tower of St Oswald's church high on its knoll. The route turns left on the B6413 to bring you back to Lazonby over a handsome, arched bridge crossing the River Eden. There's an attractive picnic spot and small park just over the bridge.

Overleaf: *Burtree and the Pennine fells from above Little Asby*

In Lazonby you turn left on the B6412 immediately after the railway bridge up quite a sharp pitch. The height you quickly gain opens up the view to the east, across to the Pennine heights of Cross Fell and Great Dun Fell. There's a choice of routes around or through Great Salkeld and Salkeld Dykes to the crossroads marked '148' (m above sea level) at GR 540 365. The battlemented church tower of Great Salkeld, fortified to protect the populace when marauders passed through, is evidence of the troubled past of the region. Once you are over the top of the ridge above Penrith the blue Lakeland hills flanking Ullswater take over the skyline. Then it's a fine swoop down past the golf course into Penrith.

Penrith is one of the sandstone towns, its buildings owing much to the eighteenth century. As a local centre it is well-stocked with shops and accommodation and, while it still has some traffic problems, they have been much alleviated by the building of the M6 to bypass the town. One souvenir of the former traversing of the town by heavy traffic is a quite intricate one–way street system which can be confusing.

If you have chosen Penrith as the starting point for your trip, the route out of the town, initially by the B5288 passes conveniently close by the railway station. Just after crossing over the M6 you turn right on the road signposted to Newton Reigny and Newton Rigg. In Newton Reigny the route forks left on the road signposted to Laithes which runs along the little valley of the River Petteril. As you turn left after Laithes, towards Blencow and Greystoke, the Lakeland hills are once more in your sights, appealingly blue and misty. Just after Little Blencow the ruined fortified manor of Blencow Hall is a prominent landmark.

In Greystoke the route goes straight on, joining the B5288 again briefly, leaving it once more by a left fork a short way out of the village. This fine narrow road climbs steadily, flanked by fields that seemed incredibly green on the day that we passed. The road crosses the A66 trunk road—fortunately at a point where you can tackle one carriageway of the crossing at a time—and then opens out to a superb view above Hutton John, backed by the hills of Martindale and Bampton Commons culminating in the peaks of High Street and Helvellyn.

There's quite a steep drop through Hutton John

to the Dacre Beck, and then the road rises and falls gently until the last downhill swoop past Wreay brings you to the main road, the A592, above Ullswater. It is possible as an alternative to take the right fork directly after the Dacre Beck at Sparket Mill and then go through Thackwaite into Matterdale. This involves an extra 10 miles, say 15km, of which perhaps two-thirds is by main road. Out of season, certainly, these particular roads are not heavily trafficked and the lakeside run is a very pleasant one. This detour also gives the chance of a visit to the waterfall of Aira Force, about 200yd (200m) from the road at GR 400 205. In either case, follow the A592, then the B5320 into the well-appointed little village of Pooley Bridge.

From Pooley Bridge there is another choice of route through to Bampton and thence to Shap. Much to be recommended if the weather is good and you have time is the bridleway track over Askham Fell and Barton Fell Common. The track is well-surfaced and quite well drained so that it is intrinsically ridable all the way, although the initial climb above the Elder Beck is quite steep. To get to the track, you take the right fork by the church in Pooley Bridge, signposted 'Howtown 3½, Martindale 4½'. At the next crossroads, marked by a signpost marked with a crown, go straight on on the road marked 'No through road'. This continues, climbing, as a surfaced road up as far as Roehead Farm; here you go through the gate marked as 'Public bridleway to Helton over Barton Fell Common' and up the gravel track over the shoulder of the hill. At the top the bridleway flattens out into a broad grassy track, marked from time to time by small cairns and occasional discreet National Park signposts. There are superb views to the right up Ullswater to Helvellyn. After a short distance along the flattish part of the track, near GR 486 226, a tremendous view opens up quite suddenly to the left, right across the Eden Valley to the Pennines; on the afternoon that we crossed, the distant hills hung blue and delicate in the autumn haze. There is an indication that you are approaching the surfaced road when you see a large and isolated standing stone to the left of the track. On the map it's marked as the Cop Stone, at GR 496 217. From here it is gently downhill for 200–300yd (200–300m) to the surfaced road. You can either turn left into Helton along the road, or continue on the bridleway which drops quite sharply to join the Helton to Bampton road about ¾ mile (1km) south of Helton. The road enters Helton by the village green, which has a superb sycamore tree, brilliantly yellow on our autumn visit, after which you turn sharp right towards the Bampton road. There is, incidentally, a pub on the lower road which skirts the foot of the village—the Helton bypass, as it were. If you've found it thirsty work over the fell it could be welcome.

The road alternative from Pooley Bridge involves following the B5320 towards Penrith for nearly a mile (rather over 1km) and then turning right into a very narrow road signposted 'Celleron and Askham'. Once more the first climb is quite a pull, up to Celleron—which is far less prominent on the ground than on the map—and then there is quite a bit of downhill to Askham. Shortly after Askham there is another choice: right to Helton or fork left by Whale and Low Knipe. Both roads are quite up-and-down, and both lead to Bampton Grange and the bridge over the River Lowther. It is also possible from Bampton to make an out-and-home excursion up to Haweswater, a round trip adding some 12 miles, say 20km, if you go right to the head of the lake. From Bampton Grange it's a steady pull up to the ridge and then a fine run along the ridge, ending in a fine drop into Shap, between beautifully-maintained stone walls.

In Shap village, turn right onto the A6 for a short stretch, and leave it to the left up a road signposted 'Crosby Ravensworth' which starts off with quite a sharp little climb. Once again when you get to the top there are fine views across to the Pennines. There is a quite steep drop into Crosby Ravensworth, where you turn right to cross the Lyvennet Beck. The climb up from the beck is quite a steady one up a walled but attractively tree-lined road to Gilts, where you come out into open country. From the summit, at the junction with the B6280 where you turn right, there's a

superb, wide and beautifully surfaced descent into Orton—one of those downhill swoops to be relished.

Orton is a rather open village, with houses set around a large water-meadow in the middle. Turn left at the south end of the village on the B6261, continuing straight on where the B-road goes right, to Raisbeck. Turn left just after Raisbeck, through a delightful short stretch of dwarf oaks and then out onto the open moor. This is sheep country—although we did see a herd of domesticated deer grazing at Holme House Farm. From here for 2 or 3 miles (4 to 5km) the road is one which has been for me, ever since I first travelled it many years ago, the epitome of the open road. Gently rising, and leaving Sunbiggin Tarn to the right, you can see the little road ahead winding away over the moor. Towards the end of the unfenced road there is a short stretch of limestone pavement—where horizontal limestone outcrops at the surface as flat-topped smooth rock with deep water-worn fissures.

At Whygill Head the route turns left to Great Asby, a rolling road between large grazing meadows, separated by stone walls. Here there are views again, this time of some of the Pennine fells further south above Brough. As we dropped into Great Asby, on an almost dead calm day, little plumes of smoke rose straight upwards from the chimneys of the trim cottages. About 1½ miles (some 2km) after Great Asby a tiny road signposted 'Rutter Falls' turns off to the left. The falls are marked Rutter Force on the map: 'force', which we also encountered in Aira Force, is the old Norse (and modern Scandinavian) word *foss*—a waterfall. Considering the small size of the stream—the Hoff Beck—the falls are quite impressive. For the hungry or thirsty cyclist there is also a small cafe across the footbridge—or through the ford—over the beck. From here it is a quite gentle 3 miles (5km) back into Appleby.

• INFORMATION •

Starting point

As described the route starts and finishes at Appleby-in-Westmorland; another convenient point would be Penrith. It would also be possible to start from Kirkby Stephen, joining the route at Whygill Head.

Access

Rail routes are Appleby from Carlisle and Leeds and Penrith from Carlisle or Lancaster. Some cycle restrictions possible. Main access roads are the A66 to Appleby and the A6/M6 to Penrith.

Accommodation

There are B&B and hotel possibilities in Appleby-in-Westmorland, Blencarn, Crosby Garrett (highly recommended), Crosby Ravensworth, Dacre (nr Hutton John), Dufton, Gaisgill (nr Orton), Helton, Kirkby Stephen, Lazonby, Orton, Penrith, Pooley Bridge, Shap and Tirril (nr Celleron). There are campsites at Greystoke, Ormside (nr Great Asby), Ousby (nr Skirwith), Penrith, Penruddock (nr Hutton John), Pooley Bridge (several in locality), Stainton and Watermillock (nr Wreay). There are youth hostels in Kirkby Stephen, Dufton and Tebay (nr Orton). If you need to consult directories or listings, check under Cumbria.

Tourist information offices

Appleby-in-Westmorland, Kirkby Stephen, Penrith, Pooley Bridge.

Cycle shops

There are cycle shops in Penrith and Kirkby Stephen. Cycle hire is also available from Harpers Cycles in Penrith.

Maps

The whole route is on os 1:50 000 sheets 90 and 91. Basic route distance is about 85 miles (140km).

Rutter Force

HEREFORDSHIRE AND SHROPSHIRE

• WEEKEND ROUTE •

The Welsh border counties of Hereford-shire and Shropshire offer some of the finest cycling in England. Many travelled cycle-tourists would rate these two counties as embracing the most attractive 'lowland' scenery in the country—and I would agree with them. Not that every bit of the route is as low as all that: the highest point, at the westernmost extremity of the route on the ridge road which runs along the boundary with Wales, is within a shade of 400 metres above sea level. For all that, the hills are wholly hills in shape and nature, not mountains, and there is a pleasing roundness to the contours. Except for that border ridge, the route lies wholly within England, yet as soon as you move west of Leominster you begin to hear traces of Welsh intonation in local speech.

This route, like the others, takes in a range of landscape. To the east and south the rolling hills and fertile valleys of Herefordshire embrace hopfields and lush grazing for the world-renowned Hereford cattle. To the north the high-er and often forested hills are separated by deep valleys. It is one of the areas of Britain which most resembles parts of continental Europe—the *bocage* country of Normandy, or perhaps the Vosges, the Black Forest and Schwäbische Alp on a smal-ler scale. These are the 'coloured counties' about which A. E. Housman's Shropshire Lad romanced. Although it is doubtful that Housman was a fre-quent visitor to the county, his title describes exactly the superb patchwork of small multi-coloured fields seen from a vantage point such as Clee Hill around harvest time.

This, too, is the region of black-and-white tim-bered villages, with Weobley and Pembridge in Herefordshire almost *too* picturesque. The towns on the route—Ludlow and Leominster—also have fine ranges of timbered buildings. It is perhaps the near perfection of placing of the towns and villages in their settings, and the har-mony of materials and style, that makes Hereford-shire and Shropshire so pleasing to the eye.

What makes the counties so pleasing to the cyclist, too, are the small winding lanes and the unexpected vistas that they continually present. The rolling countryside certainly rolls: this area, like the Cotswolds not too far away, is *not* to be hurried. There are some quite steep hills but also some fine upland runs along ridges and one or two spectacular downhill swoops.

Either Ludlow or Leominster make a suitable starting point for the route; both can be reached by rail, as can Hereford, about 10 miles (some 15km) to the south-east of the route. We chose Leominster as our starting point, partly because it was convenient, but not a little to save the joy of Ludlow until later.

• THE ROUTE •

Leominster is a fine bustling town, very much the everyday shopping and commercial centre for its surroundings, despite the presence of the much larger city of Hereford not far away. The well-proportioned main street is a riot of black-and-white timber-framed buildings, culminating in the Old Town Hall. Leominster's fortunes were founded on English wool but today cattle share pride of place in the agricultural markets of Here-fordshire and Shropshire. The town sits between the River Lugg and its tributary, the Arrow. Both rivers have names of Celtic origin: Lugg is said to derive from the same root as the Welsh *llug*—'light, shining', and Arrow from *arian*—'silver'. Together with the River Teme, above which Ludlow stands, these rivers shape and embellish the countryside through which the route passes.

Leominster should be bypassed by the busy A49, the spinal route that follows the Welsh border from the towns of Lancashire to south Wales, by the time this book is published. However, as a result of being for years traversed by this route and the A44, the town has an inescapable one-way street system. The route leaves this system to the west, almost by centrifugal force as it were, turning left just after a closed cinema into Rylands Road, signposted 'Ivington'.

After half a mile (say a kilometre) or so of housing you are suddenly in open grazing country, dropping gently to the first meeting with the River Arrow. Almost immediately you are aware of one of Herefordshire's characteristics: the rich red soil, deriving from the Old Red Sandstone beneath. From time to time harder facies, or varieties of rock type, of the sandstone form resistant hills and it is up to the flanks of one of them that the road now climbs to Upper Hill. It's not a terribly stiff climb but the road does twist and turn below the wooded slopes. Rather incongruously, as you turn a bend near Upper Hill, you are confronted by an aeroplane in front of a small engineering works.

The route crosses the old Roman road from Leintwardine ('*Branogenium*') to Hereford, now the A4110, by a left and right dogleg at the Bush Inn to turn towards King's Pyon and Weobley. The name Pyon comes apparently from the Old English *peona eg*—'gnat island'. Maybe it was too early in the season, but we passed through unscathed. King's Pyon belonged to Edward the Confessor and the nearby Canon Pyon to the cathedral of Hereford. King's Pyon has an oast house and an odd little timbered dovecote or miniature granary.

Weobley (which is pronounced 'Webbley') is *the* black-and-white village. Coming in from this direction breaks you in gently as you approach a fine timbered inn at the end of the street. Then, as you go left and right, you come on the superb centre where two rows of timbered houses either side of the broad 'square' converge on the focus of the overhanging Red Lion, framing the church spire behind. There is more black and white and cream and white down the other short streets. (If you wish to start your ride from Hereford, the road out past the racecourse, and then by Tillingdon and Wormsley Hill to Weobley is one of the most pleasant ways of joining the route.)

The route out of Weobley is by the B4230 to the north-west to join, briefly, the A4112. Here you turn left for about ¼ mile (some 400m) and then right and right again on the Pembridge road. There is a little climb up to the corner of a wood at GR 384 525; here it's worth turning round to look at the view. The magnificent line of the ridge of the Black Mountains dominates the far horizon, culminating in the sharp northern scarp—particularly striking at sunset or when early or late snow on the ridge contrasts with the colours of the lowlands.

The twisting little road leads eventually to Luntley where a signpost directs attention to a cider mill—with sampling—just on the outskirts of Lower Barewood. Don't be disheartened at your slow progress from the sign which claims the mill to be ¼ mile away—it's over three times as far! Pembridge, when you reach it, is another black-and-white village, with the little grouping opposite the church especially fine. The church has an oddity—a separate timber and wood-shingled belfry in the churchyard, some distance from the church itself.

The turning off the A44 almost opposite the church leads down to the River Arrow and its watermeadows, and a left turn soon after follows the river to Staunton–on-Arrow. Staunton's little church is very prominent on its knoll as you approach from the crossroads. Just beyond the village the route turns right for Byton along a charming but quite up-and-down little lane between incredibly green fields. It comes almost as a shock to realize at the crossroads at Byton Hand that Wales is now actually quite close, since the signpost here marks Presteigne as only 4 miles (about 6km) away; the border is in fact only about half as far as this.

The character of the countryside is changing too. The hills are becoming more dramatic, while denser, often coniferous, woodland is beginning

Overleaf: *Ludlow, seen from the west*

HEREFORDSHIRE AND SHROPSHIRE ROUTE

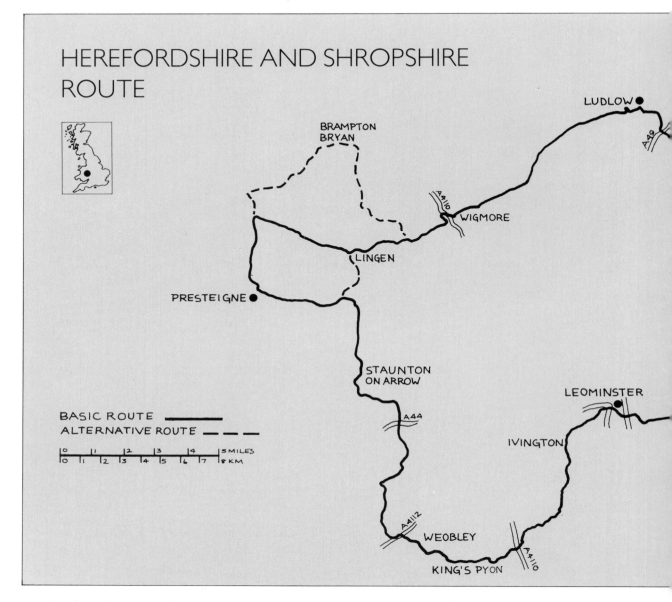

BASIC ROUTE ——————

ALTERNATIVE ROUTE — — —

to take over their tops. The geology becomes much more complex: Shropshire has exposed outcrops of some of the oldest rocks in Britain. After Byton village a short but sharp climb precedes a very pretty wooded descent to the bridge over the River Lugg and an almost alpine meadow in a clearing in the trees beside the river.

From the next junction, at GR 382 647, there is a choice of route. You can turn right to go, more or less directly on a quite switchback road, to Lingen. Or, for a glimpse of Wales, you can turn left to

follow, broadly, the valley of the River Lugg to the outskirts of Presteigne. Here, at GR 318 652, a right turn, shortly followed by a left, brings you to the foot (GR 313 658) of the long climb up to the ridge that separates England from Wales. The climb averages about 10%, 1-in-10, and takes you up close to the 400-metre mark. It begins as a hollow lane, between high banks, with an interlude at Stocken Farm with an unexpected display of bullrushes. We welcomed the rest as we watched a minute shrew run across the road, its tiny feet no more than a mist beneath it as it made for the

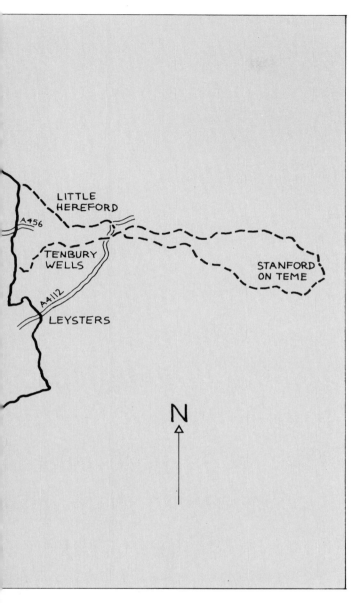

ridge road for another mile (or 1½km), turning right at the junction marked '377' (m above sea level) past Long Wood and down to Brampton Bryan. There are tantalizing glimpses of the Teme valley through the wood to begin with, and then a fine view ahead up the Clun valley to the great ridge of the Long Mynd. The easier route to Wigmore follows the quite quiet A4113, the B4530, and a short stretch of the A4110. There are a variety of less easy routes over the ridge.

Meanwhile, the direct route has reached Lingen. The village boasts a pub, the first for some while, and a small shop. It's quite a stiff pull out of the village, up to the crossroads marked as Cross of the Tree, followed by a drop through suburban-sounding Ongar Street. Here the road climbs through quite a dense stretch of forest—there's quite a steep bit at the top—and then a fine, if narrow, drop into Wigmore. Wigmore, too, is quite well provided with welcome places to eat.

By contrast with the last few miles, the route out of Wigmore—turning right at the top end of the high street past the Compasses—is quite gentle for a spell, through Leinthall Starkes and Elton. At the next hamlet, Aston, there is quite a remarkable minute Norman church: we'd have missed it but for following the route for a spell in the opposite direction and seeing the characteristic north doorway above us on the bank. What is unusual is the repetitive pattern of stylized brownish-red flowers painted as a wall decoration. They look Art Deco but are in fact Norman; they were uncovered during restoration in 1879 and restored then, together with a frieze of foliage which runs above them.

Very shortly you are in wooded country again, climbing steadily up to Bringewood Chase. Here, just before the summit, we surprised deer browsing, almost submerged in the sea of bracken on the high bank beside the road. From the top there is a superb downhill run, gently winding and beautifully surfaced. Then, just after the end of the wood, you come quite suddenly on a small common, with the classic view of Ludlow—castle, church and town, hanging beneath the backdrop of Titterstone Clee. It's a view that never fails to please, always different with the moods of the weather, the light and the season.

Although the road straight ahead also leads

distant bank. Once on the top, you are on the roof of the world, your left foot in Wales, your right in England. Ahead lies range upon range of the Shropshire hills, while to the left the view stretches from the Brecon Beacons in the south to the great dome of Radnor Forest in the west, and beyond to bluer and bluer less distinct hills.

There's quite a choice of ways down from the ridge, all eventually converging on Wigmore (GR 413 690). You can turn right, just before the highest point of the ridge, to drop straight to Lingen and rejoin the direct route. Or you can follow the

• INFORMATION •

Starting point
As described the route starts and finishes in Leominster; another convenient point would be Ludlow. It would also be possible to start from Hereford, joining the route at Weobley.

Access
Rail routes are to Leominster, Hereford and Ludlow from Newport and Shrewsbury, and to Hereford from London (Paddington), Oxford and Worcester. Main access roads are the A44 to Leominster and the A49 to Ludlow, Leominster and Hereford.

Accommodation
B&B and hotel accommodation is plentiful; possibilities we noticed include Brimfield (nr Little Hereford), Bringewood Chase, Bush Bank, Leominster, Little Hereford, Ludlow, Pembridge, Tenbury Wells, Weobley and Wigmore. There are campsites at Bush Bank, Leominster, Ludlow, Shobdon (nr Staunton on Arrow), Wigmore and Woonton (nr Weobley). The only youth hostel on or near the route is in Ludlow. If you need to consult directories or listings, check under Shropshire and Hereford and Worcester. Presteigne is in Powys.

Tourist information offices
Leominster and Ludlow.

Cycle shops
There is a cycle shop in Leominster and spares are available at Ludford Bridge Service Stn (near youth hostel) in Ludlow.

Maps
The basic route is on OS 1:50 00 sheets 137 and 149; the Teme valley detour east of Tenbury Wells calls for sheet 138 as well. Basic route distance is about 60 miles (100km).

The coloured counties: Shropshire meadows seen from Clee Hill

into the town, the most dramatic entry is to turn left, almost doubling back, down the little road that drops sharply to the bridge over the River Teme. Be careful—there is a hairpin bend part way down at a road junction! At the bridge, the walls of the castle look high above, while a little climb brings you up to the town centre. Ludlow is a planned town, built in a bend of the River Teme, with three parallel south-facing roads dropping to the river, and a network of level crossroads linking them. The castle, the church and a few of the official buildings are in pink sandstone, but it is the volume of elaborate timberwork and superb black-and-white buildings that is the most striking. Historic and exceptionally beautiful, Ludlow well merits a few hours' exploration, particularly at a quiet time.

Like Leominster, Ludlow used to have the A49 running through it, so it too retains vestiges of the one-way system that made necessary. To get onto the right road, starting for convenience from the castle and the top of the town, go down Mill Lane. After about 200yd (or 200m), just after the Blue Boar on the right, a rather insignificant little road sign 'A49 Leominster and Shrewsbury' and a large arrow on the road direct you left into what is almost an alleyway, Bell Lane. At the crossroads at the end, turn right down Broad Street under the arch of Broad Gate, one of the old entrances to the town. At the bottom turn left at the traffic lights just before the bridge, and after another 200yd (200m) or so turn right into a road that leads along the river bank and is signposted 'Kidderminster'. Like the previous one, this road too tries to sweep you round to the left, but you turn right into a very small road that continues along the river and is called, logically, 'Temeside'. This road leads you under the railway and over the bypass and then climbs to the top of Tinkers Hill. From here, and at intervals along the road, there are glimpses away to the left of the profile of Clee Hill. On the summer weekends when we explored these lanes, the hedges were adorned with great banks of honeysuckle and in places were crimson with foxgloves.

At the crossroads at GR 548 707 there is a choice of route: you can turn right, signposted 'Little Hereford', down into the Teme valley, or you can go straight on, as also signposted, to Tenbury Wells. Tenbury is another black-and-white town

and well worth a visit if you have time. It is also the gateway to a delightful stretch of the Teme valley, where an admittedly quite strenuous detour leads through a fertile red soil countryside of hop yards and orchards. In spring this is a snowy riot of blossom and young green leaf. *All* the roads in the Teme valley resemble switchbacks, but this is a particularly rewarding one as it winds through the vineyard-like orchards and past the rows of cool green hop bines. The detour needs another map—the Kidderminster sheet—from which you will see that you can make it as long as you like, although either Stanford-on-Teme or Ham Bridge, on the B4204 between Martley and Clifton-on-Teme, would seem to be natural turning points, with a variety of none too long or strenuous return routes to Tenbury. You can also make the detour almost as short as you like by turning back to Lower Rochford.

The direct route drops through orchards to the bridge over the River Teme, on a short stretch of the A456. Just after the bridge the route goes left and embarks on a fairly steady climb up a delightful little lane, with a few downhill respites as it crosses streams, to the crossroads at Leysters Pole. Almost immediately after the crossroads you turn right down what looks suspiciously like a private drive, with weathered and lichen-covered gateposts. Here there is a magnificent chestnut avenue, glowing green and luminous on the June morning that we passed through. It's a very quiet little road—a fox crossed silently in front of us at one point—with, to the right, open views to the Shropshire hills that the route crosses before Ludlow. There are a couple of farm gates, and then the road twists, drops and climbs for a while through fields of deep red earth past Whyle to Brockmanton. A right turn brings you past the unexpected black-and-white timber and plaster of Manor Farm, tucked tightly into a bend of the road on quite a steep little drop. There's an equally steep pitch up from the stream, with the reward at the top of a tremendous view over Leominster out to the hills to the west. The road winds and drops again to the stream at Tick Bridge, where we passed some lazy minutes watching some brightly-coloured and busy dragonflies dart to and fro above the water. From here a last little climb brings you to the A44 and the final downhill mile or so into Leominster.

LINCOLNSHIRE WOLDS

• WEEKEND ROUTE •

Lincolnshire, even after losing a large chunk to Humberside in the 1970s, is one of the largest counties in England. But it is one that is remarkably little visited—even taking into account seaside resorts like Skegness, the archetypal holiday camp, and Mablethorpe. At one time these were *the* seaside holiday places for East Midlanders; now the lone railway line to Skegness describes bizarre meanders as it follows a route cobbled together from the remnants of several deleted lines. Lincolnshire is traditionally divided into three Parts: Holland, the fen country to the south-east; Kesteven, the southwestern part; and Lindsey, the northern half from Lincoln up—which is the area in which the route lies.

As the name Holland would suggest, it has long been a county influenced by its neighbours across the North Sea. Long before Dutch engineers such as Vermuyden began the drainage of the Fens and the Humber marshes, the Danes had left their characteristic names scattered across the Danelaw which they occupied. The numerous villages ending in '-by' and the outlying hamlets or 'thorp(e)s', all attest to the Danish influence. Nowadays the old Danelaw is one of the most sparsely populated parts of lowland England. Even in high summer, away from the few tourist spots, you will find little traffic. On the bank holiday weekend when we explored the route there were places where perhaps half an hour passed without meeting anyone else on the road.

The Wolds, which form the upland part of the route, are relatively low flattish-topped rounded hills. The highest spot in Lincolnshire is only 168m above sea level. Once you climb from the wooded stream valleys or up the western scarp from Market Rasen you are in a countryside of soft curves and immense horizons, dominated by the changing mood and pattern of the sky. To a large extent this is corn-growing country with great fields, rolling hedgeless to the horizon, interrupted only by the small woods and copses. Harvest was in full swing when we visited the Wolds, with teams of vivid red combine harvesters cutting swathes through the yellow carpet. Partridges combed the stubble worrying at the stalks for fallen grain.

As you go eastwards the hills gradually peter out, with more woodlands and hedgerows, then these, too, shade into the flatter, drained marshland to the east. The route pays a fleeting visit to the sandy, dune-edged coast with its hardy holidaymakers and trim beach-huts before heading back to the hills. Overall this is one of the gentler itineraries: there are perhaps no more than three or four hills that the Ordnance Survey think worthy of one of their arrows.

• THE ROUTE •

Market Rasen, the starting point for the route, is very much a centre for the surrounding countryside. There is a long high street with a tremendous mixture of building styles and ages. It has much the sort of shops you would expect to find serving a rural and farming-based community—none of the big multiple stores but ironmongers, agricultural engineers, small furnishers, specialists in various types of food. It also possesses a most impressive colonnaded Methodist Church, down towards the station; at the other end of the spiritual scale, Market Rasen has a very well-known racecourse as well.

The route leaves the town by the B1203, James Bridge Street, which turns north off the High Street just east of the railway bridge. After about ½ mile (800m), you fork left on the Walesby road,

Wolds near Burwell

into the attractive mixed woodland of Willingham Forest. Then, suddenly, as you emerge from the forest, there is a tremendous view of the whole western escarpment of the Wolds—softly misty and ethereally beautiful on the August morning that we approached them. The road winds up through the compact stone village of Walesby, and then up a short, somewhat stiffer climb past the second of Walesby's two prominent church towers, set above steep dimpled meadows of incredible greenness.

At the top you have the first experience of the rolling openness of the wolds: you could almost be forgiven for thinking of them as nearly flat, because the view in all directions merely takes in the tops of the gently rounded humpbacks of the hills, a wide horizon beneath an enormous sky. But then a closer look shows the woodlands nestling in the quite steep-sided little valleys, and the near-hidden farms and hamlets. From the ridge road between Walesby and Stainton le Vale you can see north-east as far as the distant blue line of

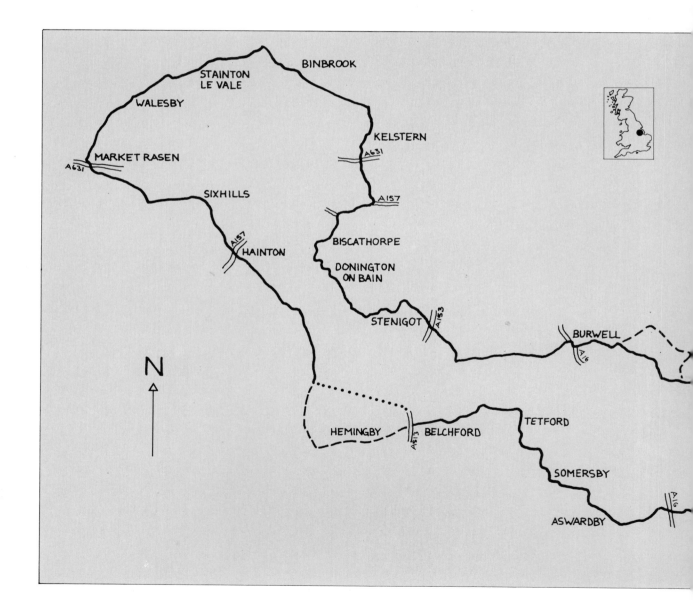

the sea 20 miles (some 30km) away. In fact, at
157m above sea level, a touch over 500ft, this road
passes over the highest point of the whole trip
and offers some quite amazing views.

A narrow lane brings you to the hamlet of Stainton le Vale and then, forking right just after the
church, into an unfenced stretch between rolling
cornfields. The sides of a miniature cutting on the
little hill up towards Binbrook were a sea of blue
harebells as we climbed. Binbrook has continuing Air Force associations, and there is a

roadside memorial to Australian airmen who
served there. It is a spacious little village,
pleasingly set around a small square, suggesting
that it may well have been a modest market town
at some time in the past. The route leaves Binbrook by the Louth road, past the honey-coloured
stone church, and then up the steady climb of
Limber Hill.

This is one of the parts where the roads and
fields are still hedged, and there is a fine impression of the giant patchwork of the fields. At the time
we passed there were the two very different
golds of standing and harvested corn, the green
of grassland and the brown where harvest had
already passed and the plough had taken over.
Just after the water tower at the top you turn right
through the hamlet of Kelstern and then past the
lost village of Calcethorpe, now only a farm and a
couple of cottages. There is a steady climb up to
the A157, where you turn right to swoop down to
the valley.

Just before the bridge at the foot of the hill, turn
left onto a very small road signposted 'Gayton le
Wold and Biscathorpe' which climbs gently over
the shoulder of the hill and then drops to the
gated section across the open grassland at Biscathorpe Park. Here, just before the church,
there are *two* fords, in quick succession—the first
through the brook that comes down from Calcethorpe, the second the River Bain. At the
second ford—one of the utterly inconsequential
things that you notice from a bicycle—there was
a pair of child's shoes with minute yellow socks
tucked in them very neatly parked on the footbridge; we wondered vaguely whether to look
for the body, and then saw the owner paddling a
little way downstream. A trivial observation, but
delightful nevertheless!

From the road beyond Biscathorpe there's a
view down to the left of the little lake—marked
'Fish Pond' on the map—and then a gentle drop
into Donnington-on-Bain. The first impression of
Donnington is of bright orange pantiles, a common feature of the wolds, and of the squat church
tower, only a little higher than the roof. Donnington also boasts the first pub you will have passed
in quite a while—and the last for quite some
distance.

The most pleasant way up from the Bain valley
is to turn left at a little chapel up a road signposted

LINCOLNSHIRE
WOLDS ROUTE

BASIC ROUTE ————
ALTERNATIVE ROUTE — — —
UNSURFACED OR .....
BRIDLEWAY

• INFORMATION •

Starting point
As described the route starts and finishes at Market Rasen. It would also be possible to start from Lincoln, joining the route at Market Rasen, or from Louth, joining at Donnington on Bain or Belleau.

Access
Rail access is to Market Rasen from Nottingham, Newark on Trent and Lincoln or Cleethorpes and Grimsby. Some bicycle restrictions. Main access roads are A46 to Market Rasen or A16 to Louth.

Accommodation
Accommodation is quite sparse; we could find only the following B&B and hotel possibilities, hardly any of them directly on the route: Chapel St Leonards, Claxby (nr Walesby), Hainton, Louth, Scamblesby (nr Belchford), Spilsby (nr Welton le Marsh—well, fairly near), Welton-le-Wold (nr Calcethorpe) and Withcall (about 4 miles (6km) from Donnington on Bain). There are campsites at Chapel St Leonards and Market Rasen, and also at Huttoft (about 3 miles (5km) from Anderby Creek), Ingoldmells (about 3 miles (5km) from Chapel St Leonards) and Middle Rasen (about 3 miles (5km) from Market Rasen). There is one youth hostel which is generally open only on Saturday nights (at other times only if booked in advance), at Woody's Top near Ruckland. If you need to consult directories or listings, check under Lincolnshire.

Tourist information offices
None on the route; the nearest are in Lincoln, Louth, Spilsby and Horncastle.

Cycle shops
There is a cycle shop in Alford, otherwise the only one we can find is in Spilsby. There is cycle hire at Pedalwise in Lincoln, where there are also several bike shops.

Maps
The whole route is on OS 1:50 000 sheets 113 and 122. Total route distance is about 90 miles (145km).

Windmill in motion at Alford

'Raithby 4½, Louth 7' which climbs up past Steni-got House through attractive, and on a hot day more than welcome, mixed woodland. Turn left at the T-junction at the top of the hill, then right at the crossroads. The ridge road here is rather feature-less until you cross the A153. However, the other ridge road past Maidenwell and Farforth, which turns left at GR 297 786 is a delight. As it switches from side to side of the contours you get views to right and left, with especially attractive glimpses of the wooded valley below Ruckland, cool green below the gold of the harvest when we passed. Then as the road comes over the brow of the hill there is one of the most exquisite views in the wolds. The road goes ahead down a gently curved valley with the perfectly-placed tower of Burwell church equally framed by sweeping con-tours and artfully-placed woods.

Burwell, with an unusual octagonal church hall, marks the edge of the high wolds and from here through to Alford it is a country of copses, hedge-rows and meadowland. The road winds and twists in a series of inexplicable bends, a fine example of Chesterton's Rolling English Drunkard's art. To maintain the octagonal theme there is an octagon-al dovecote opposite the church at Belleau; it seems possible that these buildings were in-spired by some of the eight-sided features on nearby cathedrals and great churches.

Alford, the second-largest town on the route, was all a-bustle with a bank holiday fair as we passed through. It, too, is very much a rural and agricultural centre. The most noticeable feature, though, as we approached the town was the working windmill, at the junction of the A1104 and the A1111, GR 457 766. From quite some miles away we could see the glint of the five white majestically-turning sails, high above the roofs of the town. The mill is owned by the Lincolnshire County Council and is at times open to the public.

The route from Alford is by about a mile (1½km) of the A1111 to Bilsby and then on the B1449; it's possible to bypass the main road on a minor road by Bilsby Field—but then that bypas-ses the windmill as well. By now the countryside is absolutely flat, the fertile fields on reclaimed marshland. The route follows the B1449 to the A52, goes left on the main road for just over ¼ mile (some 500m) and then turns right through Anderby to reach the sea at Anderby Creek.

The beach here is a mixture of sand and shin-gle, with the long fingers of the wooden groynes stretching out to the water to hold back the drift of sand. North Sea coast resorts are often euphemis-tically described as 'bracing' and even on this August Bank Holiday afternoon families were sheltering from the breeze behind gaily coloured windbreaks. The dunes here rise to some 10m, so that the road along the old Sea Bank has views inland but none out to sea. The next village down the coast, Chapel St Leonards, has the trappings of a small seaside resort. Neat rows of white beach huts top the dunes and there are candy-floss and trinket stalls—but most welcome to the cyclist are likely to be the numerous eating places.

The way out of Chapel St Leonards is by way of Hogsthorpe, then left and right briefly on the A52, turning off the main road at GR 534 717. The flat road through Sloothby is an attractive marshland route, with mixed fields of grazing for sheep and cattle, and barley or wheat. In Sloothby the route bears left to Welton le Marsh, the last marshland village. The turning by the church, Mill Lane, could be easily missed, but follow it over the slight rise of Candlesby Hill. Here, just as you come over the brow of the hill, you can see the faint pencil of Boston Stump nearly 25 miles (40km) away on the horizon to the south-west.

The landscape changes quite abruptly here to low but undulating wold. The next few villages—Grebby, Skendleby, Langton, Aswardby, Harrington—are all marked by a succession of halls and manor houses, so that you have the impression of continuous rolling parkland, with fine tree-lined roads. Langton is distinguished by an unusual Georgian brick chapel. As the road leaves Harrington it plunges into a green hollow, with a whitewashed thatched cottage, rather un-usual in these parts.

A fine avenue of oaks leads to oddly-named Bag Enderby, where the little church lies in a small square of roads, signposted to the Tenny-son monument. The poet Tennyson was born at the next village, Somersby, where his father was rector of both parishes. He spent his childhood here, and his poem 'The Brook' ('I come from haunts of coot and hern ...') is thought to have been inspired by the nearby River Lymn. In the church at Bag Enderby there is a display by children from a local school identifying places on the stream as they appear in verse.

From Bag Enderby the route turns right just under Tennyson's father's church at Somersby through a winding lane to Tetford—a village with the first pub and small shop for miles. The climb up to the ridge at Tetford Hill is a steep one, meriting an Ordnance Survey arrow, through groves of ashes. The view opens up as you climb to the Bluestone Heath Road, where you turn left. This is one of the old wold ridge roads, said to take its name from 'bluestones' or sarsens: the only flaw seems to be that there aren't any near it. There is an 'official' viewpoint at GR 315 763, with an explanatory panel—and an almost certainly erroneous explanation of the name of the next village, Belchford. The view is certainly a fine one, right across the broad valley to the next ridge of the wolds. As we watched in the warm evening sunshine the combine harvesters, whose hum had been with us all the time we were on the high wolds, made their last sweeps round the giant fields and headed for home.

There is a choice of routes after Belchford once you have reached the A153 at GR 274 753, Foxendale. The road straight on leads through Hemingby to the old road of High Street, where you turn right on the outskirts of Baumber towards Market Stainton. The alternative is to turn right on the A153 for about ½ mile (some 800m) and then to follow the Roman road from GR 272 761 to GR 225 774 at Stoup Farm. It is clearly signposted 'Public Bridleway to Great Sturton 4½ (Roman road)' and begins as a grassy track; from Asterby Grange it is metalled as far as the road at '97' (m above sea level). The next part is a rather more rutted, grassy track, falling gently to the River Bain, here artificially straightened between banks and crossed by a most un-Roman concrete bridge. The memories of this spot are of silence but for peewits wheeling overhead with their thin call, while moorhens scurried away as we peeped over the rim of the river bank. There is a rather poorly-drained stretch for a short distance beyond this—probably inadvisable in wet weather—but it soon climbs away to become a firm-based gravel track. On several stretches there are welcome signs that trees are being planted beside the track, one hopes in some form of penance for having grubbed up the once healthy and abundant hedges.

The next section of the route, past Market Stainton and through Benniworth and South Willingham serves to underline how sparsely populated the old Danelaw is: don't depend on any of these villages, hamlets really, for food or drink. There *is* actually a pub at Hainton; here you briefly join the A157—and then go off the Skegness map, at GR 180 848, rejoining the Grimsby one just under a mile (rather over 1km) later at GR 174 860, still on the same road. Sixhills, at the top of a slight rise is another shopless and publess hamlet. At the next junction, fork left: don't follow the wider road that bears right and is signposted to Market Rasen—that would take you out onto the A631—but go down towards Little London. This is a beautifully surfaced gently downhill run, after which you turn right through the wood, past the golf course and racecourse, down into Market Rasen once more.

PEAK DISTRICT

• WEEKEND ROUTE •

Although the Peak District is still in the Midlands and geographically some way further south than the farmlands of the Lincolnshire Wolds, this route gives a first taste of the grander and sterner landscapes of the north. The reason, once more, is a geological one. Like perhaps half of the routes this one is in limestone country, but gone are the softness of the chalk and the golden stone of the Cotswolds and Rutland. This rock is the hard Mountain or Carboniferous Limestone of an earlier age, interspersed in places with even harder gritstones, at one time used to make the millstones which are now the National Park's symbol. These grits give severe and tumbled landscapes where they outcrop and change the whole feel of the country, almost within yards. In the main they outcrop to the west in the Edges above Buxton and in the magnificent Roaches above Leek.

From the early days of the outdoor movement the area has been a centre for walking: the Ramblers' Association had its origins in agitation to secure access to the Peak District moorlands. Several million people live in the cities surrounding the Peak and so the area became the traditional 'lung' for those who sought in walking the moors and dales a fresh-air escape from the industrial towns. Even the most determined cycletourist has to concede that many of the intimate details of the deep dales as well as the high moorland of the Dark Peak can indeed only be discovered by the walker. As with some of the other routes it is the openness of the upland landscape which appeals together with the sudden glimpses down into the sharp-cut and often wooded dales. Most of the seasonal changes of colour, particularly the brilliant purple of the heather on the western moors at the end of the summer, are also to be found in the high places. This route therefore follows a roughly circular path, much of it along upland ridges, to take in the range of terrain that the southern half of the Peak District National Park embraces.

As the first National Park in Britain, the Peak District has a well-developed system of trails. Three that could interest cyclists are on former railway lines: the High Peak Trail, the Tissington Trail which joins it, and the Manifold Valley. The route gives a chance of sampling the first two, while the Manifold would be a simple detour. As far as possible the route avoids the 'honeypot' areas on which the swarms of visitor bees converge. However, as in Dorset and the Cotswolds, the known attractions become very crowded in the main holiday season and at summer weekends. Even on fine winter weekends such villages as Hartington and dales such as Dovedale and the upper Manifold become quite busy.

Parts of the route are undeniably hilly—low gears and patience are essential. To compensate for the climbs, though, some of the runs along ridges are utterly superb—in particular, the tremendous one along Morridge from Upper Hulme to Waterfall and Waterhouses, which we followed on a memorable golden evening as the towering thunderheads of a passing storm rolled away.

The literal high points of this route are further above sea level than on most of the other 'weekend' routes. This means that the weather begins to show the effects of altitude that you find in mountain country. It can be appreciably colder and windier on the tops than in the valleys. The hills of the Peak District are also the first that cold east and north winds from the Arctic meet. In winter some spots, though spectacular and rewarding, can be quite bleak. In overcast condi-

A wintry view from the Tissington Trail, in the Peak District National Park

tions this is even more true. Adequate clothing is essential then and even in late spring or early autumn gloves and hats can be very useful. The panoramic views and the magnificent shapes and changing colours of the hills make it all more than worth the effort.

• THE ROUTE •

Unlike the other routes, this one has no natural starting point in a town. Buxton—the spa, Leek—once a centre for silk manufacture, and Ashbourne all lie a few miles off the route, and any of them could be a starting point. It seems more likely, though, that you would start from one of the villages with accommodation, such as Hartington, Waterhouses or Ilam. We followed the route round from Ilam, where an excellent small campsite in a copse high above the village brought us, on different occasions, a superb sunset, a brilliant full moon, a bright frosty morning with a dusting of snow on the tops and a soft early autumn dawn. So Ilam—GR 135 508, 4 miles (6km) north-west of Ashbourne—seems as good a place as any to start.

The road leaves Ilam eastwards, first following briefly the River Manifold on its way to join the Dove, below the distinctive pyramid of Thorpe Cloud. The word 'cloud' which you will find in several hill names hereabouts means literally that—a hill; it comes from the same root as the now much more humble 'clod'. The road climbs abruptly from the foot of Dovedale into the open village of Thorpe, and then on to a staggered crossroads by the Dog and Partridge. Here there is a fundamental choice: whether to follow the Tissington Trail or the alternative road route. It's almost a pity to have to choose; the Trail offers gentle gradients and freedom from motor traffic but bypasses the rest of life, the road route takes in attractive villages and more variety, but is undoubtedly a good deal hillier. The routes reunite at Parsley Hay above Hartington.

The Tissington Trail

The Tissington Trail follows the route of the London and North Western Railway's Ashbourne to Buxton line, opened in 1899 and closed in 1967. The Peak National Park authority soon after acquired this line and the High Peak mineral line which joins it just below Parsley Hay, together with the station properties. The trails have been given a smooth ash and gravel surface and are open to walkers, cyclists and riders. The Ashbourne to Thorpe section would of course make a good link from Ashbourne to the route; there are further points of access at Tissington and Alsop-en-le-Dale, which could be reached directly by a fine if tough little hill road direct from Thorpe. There is also an access point to the High Peak Trail at Longcliffe, though it might involve a bit of a haul up an embankment for bicycles.

The trails give, of course, fine traffic-free riding but can be quite crowded with (quite legitimate) strollers, particularly near the access points. The surface is fine in dryish weather, although we found it a little heavy when it had just melted after frost. The trails have the advantages and disadvantages of all ex-railway routes. Although the gradients are shallow they can be quite relentless, and one or two stretches near the top end could be quite dispiriting if the going were at all sticky. In addition, the views of course disappear when the route goes into cuttings: you could, for example, easily miss Tissington if you didn't know it was there. That said, the views from the many embankments are very fine, and in conditions like the brisk February day when we followed it, with a thin tracery of snow beside the stone walls of the fields below, utterly exhilarating.

The alternative road route

From The Dog and Partridge, the Tissington road crosses the A515 to plunge into what looks like a private road but isn't, through a particularly fine avenue of trees. Tissington is a typically compact stone village, but its main fame derives from the ancient Ascension Day 'well-dressing' ceremony which takes place each year, when the village's wells are decorated with numerous tableaux of biblical scenes. The pictures are made up from tens of thousands of flower petals pressed into damp clay and held in a wooden frame. Nearly a couple of dozen other Derbyshire villages have similar traditions, some on different dates. These old and fascinating ceremonies are thought to have pre-Christian origins as propitiation to deities who presided over the water supply, but the precise reasons for their annual occurrence remain unclear.

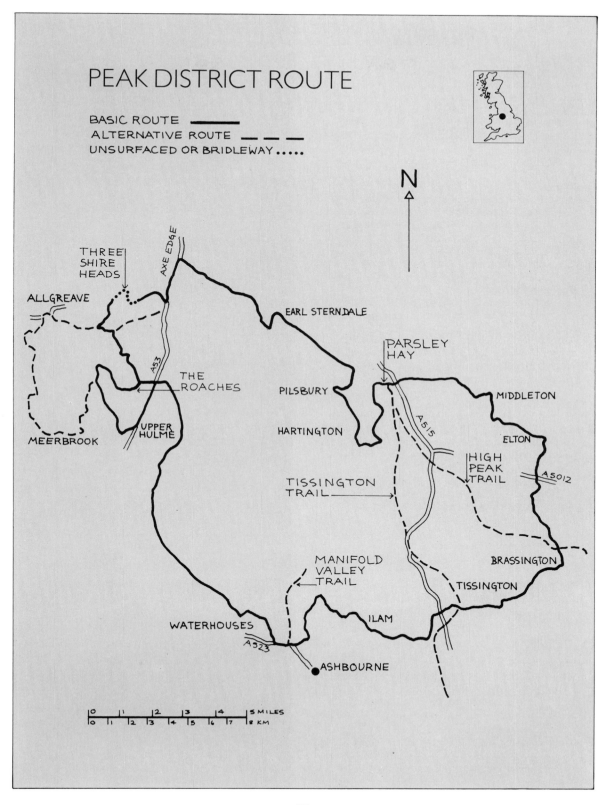

PEAK DISTRICT ROUTE

BASIC ROUTE ——————
ALTERNATIVE ROUTE — — —
UNSURFACED OR BRIDLEWAY .....

N

THREE SHIRE HEADS

AXE EDGE

ALLGREAVE

EARL STERNDALE

PARSLEY HAY

A53

THE ROACHES

PILSBURY

MIDDLETON

A515

UPPER HULME

HARTINGTON

ELTON

MEERBROOK

HIGH PEAK TRAIL

A5012

TISSINGTON TRAIL

MANIFOLD VALLEY TRAIL

BRASSINGTON

TISSINGTON

WATERHOUSES

ILAM

A523

ASHBOURNE

0   1   2   3   4   5 MILES
0   1   2   3   4   5   6   7   8 KM

• INFORMATION •

Starting point
As described the route starts and finishes at Ilam; another convenient point would be Hartington. It would also be possible to start from Ashbourne, joining the route at Tissington by the Tissington Trail; from Matlock, joining at Longcliffe or Elton; from Buxton joining at Axe Edge; or from Leek, joining at Meerbrook or Morridge.

Access
There is no direct rail access to the route: the nearest railheads are Matlock (from Derby) and Buxton (from Manchester (Piccadilly) and Stockport). Possible bicycle restrictions. The main access roads are the A6 to Matlock and Buxton, the A515 to Ashbourne and the A53 to Leek.

Accommodation
B&B and hotel accommodation is plentiful, quite a lot of the smaller B&B places do not appear to be on any listing; among others we noted Ashbourne, Elton, Grindon (nr Waterfall), Hartington, Pethills (on route from Morridge to Waterfall), Thorpe, Waterhouses. There are campsites at Blackshaw Moor (1 mile (1½km) S of Hulme End), Bradnop (1 mile (1½km) on Leek side of Morridge ridge road), Brassington, Fenny Bentley, Hartington, Ilam and Youlgreave, plus a number of farms who will informally accept the odd tent for a night or two. There are youth hostels at Ilam, Youlgreave, Elton, Hartington, Gradbach and Meerbrook. If you need to consult directories or listings, check under Derbyshire and Staffordshire. Some places at the extreme W of the route may have postal addresses in Cheshire.

Tourist information offices
Leek, Ilam, Ashbourne, Hartington and Buxton.

Cycle shops and hire
There are cycle shops in Leek and Ashbourne. Bicycles may be hired in Ashbourne, Parsley Hay and Waterhouses: these are all on the trails following the line of former railways.

Maps
The whole route is on OS 1:50 000 sheets 118 and 119 or on the single 1:63 360 Tourist Peak District sheet—not quite as easy to follow on the road. Basic route distance is about 70 miles (110km).

At Three Shire Heads

There is a second chance to join the Tissington Trail in the village, but the road alternative winds over the hill and then drops precipitately to the B5056 in the valley bottom. Don't drop too eagerly, though: there's quite a deep cobbled ford at the bottom with, fortunately, an alternative footbridge if it appears too deep to negotiate. A left-and-right crossing of the B-road brings you up a steady climb to Bradbourne. From here to Brassington the landscape changes into lusher and more intimate grazing or cultivation. Beyond Brassington, however, the hillsides show the characteristic pockmarked effect that is the legacy of the lead-mining which was carried out round here from Roman times. Nowadays most of the mineral extraction is limestone quarrying, though there are some more specialized minerals to be found: I have memories of being involved with a largely unsuccessful project to extract magnesium metal from the dolomitic rocks a couple of miles (some 3km) east of Brassington.

Beyond Longcliffe once more the country changes to open rolling fields, but fields nevertheless neatly and strictly confined between their stone walls, with the occasional rocky outcrop. The road continues across the Roman-sounding 'Via Gellia', the A5012, whose name derives from Victorian pretentiousness rather than antiquity. From just above the next village, Elton, the view opens out northwards over the quite different eastern part of the Peak. Beyond the tree-filled nearer dales such as Lathkill and Darley Dale, you can see further forests around Chatsworth, and even beyond them the barer hills of the moors above Sheffield and reaching up to the range of the Dark Peak.

Elton, too, is an attractively solid and compact stone village. Here the route goes left to Dale End and then, after quite a stiff little climb where you fork left at an almost unmarked junction, the minute road almost contours, falling very gently, to Middleton. This village—in full Middleton-by-Youlgreave, emphasizes the sign, to avoid confusion with the other one near Wirksworth—has all the signs of an estate village: a not unpleasing uniformity of style and an attractive grouping round a lime tree on the village green by the entrance to the big house. The road climbs quite steeply out of the village to the windy ridge of Long Rake and then, crossing the A515, to Parsley Hay to meet the Tissington Trail.

From Parsley Hay there are two choices; you can either drop into Hartington or, if you want to bypass the village and hang on to some of your height, you can turn right at the T-junction at GR 137 637. The routes meet again at the next crossroads, above Mosey Low. There are also two routes into Hartington, both of them offering tremendous downhill runs into the village, although the right-hand fork climbs rather first. This is definitely limestone wall country, with the stone grey or near-white in places, the greyness frequently relieved at the time that we passed by the bright yellow of the unwelcome ragwort.

Hartington is the largest village actually on the route, and an alternative possible starting point. It is a very popular village in summer, and even on fine weekends in winter, for it is a good centre and has an extensive choice of eating places, shops and accommodation. The route leaves the village by the small square in the centre, up a narrow road signposted to Pilsbury. It is marked as a gated road; in fact it is a *very* gated road, with about half a dozen of them. After an unpromising start through rather an untidy straggle of caravans and the like it turns into a fine, open, unfenced little road, rising and falling on the slope above the tumbling River Dove. Pilsbury proves to be no more than a farm and its outbuildings, followed by a sharp bend and a very steep couple of pitches up the flank of the hill.

From the crossroads at GR 127 647 the ridge road runs into Earl Sterndale, passing an intriguing little gorge up which the road from Crowdecote climbs between High Wheeldon and Aldery Cliff. Earl Sterndale is quite a long village, with welcome seats on the village green. Just past the village, the route turns left down the B5053 to Glutton Bridge through another miniature gorge. There's yet another on the small road which turns right just before the actual bridge, where, just after Dowell Hall, the road passes through a narrow cleft.

The climb brings you out onto barer rough grazing country. For a short spell you have left the walls, while the harsh outlines of the gritstone edges have become prominent. The next stretch involves about 1½ miles (some 2km) of the main A53, close under the black bulk of Axe Edge. There is a choice of route here: you can turn right at New Lodge Farm (GR 031 680) to take, eventually, the track to Three Shire Heads, or follow a surfaced route by taking the next right turn through Flash, one of several claimants to be the highest village in England. The hospitable Travellers' Rest, between the two turnings, has saved us from dehydration or exposure on many occasions, while Flash village has a store and off licence, the first for some miles of the route.

The Three Shire Heads route follows the surfaced road, marked as allowing no access for motor traffic at GR 018 680, down the bracken and heather-covered little valley by Hawks Nest, continuing to bear right as it becomes a sandy track between stone walls. There follows a short rough stretch as the path drops to the delectably-sited arched bridge over the infant River Dane, which falls in a series of pools and cascades. The three shires which meet here are Staffordshire to the south and east, Cheshire to the west and Derbyshire, unexpectedly to the north. The route crosses the bridge and follows a firm track which climbs steeply up the bracken-covered slope, with the stream far below, reaching the surfaced road after about half a mile (800m).

On reaching the road, the route turns sharp left, almost doubling back, to follow the narrow twisting switchback gated road until it, too, meets the next road at a similarly acute junction (GR 996 665, about ¼ mile, 400m, off the edge of the Buxton map: you will only need the Potteries sheet if you intend to follow the next optional detour). Here there are two possibilities—either to follow a (relatively) direct route back to Ilam, or to add on nearly 12 miles, some 18km, by following a rather hilly but scenically spectacular route via Gun Hill and the Roaches.

The direct route turns left to drop to a curving bridge back over the River Dane and then to turn right at Greens up the charmingly-named Green Gutter to Goldsditch Moss. Here you emerge quite suddenly onto the craggy gritstone country, with the jagged ridge of the Roaches to your right. The soil is more acid, too, and the hillsides are a mass of heather, brilliantly deep purple when we passed, glistening with the drops of a recent shower. A clutch of partridge chicks scattered as we approached, scampering along the road, seemingly unable to fly until, as at a signal, they all took off in a bunch over the low wall. From here

there's a steady climb across the purple moor to the junction at GR 017 636, just past Newstone Farm.

From this point it is possible simply to turn left up to the main road, the A53, at the Winking Man. It is also possible to follow a 7-mile (11km) circuit to take in the Roaches by bearing right over to the main road by the outcrop of Ramshaw Rocks. Follow the main road downhill for about ¾ mile (1km) to Upper Hulme where you turn right by a telephone box, passing the Old Rock Inn, then right again, just after the Methodist chapel. You may wonder if it's the right road, since it appears to go through the middle of a largely disused factory. It climbs, sharply at first, then more gently, to wind along below the crags of Hen Cloud and the Five Clouds, a popular rock-climbing spot. A final steep pitch through open grassland after a gate brings you to Roach End, with a spectacular view from its 403-metre vantage point over the ridges above Congleton and the Cheshire plain. The run down from the top to GR 017 636 is pure delight, through brilliant banks of heather with tremendous views over the Edges and hills to Buxton and beyond.

The longer detour that takes in Gun Hill bears right after the gated road from Three Shire Heads up a quite steep little pitch, followed by a long sweep down, with the steep, wooded valley, or 'clough' of the River Dane below to the left. At Allgreave, a grey, stone hamlet brilliant with orange nasturtiums when we went by, you briefly join the A54, bearing left downhill to leave it again just after the bridge. There's no disguising the fact that the next part, through Wincle and Danebridge to Gun End is hilly: there are half a dozen of the Ordnance Survey's arrows, plus several they seem to have missed. But the twisting road is a delightful wooded one, quite different from the open moorlands and upland grazing of the rest of the route. The climb over Gun Hill is steady rather than steep, while from the top, at GR 970 608, there are sweeping views southwards. There are more views, on the whole wall of the Roaches, on the way down to Meerbrook. A left turn in Meerbrook at the old school, now a youth hostel, leads to the stiff climb up to Roach End.

All these possible routes converge at the Winking Man on the A53 at GR 026 637, to embark on the superb Morridge ridge road. The road

Opposite: *On Morridge, looking towards the Roaches and Axe Edge*

Below: *An ancient roadside distance marker*

rises relatively gently round the edge of the valley with open views to the right all the way, first over the Roaches, and then, as the road bends, over range after range of the Staffordshire hills. Ignore all left turnings until you reach the junction at GR 028 595, marked '463' (m above sea level), where you bear left for the magnificent ridge run to Waterfall. By now views have opened to the east, too, over the succession of folds and dales, and with the road gently downhill you could be forgiven for thinking this is ideal cycling—particularly if you strike an evening like ours with majestic white cumulus clouds and patches of sunshine marching across the skyscape.

Although the road after the B5053 is marked uncoloured it is a perfectly good, if narrow, surfaced road, with one or two ups and downs, through to Waterfall. Just after Waterfall you follow the road marked as 'Single track road'—which it certainly is, and with a few holes and grass down the middle, too. It certainly doesn't need much to block it but we didn't mind waiting for the cows to cross on their way back from milking. The road reaches the main road with a sharp bend and a 16%, 1-in-6, gradient.

Waterhouses straggles along the main A523, with a selection of accommodation available. It is also the point at which you can begin the Manifold Valley Trail, another converted railway which actually for its first part follows the River Hamps. Unlike the other trails this one is hard surfaced, although still restricted to use by walkers, cyclists and riders for much of its length. It offers a fine mix of river valley and woodland scenery—and even a short tunnel towards the top end. The upper part, from Wettonmill northwards, does tend to get quite crowded at popular times. You can join the trail at GR 091 501 in Waterhouses, and it leads eventually to Hulme End, just below Hartington. If you leave it at Weags Bridge it offers an alternative, if very hilly, route back to Ilam.

The finale of the road route is not one to miss, though. The route leaves the main road just up from the start of the trail, on a small road signposted 'Calton'. In Calton itself you bear left up a fine narrow lane between trim stone walls which climbs steadily to open country, with views over the Hamps and Manifold valleys. Then, over the brow, begins a beautiful descent through open grazing to the steep-sided valley of the River Manifold—look out for the unexpected gate at Throwley Hall Farm, though! A last little rise through a line of elms brings you back to the suggested starting-point of Ilam.

RUTLAND

• WEEKEND ROUTE •

R ecent maps would have you believe that there is no such county as Rutland. They might tell you that Rutland is merely a district of Leicestershire, or point to Rutland Water, the reservoir to the east of Oakham which flooded some six square miles (15sq km) of the county. This was done around the time in the 1970s that Rutland was officially subsumed into Leicestershire—almost as though the point had to be hammered home to the recalcitrant Rutlanders. But the Rutlanders remain fiercely defiant. 'Rutland' signs appear at the county boundary and the rebellious village of Belton had itself renamed Belton-in-Rutland by no less a personage than the Duke of Rutland himself. So we may say that this route embraces three counties: Leicestershire, Rutland and Northamptonshire.

The countryside divides into two main parts. To the north and west lie the rolling wolds, and south and east of them, beyond the valley of the River Welland, the gentler sweeps of the Northamptonshire hills, part of that great limestone belt that sweeps across southern England and on which two of our routes lie. But the contours are much gentler here than in the Cotswolds, although the map's telltale steep-hill arrows do crop up here and there. And, although the stone-built villages rival for handsomeness their more famous and more crowded cousins in the Cotswolds, the limestone and ironstone is somehow less omnipresent: there are few stone walls except in the villages, and the nearness of brickfields breaks the stone monopoly.

What makes the area superb for cycling is the remarkable network of quiet little roads and the unexpected variety of its intimate landscape. For every delectable little lane that the route steers you towards, there will be half a dozen tantalizing alternatives, notably in the wolds. Many of them are hedgeless, between high walls of corn or across sheep-shorn turf. But these are not the hedgeless prairies of modern mechanical agriculture: the frequent sight of the old ridge-and-furrow pattern criss-crossing the pasture and ignoring later field boundaries demonstrates that this is the true and traditional openness of unenclosed rural England.

• THE ROUTE •

Oakham, our starting point, was the county town of Rutland. It is a workmanlike and bustling little place, still retaining its county capital trappings. There is the Rutland Museum and the remains of a castle, whose Great Hall houses an unusual collection—of horseshoes. It is said that the custom of depositing a shoe originated when travellers were required to leave some bond against their leaving with an unpaid bill. A horse minus a shoe was effectively immobilized. Later, leaving a shoe at Oakham became a ritual for titled and royal visitors—and the horseshoe became the county's symbol.

The route leaves Oakham at the west end of the main street, the A606, just after the railway level crossing at the station, following the unclassified road west to the rather complex village of Knossington. On the outskirts of the village, GR 805 089, a very narrow short cut to the village centre turns off, looking like the entrance to somebody's garden. The road is so narrow you can stand in the middle and touch the lush grass on both sides. Ironically there's a 30 mph speed limit at the bottom!

The route bears to the left in Knossington and out to the crossroads at Furze Hill, where you can go straight on to Owston and Maresfield, or turn left for a worthwhile detour by Launde Park. This

Overleaf: Norcot windmill

road leads through a fine grove of chestnuts in Owston Woods and then, after left and right turns, onto a veritable switchback. A series of ponds, the haunt of anglers and grandiosely named Launde Lakes, marks the entrance to Launde Park, the first of several such open grassland stretches on the route. Open grazing means gates: we found such a variety of gate fixings on this route, and permutations of gates opening forwards, backwards or both that we feel a diligent rural historian could well work them up into a PhD thesis.

The road continues up and down westwards from Launde, but the country has changed into a landscape of hedges, small lush grazing fields, and copses. On the flank of Whatborough Hill (GR 763 057) you follow a right turn marked 'Gated road to Marefield'. Marefield proves to be no more than a few cottages, followed by more open grazing; we had to slow down while sheep made up their woolly minds whether to scatter to right or left. *We* knew we were going left, though, and then right after the gate by the brook up a quite earnest little climb to the B6047.

Here the route goes right again, giving two choices, both of which pass through very similar open parkland. Both parks, too, were created on the sites of villages they displaced. This part of Leicestershire lost quite a few villages by this process of 'emparkment', as well as others by clearances for sheep farming in the heyday of English wool. On the days that we passed, Lowesby (first left) offered grazing sheep and pale cattle, while Baggrave (second left, then left again) offered only sheep; both offer a superb run down and brief exhilarating climb from the valley of the infant Queniborough Brook which later joins the Rivers Wreake, Soar and Trent. On a clear day you can see from this ridge over to the west the blue line of the hills of Charnwood Forest on the horizon.

From the end of either road you can go direct to the crossroads at GR 723 050 above Lord Morton's Covert or, if there's time, go through Hungarton and then follow the interesting bridle route which passes by Quenby Hall. This begins as a surfaced road, signposted as 'Public bridleway to Quenby Hall only'. The surfaced drive curves round to reveal the imposing brick facade of the seventeenth-century hall, which has been de-

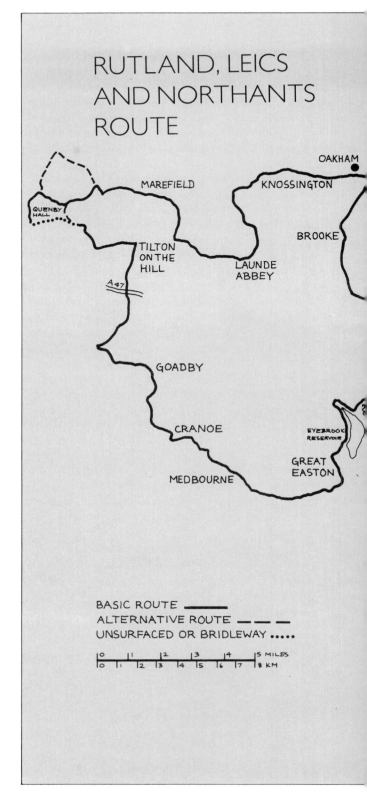

RUTLAND, LEICS AND NORTHANTS ROUTE

BASIC ROUTE ———
ALTERNATIVE ROUTE — — —
UNSURFACED OR BRIDLEWAY •••••

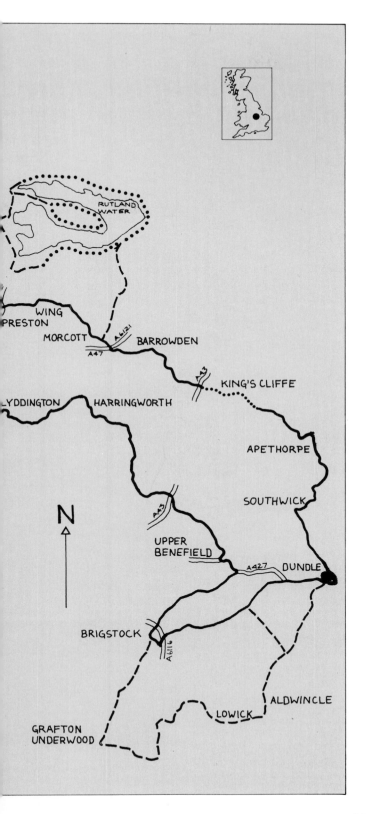

scribed as the finest Jacobean house in Leicester-shire. Just before the wrought-iron gates an arrow on the road directs you to the right; the bridleway goes through a red-oxide-painted gate beside the wall of the garden. Skirt this wall across the open grassland and at the far corner you strike out directly to the track which is the eastern continuation of the drive. The official line of the bridleway goes just to the right of the scattered oaks, turning left about 45° from the line of the wall. There are about three field gates to open and close before you reach the public road once more.

After the Lord Morton's Covert crossroads there's a further choice: left leads to Tilton-on-the-Hill, right and left to Billesdon; both offer the chance of food. From Tilton there's a fine, narrow gated road south to Skeffington and then, after the A47, more gates and a delectable little road, with yet more gates, that emerges into Rolleston Park along a magnificent avenue of chestnuts. There is *no* inn at New Inn so, in disdain, the route goes sharp left without emerging onto the B6047, across the edge of this pleasant sheep-filled open park. If you've come from Billesdon, this is where you leave the B-road. Another fine open stretch—this time through cornfields—follows, passing another emparked and lost village, Noseley.

After the feast of a swooping drop comes the reckoning with a steep little climb up to Goadby and then the reward of another attractive open stretch into Glooston—gold with ripening corn when we passed and backed with the cool green of a line of poplars by the stream. The small hamlet of Glooston has a very handsome run of ironstone cottages and, unexpectedly perhaps, a restaurant and pub. All are down the dead-end road to the right. The route turns left, to Cranoe, of which the first glimpse you get is the tower of the little church, apparently almost below road level, before you sweep round beside it. Cranoe means 'the hoe [or spur of land] frequented by crows', although we didn't see any there.

A left turn at the crossroads and a right at the next take you to Slawston. As you leave Slawston there's a fast downhill stretch from which, to the left, an alignment of willows and poplars down by the stream is echoed by a line of trees on the hill above. The next village, Medbourne, is quite different, spacious, with a great deal of green and

• INFORMATION •

Starting point

As described the route starts and finishes at Oakham; other convenient starting points would be Uppingham and Oundle. It would also be possible to start from Leicester, joining the route at Hungarton; or Stamford, joining at Barrowden, the Luffenhams or King's Cliffe.

Access

Rail routes are to Oakham from Ipswich, Cambridge, Ely and Peterborough or Birmingham and Leicester, and to Leicester from Sheffield, Nottingham or London (St Pancras). Some bicycle restrictions. Main access roads are A606 to Oakham and A47 to Uppingham. The A6 passes just to the south of the route, and the A1 just to the east.

Accommodation

There are B&B and hotel possibilities at Belton-in-Rutland (nr Uppingham), Launde, Oakham, Oundle, Rockingham (nr Great Easton), Uppingham, Whissendine (4 miles (6km) N of Oakham) and Wing. There are camp sites at Belton-in-Rutland, Langham, Oundle, Tilton-on-the-Hill, and Uppingham. There is no youth hostel on or near the route. If you need to consult directories or listings check under Leicestershire and Northamptonshire.

Tourist information office

Oakham.

Cycle shops and hire

There is a small bike shop in Oakham, otherwise the nearest are in Leicester and Market Harborough. Rutland Water Cycling operate a hire service from Whitwell car park on the N side of the Water, from March to October, and at weekends until Christmas. Their satellite at Normanton on the S side of the Water is open at weekends and holidays from Easter to September. Their leaflet shows routes round the Water—and features neatly-named 'thirst-aid stations' en route.

Maps

The whole route is on OS 1:50 000 sheet 141. Basic route distance is about 95 miles (150km).

Normanton church (now a museum)

with cottages set well back either side of a brook that runs through the middle. Leading up to the church is a newly-restored packhorse bridge, said to date from the thirteenth century; the little river seemed tranquil enough as we crossed it, but villagers spoke of its rising in winter far above the concrete road bridge which normally goes over it.

The route bears left at the southern end of the village, over the shoulder of the hill to Drayton and Great Easton. There's quite a determined climb on the road north out of the attractive golden stone cluster of Great Easton. Towards the top of the hill a small road turns off to the right, climbs briefly and then gives way to an unexpected view. Below lies the considerable blue expanse of the Eyebrook Reservoir, old enough now to have become part of the landscape and an established haunt of anglers, at the southern end, and water birds at the other. Particularly at the north-westernmost tip you can see in the shallows large flocks of geese, gulls and smaller birds.

At the end of the lake there are two choices. Straight ahead leads to the B664 which climbs a miniature continental pass—only about 90m but with a superb hairpin bend—to the pleasant and compact town of Uppingham. Here there is quite a choice of shops and places to stay and eat. Uppingham, with its public school, is one of three scholarly towns on the route. The right turn leads round the head of the lake and then up quite sharply through the hamlet of Stoke Dry. The church halfway up the hill has thirteenth-century wall paintings, the main one showing St Christopher and the martyred St Edmund (of Bury St Edmunds). Interestingly the figures loosing their arrows at poor Edmund have American-Indian-style feathered headdresses, and this has been adduced as evidence of a Viking folk-memory of such people from tales of pre-Columbus Norse travels to America.

At the top of the hill the route crosses the A6003 and swoops down to Lyddington, a superb deep golden-brown ironstone village. There are some very handsome buildings lining the long village street. Towards the southern end, a turning by an odd little octagonal tower leads to the fine church and the striking Bede House. This house, once the palace of the bishops of Lincoln was converted in 1602 into an almshouse for 'twelve men and two women'. Residence presumably entailed a commitment to devotions, since the term 'bede' derives from the Old English *gebed*—prayer.

A road at the south end of the village goes down to the B672 in the Welland valley. Ahead is the remarkable Welland Viaduct, a brick structure of eighty-two arches which carries the Oakham to Kettering railway high across the River Welland. The arches are all numbered and you fork right to pass between the 59th and 60th arches, to Harringworth. As well as being in the shadow of Britain's longest brick viaduct, Harringworth's other claim to fame is that the village pub, the Red Swan, proclaims that it has won prizes for the best steak-and-kidney pies in Britain.

There's quite a sharp little climb up from the centre of Harringworth between high banks and once over the top you turn, opposite a small obelisk commemorating a wartime American air squadron, down a narrow lane to Deene. This estate village stands beside Kirby Hall, a large Elizabethan mansion built of the local stone and noted for the richness and variety of its architectural detail. It is set in an attractive park with an ornamental lake and is open to the public.

The route crosses the A43 in a right-and-left manoeuvre to follow a small and gently rolling lane to Upper Benefield, a soft grey village with a simple tall-spired church. Here there's a choice: the A427—which doesn't appear to carry a great deal of traffic—leads direct to Oundle, or a turning off it at Lower Benefield offers a detour through rolling farm country, before striking back to Oundle.

This detour leads first to Brigstock, where there's again a choice. The shorter route involves turning left in the village on Tunnel Hill which becomes the old Lyveden Road and then wheeling the bicycle over the footbridge to the actual Lyveden Road.

The road is one of those open rolling ones with surprisingly wide vistas over cornfields and, when we were there, beans. There's a fine line of new poplars on one stretch giving the whole scene a French air. To the right of the road, and reached from a bridleway which leaves it at GR 982 861, lies Lyveden New Building, or Lyveden New Bield as the signposts call it. It is only 'new' in the sense that it is newer than the building it was intended to replace. Begun in 1594 it was never finished and the stone shell stands in eerie loneliness among the trees.

A little further on along this road, at GR 995 868, it is possible as an alternative to the direct route to Oundle to follow a 'byway', marked as a black dashed line on the map, over Winning Foot Hill. The first part of the track is grassy (and might be a little tricky in wet weather) but becomes a firm-based stony track at the top of the field and later on is surfaced. It's a very quiet place: rabbits scampered into their hedgerow burrows as we approached and pigeons cooed from the woods—why *do* pigeons and doves always sound distant, even if they're close at hand? The byway reaches the Aldwincle to Stoke Doyle road at GR 016 846, where you turn left for Oundle.

The longer detour from Brigstock, goes by way of Grafton Underwood (where we saw deer crossing the road), Slipton, Sudborough and Lowick to take in more of the Northamptonshire uplands. The uncoloured road on the map which leaves the A6116 at GR 980 807 is the old road out of Lowick and remains as a surfaced bridleway through to the Aldwincle road. This detour gives broad views over the valley of the River Nene on its way up to Wadenhoe, Stoke Doyle and then Oundle.

Oundle is a warm-grey stone town, compact and dominated by the tall steeple of St Peter's church. There are several handsome Georgian buildings along the main street and around the market place, but the town's main charm lies in its being all of a piece—planted long ago, as it were, and now grown to a harmonious maturity. There is also, one should add, a good selection of shops and eating places.

The best way out of Oundle is to turn up past the public school towards Glapthorn, bearing right to climb past the water tower and then down by Southwick to Woodnewton. From here the route follows the valley of the Willow Brook, fringed with lines of poplars as well as willows, through two very different villages. Apethorpe is a typical estate hamlet, with uniformly designed houses, quite a bit of thatch, grouped round the little road that leads to the drive of Apethorpe Hall. The next village, King's Cliffe, on the other hand, is a quite substantial but close-packed stone place, almost a small town.

At the west end of King's Cliffe village where the two almost parallel streets, West Street and Wood Road, meet (GR 001 972), turn right into Wood Lane and continue up the limestone track at the end of the surfaced part. To begin with it's a bit rutted but once you get to the timber yard it becomes a very fine stone surfaced track. This is a superb ride through mixed forest for about 1½ miles (over 2km) until you reach the surfaced road again at Top Lodge. A brief drop and climb bring you across the busy A43 and into more forest. This is Wakerley Great Wood, a remnant of the old Rockingham Forest—one of three royal forests which up to the early middle ages reserved between them most of Northamptonshire for the monarch's deer-hunting pleasure.

A twisting drop brings you into Wakerley itself, with a right turn to Barrowden. The route out leads past an externally well-preserved windmill, now apparently a private house. A left turn on the A47, a right shortly after on the A6121 and an almost immediate left bring you into Morcott, a compact stone village. The colour of the stone is beginning to change back to the honey-brown once more, and by the next two villages, Wing and Preston, the change is complete.

From Morcott it is also possible to make a detour by way of the Luffenhams and Edith Weston to circumnavigate Rutland Water. It could also be reached direct from Oakham at the end or beginning of the main trip. This reservoir is one of two on the routes in this book—the other is Kielder Water in Northumberland—to claim to be the largest man-made lake in Britain; Rutland Water even claims to be the largest in Europe. It seems likely that while Rutland Water may indeed have the largest man-made *surface area* of water, many others by being appreciably deeper can reasonably claim to hold more water. There is a waymarked cycle route, part on tracks, part on shared pedestrian and cycle paths, part on minor roads, that goes all the way round the lake and takes in the Hambleton peninsula that thrusts out into the middle. It never strays far from the lake shore. The total distance is some 40km, although there are obviously shorter possibilities. A detailed leaflet is available from Rutland Water Cycling, who have a couple of cycle hire centres at Whitwell and Normanton.

At Wing there is a turf maze beside the road.

The precise purpose of such mazes—a sinuous turf bank which leads in a succession of doubled-up coils from the entrance to the centre of the circular pattern—is unknown, but they are believed to have had connexions with spring fertility rites. As with many pagan relics, when Christianity arrived the church claimed mazes for their own and it is this later interpretation which the local history society's plaque beside the Wing maze prefers.

Preston, on a loop road on the far side of the A6003, is a lovely ironstone village, all of a piece with some handsomely-proportioned buildings, and bright with summer flowers on the day we passed through. They do cream teas in the village hall on summer Sundays, too! The route leaves Preston at the south end, without going back onto the main road, by a right turn which brings you out on an open little road to Ridlington. The road is quite a switchback with a tremendous swoop down from Ridlington to the infant River Chater, followed by a climb and another drop to Brooke, with its rather stumpy little church tower. From the top of the ridge as we passed there were golden cornfields almost as far as the eye could see. There's a long steady pull up out of Brooke and then, as you breast the top of this last hill, there is a panorama with Oakham laid out at your feet and a wide sweep over Rutland Water to your right.

The picturesque village of Preston

WEALD OF KENT AND SUSSEX, AND ROMNEY MARSH

• WEEKEND ROUTE •

The name 'weald' is an old Anglo-Saxon one, meaning 'wood',—essentially the same word as the modern German *Wald*. Although over the centuries since the Weald received its name much of the woodland has been felled, trees are still the essential feature of the region. These are not only the mature forest trees but hedgerow trees and shrubs and the neat coppices of sturdy saplings. The sheer intricacy of the landscape fascinates with its continuous cameos of ridge after wooded ridge. This abundance of woodland meant that parts of the Weald were among the hardest hit by the great storm of October 1987 when some 15 million trees were blown over or shattered, barely a week after we had surveyed most of the route. The worst of the scars will take decades to heal and generations to replace but the essential 'wealdness' is still there for the discovery.

For once this is a southern-England route that is *not* on chalk or limestone. The Weald consists of sandstone ridges and clay lowlands, following a basically east–west trend. The more acid soils support other trees in place of the beeches so characteristic of the chalk hills to the north and south: the Weald is rich in oaks, chestnuts, hornbeam and hazel. Before coal and the Industrial Revolution moved the focus of industry further north, the Weald was the source of oak for shipbuilding and of charcoal used for smelting the ironstone nodules found nearby. Names such as 'Furnace Mill', 'Furnace Farm' and 'Forge Farm'

along the route, and others such as 'Hammer Mill Farm' near to it, are virtually the sole reminders of this activity.

Nowadays the Weald is very genteel country: the small copses and forest lead to neat fields, precise orchards and the increasingly rare hopfields, features which have earned Kent its 'Garden of England' title. Many of the characteristic white-cowled oast houses—for the natural drying of hops—have now been converted into picturesque if unusually-shaped desirable residences. The attractions of the area make it a sought-after place to live for many who work in London, while Kent also lies astride the routes to the Channel coast. The major trunk roads, such as the A21, do at busy seasons form quite real barriers, so the route has been chosen to cross them only where it cannot be avoided, and then at points where the traffic is necessarily slowed through a village.

The general affluence of the area means that some of the smaller roads, particularly some of the B-routes, are also quite busy. The route follows almost entirely very minor roads and one superb and eminently ridable bridleway through Bedgebury Forest. Inevitably these smaller roads are less engineered than the main ones and there are some quite steep but short climbs, particularly where the route crosses the east-west grain of the ridges. Hills just cannot be avoided if you are to find the best of the Weald and to follow the quietest of its roads. Although the level of local traffic is maintained all year round, there is also quite a lot of tourist traffic, and crowding of the popular towns, villages and sights, during the summer months. Given the wooded nature of the Weald and the variety of its broad-leaved trees, spring and autumn or even early winter are *the* seasons for following this route. Each season has its special feature but in spring great spreads of bluebells carpet the open Wealden woodlands. Perhaps the only benefit from the 1987 storm is likely to be the heightened displays of bluebells in the newly-opened shade.

The south-eastern part of the route is utterly different. Between the Weald and the sea lies one of England's relatively few utterly flat areas. This is Romney Marsh, an area which has been land for no more than a few centuries. Now the marshes are mostly rich but exposed grazing, or given over to intensive cultivation. As with all very flat areas, the sky dominates the landscape, either as the immense dome above or reflected in the innumerable dykes and waterways. But, as I've said before, despite non-cyclists' folklore and fascinating as they may be for a few hours, dead flat landscapes do not make ideal country for cycling. After the trip across the levels I am sure you'll welcome the route's return to the little hazel-lined lanes of the Weald, even if they do require a little more work on the pedals!

• THE ROUTE •

Either Tunbridge Wells or Frant station make suitable starting points for the route. Tunbridge Wells was essentially an eighteenth-century spa town—indeed at one time it rivalled Bath for society patronage. Now, although some of the features, notably the colonnaded promenade of the Pantiles, remain, Tunbridge Wells—like so many towns within daily travelling distance of London—has grown enormously into a residential area which spreads over quite a bit of the surrounding countryside. The simplest way to leave the town, although not the quietest if you know its intricate minor routes, is to begin by following the A267 Eastbourne road and then after about ¾ mile (say 1km) bearing left on the B2169, signposted for Lamberhurst.

The route leaves the B2169 just east of Bells Yew Green at GR 615 359 to turn right down a lane signposted 'Narrow road'—a completely accurate description, which applies to quite a bit of this section of the route. Many of the lanes, too, are winding and quite up and down. On this one you plunge immediately into the typical Wealden mixture of small fields and woods, with deep, hedged banks to the roads. The road climbs away from the stream at the foot of the first hill through another typical feature—a near arch of hazel and chestnut saplings. On the October day when we passed squirrels hurried from bank to bank, foraging for autumn produce, totally disinterested by our noiseless passing.

The first turn is to the left into Whitegates Lane, following signs through to Sparrows Green. There's a complex network of roads here: at a little grass triangle with a green lamp-post, follow the sign to the Turners Green road, to go straight across the B2100 at Primmers Green. A sharp drop brings another sudden change as the country becomes open ploughland just before the climb to Wadhurst and the left turn onto the B2099. After about 1½ km, turn right onto a road signposted to Stonegate. This road follows the ridge and from time to time gives fine open views to the left over the extensive and picturesque wooded ridges of the Weald.

In Stonegate a left turn and a right about 1km later bring you down a pleasant road to cross the River Rother for the first time, at Crowhurst Bridge. Even here, barely 7 miles (some 12km) from its source, the river was swollen brown with the autumn rains when we passed. A steady climb brings you up to the ridge and Burwash— *Burg-ersc*, 'the tilled field by the fortified place', say the etymologists. This attractive, if popular, village has fine examples of the deep-red, hanging pantiles and weatherboarding typical of the area. It, like several others, suffers from sitting astride a quite busy main road.

The route turns left just past the pointed-spired church. At the foot of the hill a turning to the right leads to Bateman's, Rudyard Kipling's home for over thirty years. It is preserved much as Kipling left it and is open to the public. The original Bateman, who built the house in the seventeenth century, made his money from iron smelting, in the days when the Weald provided much of England's iron. At the corner at GR 679 226 the route leaves the obvious road to drop down a narrow

• INFORMATION •

Starting point

As described the route starts and finishes at Tunbridge Wells or Frant station. It would also be possible to start from Rye, joining the route at the Royal Military Canal.

Access

Rail routes are to Tunbridge Wells and Frant from London (Charing Cross or Waterloo) and Hastings, or to Appledore from London (Charing Cross or Waterloo), Ashford and Hastings. The main access road is the A21 to Tunbridge Wells.

Accommodation

There are B&B and hotel possibilities in Lydd, Robertsbridge, Rye, Stone-in-Oxney, Tenterden, Tunbridge Wells and Wadhurst. There are campsites at Bodiam, Burwash, Ewhurst Green, Flimwell (nr Lamberhurst), Frant, New Romney and Peasmarsh, plus Biddenden and Tenterden (both about 5 miles [8km] from Rolvenden Layne). There is no youth hostel on or particularly near the route: the nearest is at Guestling, nr Hastings. If you need to consult directories or listings, check under East Sussex and Kent.

Tourist information offices

Tunbridge Wells, Cranbrook, Tenterden and Rye.

Cycle shops

There are cycle shops in Robertsbridge, Rye and Tunbridge Wells.

Maps

The whole route requires three maps, OS 1:50 000 sheets 188, 189, and 199. Basic route distance is about 100 miles (160km).

Bodiam Castle

lane—effectively straight on, but a left turn off the larger road. After just over ¼ mile (about 500m) you take a very small right and not entirely obvious turn, opposite a house called Woodmans, to follow this switchback lane up to Oxley's Green. Here you turn left at the Fuller's Arms for the fast run in through the woods to Robertsbridge.

Robertsbridge is an attractive large village, but another to be bisected by a busy main road, in this case the A21. There is some very fine weatherboarding, more hanging tiles and timbering and a remarkably ornate United Re-

formed Church. The route goes left on the A21 for some 600yd (550 or so m), and then turns right for Salehurst; the turning, which is opposite the New Eight Bells, is not signposted, although there is an advance warning sign which could send you mistakenly down a dead end. In very dry conditions you can alternatively reach Salehurst by a bridleway bridge over the River Rother. To get to it you turn down Fair Lane, which is almost opposite the road by which you enter Robertsbridge.

Just after the church in Salehurst follow the signed lane to Bodiam to the right; at the top of the

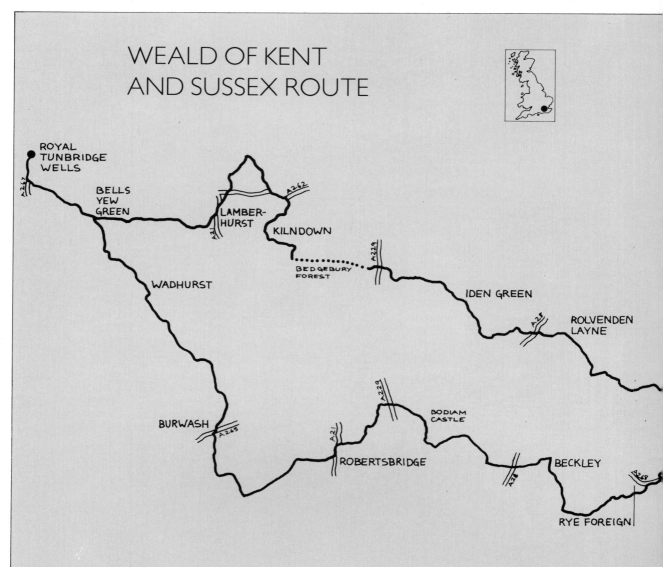

WEALD OF KENT
AND SUSSEX ROUTE

ROYAL TUNBRIDGE WELLS

BELLS YEW GREEN

LAMBER-HURST

KILNDOWN

BEDGEBURY FOREST

WADHURST

IDEN GREEN

ROLVENDEN LAYNE

BURWASH

BODIAM CASTLE

ROBERTSBRIDGE

BECKLEY

RYE FOREIGN

quite stiff hill up from the stream, you can go either way—Bourne Lane to the right looks more interesting but hillier. Take care at the crossing of the A229 at the Curlew as the rather macabre sign opposite would suggest. From here it's downhill into Bodiam.

The fourteenth-century castle at Bodiam is a gem—to my mind, easily the most castle-shaped castle in the country, and very properly set in a brimming moat. It now belongs to the National Trust; the grounds are open all the time and the castle itself most days from Easter to the autumn.

BASIC ROUTE _____
ALTERNATIVE ROUTE _ _ _
UNSURFACED OR .....
BRIDLEWAY

Go there early or very late in the day, or midweek out of season, if you want to walk round and savour the feeling of the place. It does become rather crowded in high summer or at weekends.

Once over the River Rother again the route turns left in about half a mile (some 800m) to Snagshall and the very neat village of Ewhurst Green. From this low ridge there are glimpses across the Rother valley to Bodiam and the castle—depending on your height and the state of the hedgerows. Although not far above sea level the road does dip and climb quite a bit, between orchards, fields and woods to reach the junction at GR 815 238, marked '42' (m above sea level). Here you turn right along the lane marked 'Staple Cross Private Road' (it isn't private any more), past the neat hedges and fences at Tufton Place. At the end turn left towards Mill Corner, keeping right at the next fork to go straight across the A28.

On the hot July day that we first followed this road, the next section was a quiet oasis of wooded shade, leading to the outskirts of Beckley. Here, about a quarter of a mile (400m) after a spired church on the left, turn right at GR 846 237 to follow another succession of narrow lanes. On that high summer day the hedges were a profusion of wild roses. After about 2 miles (roughly 3km) at the junction marked '77' (m above sea level), at GR 853 210, turn left. This stretch is quite hilly but there are superb Wealden views on the open stretches, picturesquely punctuated with oast houses. After the climb up past The Hermitage you eventually reach a junction at the entrance to Peasmarsh Place, GR 882 217, where the route goes right to pass through a magnificent stretch of chestnut woodland. We were very tempted by the sign listing local produce—clotted cream, cherries, strawberries, apples—but continued to join the A268 at Rye Foreign, where the route turns right.

After about ½ mile (800m), at GR 902 227, turn left down another chestnut-fringed lane skirting the wood, then through neat orchards to the village of Iden. Here a right-and-left crossing of the B2082 takes you down a little lane signposted 'Houghton Green and Appledore'. The country-

Overleaf: *St Thomas à Becket church, Fairfield, on Walland Marsh*

side changes quite abruptly as the road drops down from the edge of the hills to the Royal Military Canal which bounds the flatness of Walland and Romney Marshes.

The Royal Military Canal was hurriedly constructed during the Napoleonic Wars to stem the advance of any French landing on the flat sands bounding the Marsh or on Dungeness. As has been observed, it would seem as well it was never put to the test: any half-competent invader would have crossed it in ten minutes. Now much of it stands grass-grown and choked—a haven for wildlife. The first part the route encounters, though, is very much a flowing watercourse for it forms almost the last few miles of the River Rother. On the day that we passed brown water tumbled seawards between the brimming banks as the autumn floods drained away.

The route follows the canal for some 5 miles (8km) to Appledore, a trim little weatherboarded village whose name is almost unaltered from the Old English word for an apple-tree— *apuldor*. Here a right turn over the bridge and a second immediately after brings you out onto the open solitude of Walland Marsh. The little road winds and twists its way across the dykes— romantically named 'sewers' in this part of the world. It's a place of great quietness; several times as we approached dignified grey herons would silently fold their legs and fly in their unhurried way to some less disturbed spot. At other times there were fields full of plovers, while swans and coots populated the drains and streams. Although this and Romney Marsh proper have a few straight roads, they lack the formal rectilinear geometry of the Fens, and your direction is continually changing.

After a couple of miles you pass the intriguing little church of St Thomas à Becket at Fairfield, superbly set in waves of rolling meadow and water, surrounded by grazing Romney Marsh sheep but by no apparent parish to support it. A rather less likely landmark is a Filipino boutique as you reach the A259! The route goes right on the A259 for some 200yd (200m), to turn left off it by the Woolpack Inn. From here, there's a choice of routes across the fertile fields to Old Romney, with its old and new churches token that it was once a much larger place.

It is possible to extend the exploration of the marsh much further, to take in St Mary in the Marsh and Newchurch, or to visit the coastal resorts of St Mary's Bay and Dymchurch with their classic narrow-gauge railway. The basic route, however, crosses the A259 to join the B2070 at GR 039 264 south-east of Ivychurch. Turn left through this straggling village and then turn left to leave the B2070 at GR 022 285, just after a white house which is also a sub-Post Office, down an unsignposted road. There's a very sharp, and again unsigned, right turn after about 300yd (250m). A right-and-left dogleg at the A2070 takes you along a superb winding and narrow little lane. On the autumn afternoon that we passed, the high hawthorn hedges were weighed down under the burden of their bright red berries. The road crosses the canal once more and begins to climb very gently to Appledore Heath, and then straight on to cross what appear to be the combined Reading, Tenterden and Cradlebridge Sewers at Stone Ferry.

The ferry is long replaced by a bridge, from which the road climbs up to the Isle of Oxney— the 'Isle' is really redundant since Oxney means, literally, 'the island where oxen were kept'. In the days before the marshes were drained it would indeed have been an island. It is worth making the detour round to the left by the church in Stone-in-Oxney, since the Glebe Land opposite it is now a National Trust open space with broad views over the marsh. From here the route begins to head back westwards, joining the B2082 by the prominent and well-restored windmill at The Stocks to follow it through to the corner marked '41' (m above sea level) at GR 889 283. Here a left turn brings you down to the Rother valley again and on to Wittersham Road station. If you imagine here that you are hearing the noise of steam whistles you are probably not mistaken: the station is at present the western terminus of the Kent and East Sussex preserved steam railway.

On the outskirts of Rolvenden Layne a left turning signposted 'Newenden' leads down to the A28 through what is almost a tunnel of beech, hornbeam and chestnut. You turn left for a short way and then right to plunge into another thicket of hazel and chestnut, with a particularly superb bit at a miniature hairpin bend. From the junction at Devenden, GR 827 304, there is quite a choice of routes through a near maze of narrow and delightful, if rather up-and-down, lanes. We chose the orchard option, turning right at the junction marked '24' (m above sea level), at GR 815 298, through Standen Street to Iden Green, and then along the remarkably boisterous little road to Four Wents, GR 766 327. Here the route goes right to go almost straight across the A229 at Tubslake.

This is the beginning of the bridleway through Bedgebury Forest. The forestry road is in parts surfaced, in others firm but gravel-based, and easily ridable throughout at any time of the year. Although the plantation is mostly coniferous there are fine stands of broad-leafed trees, including some magnificent chestnuts. This superb track is quite the quietest part of the Weald section of the route: we paused on the way through after dusk one autumn evening just to listen to the soft sounds of the nocturnal creatures stirring for their nightly foraging. Just off the track, to the left after about 2 miles (or 3km) lies Bedgebury Pinetum, a collection mainly of conifers but also including some maples and similar species which make a brilliant autumn display. Unfortunately about a fifth of the painstakingly tended collection perished in the October 1987 storm but the majority remain to give an impressively varied show.

The forest road joins the B2079 at GR 715 342. There is a choice of routes from here to Lamberhurst: certainly the direct one, using the A21, is to be avoided. The most attractive that we found was to leave the B2079 at Bedgebury Cross, and then go by way of Kilndown and Riseden to the crossroads at GR 713 368. Here there is a small vineyard in a former hopfield—as well as hopfields still in use. The route turns left here to join the A262. If traffic is light it is possible to follow this road through to the junction with the B2162, along which you turn left for Lamberhurst. Alternatively the detour which forks right about ¼ mile (400m) after the bridge takes in some pleasant roads and one or two fine oast houses before joining the B2162.

Lamberhurst is a pleasant and typically Wealden village, boarded and tilehung, but one that—like Robertsbridge—suffers from the presence of the A21, cutting a swathe straight through the middle. Lamberhurst is perhaps best known nowadays, though, as the home of the largest vineyard in England. Except for one or two outposts, viticulture in Britain, believed to date from Roman times, largely died out with the dissolution of the monasteries in 1536. It was not revived until some forty years ago and now the English Vineyards Association has some 550 members, who between them cultivate some 1000 acres, around 400 hectares. At the last count some 48 acres, about 19 hectares, were under vines at Lamberhurst. The entrance is just off a small common at GR 672 357. There is a 'vineyard trail' for visitors which highlights points of interest—and of course tasting and sales.

The return route to Frant or Tunbridge Wells is first to Hook Green, either by the direct B2169 or by way of a sunken orchard-lined lane past Mount Pleasant. From Hook Green the B2169 climbs gently through mixed woodland to Frant station, and so on to Tunbridge Wells.

THE FIVE LONGER TOURS

The five longer tours are dealt with rather differently from the shorter 'weekend' routes; to have covered them in the same degree of detail would have used far too much space. Each tour chapter is broken down into three parts: first a general preamble setting the scene and drawing attention to any cycling points; next a necessarily terse route description; and finally a selection of what I feel to be the highlights of the trip, covered in more detail. In each case I have suggested a route, and some detours, which I know to be attractive. But in many places there are alternative excursions and explorations—which will be obvious from the map—and equally possible short cuts. Treat the suggested route as a guide. And if the helter-skelter route description sometimes makes it appear that you should reach and leave some delectable spot or charming village almost in the same breath, as it were, please accept that it's a result of the need for brevity. *Bonne route!*

In the route descriptions, in order to save space, I have used a number of abbreviations:

N S E W signify north, south, east and west, alone or in combination

L and **R** indicate left and right

a **uc** road is an unclassified road, i.e. one that is neither class A nor class B; in some cases I use the term **minor road** to indicate one even smaller

(**m above sl**) shows that the number referred to is a spot height at that number of metres above sea level

lc means level crossing

In the information listing accommodation addresses are restricted to B&B places on or very near the route. You may assume that there are in addition hotels in the principal towns. The cycle shop net is spread rather further afield—on the basis that if you found yourself in urgent need of spares you would be prepared to go out of your way to get them.

EAST ANGLIA

• LONGER TOURS •

East Anglia, the country of the eastern English in the days when they had largely to be distinguished from Saxons and Britons, embraces the modern counties of Norfolk and Suffolk (literally the 'north and south folk') and parts of north Essex and eastern Cambridgeshire. Others spread the borders even further: I have seen East Anglia defined as 'everything east of the A1 and south of Boston', but for me East Anglia really begins where the chalk hills and the Brecklands begin to rise, if only ever so gently, from the complete flatness of the Fens. For me the Fens have always been a land apart, so my East Anglia begins at Downham Market and Newmarket.

It's only when you look at a relatively small-scale map of England that you begin to appreciate how large even my East Anglia really is. Norfolk is one of England's largest counties and Suffolk is quite well up the list; from an arbitrary southern boundary around Chelmsford to the north Norfolk coast is nearly 100 miles (over 150km), while Downham Market is 60 miles (100km) from the east coast.

There's a popular belief that East Anglia is flat and therefore ideal cycling country—and, indeed, I have been unable to find a single Ordnance Survey steep-hill arrow on the route, nor that many anywhere on the map. But in fact it makes very pleasant cycling country because it *isn't* dead flat but has just enough rise and fall to give variety and a pleasing roundness. Some of the drops and short climbs on the little river valleys may surprise you. It is, though, certainly easy cycling country, given the absence of strong winds. It is also about the driest part of the British Isles, although cold northerlies and easterlies coming unchecked off the North Sea can make winters quite bleak. It is very much spring and summer country.

Here, perhaps more than anywhere, you are very conscious that the landscape is man-made. The appeal lies in the pleasant villages, the curving alignments of willows and poplars along the streams and the winding lanes. In southern Norfolk, the northern part of the route, there are quite large forested areas. The general underlying rock is the chalk; the rolls and swells are the gentler extension of the Chilterns and the hills of the Bedfordshire and Cambridgeshire 'weekend' tour. The nature of the surface, though, is much modified by later overlying clays, sand and gravels, giving quite different character to different areas. Where they occur, as in the great tract of the stony Breckland, the sands and gravels give rise to heathland, much of it now under trees. Near the east coast sands once again give heaths and groves of birch and pine. There *is* variety, plenty of it, in East Anglia if you follow the little roads. There is also water. The popular Norfolk Broads—which the route does not reach—are of course well known, but there are many winding streams and placid rivers. The route visits the valleys of the Lark, the Little Ouse, the Waveney, the Alde and the Deben—and several more. It is perhaps paradoxical that the undramatic landscape of the East Anglian rivers, like that of Flanders and Holland on the other side of the North Sea, has produced more great landscape painters than any of the more conventionally picturesque mountains and hills.

Much of Suffolk, particularly, owed its early prosperity to medieval wool—the same trade that made the Cotswolds and Leicestershire rich. The fruits of this affluence remain in some of the great churches and the handsome vernacular buildings of the now often quiet towns. Some of the small towns and villages, though—Lavenham, Clare, Kersey, Finchingfield and so on—are undoubtedly well-trodden tourist spots and uncomfortably crowded on summer weekends but I make no excuse for including some of these gems on the route. Any visit to East Anglia would be incomplete without them, and it is well worth getting there early in the day, or mid-week, to see them in some peace and quiet.

Modern East Anglia is largely arable farming and in some places increased mechanization has brought larger and larger fields with the wholesale removal of hedgerows. There are now some signs that this is at least slowing down and one hopes that campaigns to replace hedgerow trees and coppices will bear fruit. England is already the least-wooded country in Europe, with a high dependence on hedgerow trees in the absence of forests. At least some of the plantations of willows and poplars of the last forty years are now maturing and bringing fresh leaf to the landscape.

As I hinted earlier, the size of East Anglia makes any suggested route no more than a sample. As it stands, the route covers around 200 miles (rather over 300km), and little impromptu detours could add a third as much again. Much has been left out because of the sheer distances involved: indeed, the visit makes little more than a token visit to Norfolk. Given 200 more miles it could have taken in something of the north (and, surprisingly, west) Norfolk coast and the Broads. They will have to wait for another trip.

• THE ROUTE •

Leave **Saffron Walden** N by the B1052, Linton, road, turning R after about 300yd (250m) into uc road to Church End, Ashdon and Bartlow. Continue, crossing dual-carriageway A604 (R and L), to **West Wratting**. Turn R on B1052 through Weston Colville and Brinkley to join B1061 to Dullingham. In centre of village (GR 630 579) turn R on uc road to Stetchworth, and at N end of village bear R round Stetchworth Park to Cheveley. Turn L to junction with B1063, then R into Ashley. In centre of village continue straight on where B-road goes R, through Gazeley to junction at GR 717 649. Bear R on minor road through Needham Street to go L and R on B1506 to pass under A45.

Bear L off B1506 slip-road to A45 to take uc road to **Lackford**—this is part of the old Icknield Way, the pre-Roman road which continues the line of

the Ridgeway (see the Berkshire Downs 'weekend' route) up into East Anglia. In Lackford turn L on A1101 for rather over ¼ mile (500m) to cross River Lark, then R on uc road to West Stow. Turn L in village, then follow road round, briefly joining B1106, to Ingham. Cross A134 to T-junction at GR 866 708; here either L and continue bearing R, or R and continue bearing L, to Great Livermere and Troston. Turn L to Honington, crossing A1088 across The Black Bourn. At GR 917 750, fork L to second fork at GR 959 800 at Knettishall Heath. Bear L across heath to join A1066, then L for about 1¼ miles (2km) to turn R on uc road through the large and scenic **forest** (*see 1 below*) where the A1066 goes sharp left.

At end of forest drive bear R to join B1111 to Garboldisham, crossing A1066 to junction just before crossing of Little Ouse River (GR 003 801). Turn L on uc road through Blo Norton on streamside road to junction marked '26' (m above sl). R on B1113 over bridge at which both **River Waveney** (east-flowing to North Sea) and Little Ouse River (west-flowing to the Wash) appear to rise, then L on uc road to Palgrave (possibility of visiting Diss). Cross A143, L and R over level crossing, then L across B1077 to join B1118 to Hoxne, then follow succession of roads roughly following River Waveney through Shotford Heath, Withersdale Street and Mendham to GR 288 842. Bear R through St Cross, St Margaret and All Saints South Elmham to Rumburgh (there appear to be *seven* South Elmham churches of differing dedications ringing the former Bishop's Palace there—almost an embarrassment of riches!).

At GR 353 803, S of Rumburgh, bear R through Linstead Parva and Cookley to Walpole. L in village on B1117, then R after about 200yd (200m) and immediately left to Bramfield. L on A144 and R after about ¼ mile (400m) through Blackheath, bearing R and R to cross A12 at Red House Farm to Newdelight Walks (possibility of detour to the village of Walberswick and **Southwold** town— *see 2 below*).

From Newdelight Walks follow B1125 S for rather under 2 miles (2½km) to GR 448 700, where bear L across Westleton Walks (*see 3 below*) to Eastbridge. Bear R in village to Theberton, cross B1122 (R and L) to take uc road to outskirts of Saxmundham. Cross A12 (R and L) and follow through to join B1119 to Rendham and **Framling-**

The open road near Bramfield

ham. Leave Framlingham s on B1116 to Broadwater, then bear R on uc road to Easton and Letheringham. Follow minor roads w by Hoo and Friday Street to Cretingham and Framsden. After Framsden turn L on B1077 and continue for a short distance to Helmingham.

At s end of Helmingham village bear R on uc road beside Helmingham Park through Gosbeck to Hemingstone and Dunston's Corner (GR 135 535). Turn L to Claydon (this bit is on the corner of three maps so is a little tricky to follow: indeed, it's much easier on the ground), and in Claydon turn acutely R on B1113 to pass under A45. Immediately after underpass and river bridge turn L on uc road, then L again to join A1100 for about ½ mile (800m). At GR 120 487 turn R on uc road for Little Blakenham and Somersham, then sharp L to Elmsett and **Hadleigh** (*see 4 below*).

From Hadleigh, follow uc road N to GR 024 444, then L to cross A1141 to Kersey (*see 5 below*). At top of Kersey village street (GR 000 443) leave w to Rose Green, then N at Bull's Cross Wood (GR 957 442), crossing B1115 to A1141 at Brent Eleigh. At NW end of village turn R on uc road to Preston, bearing L to **Lavenham** (*see 6 below*). Leave Lavenham s by B1071 past church, then fork R at GR 913 484 on uc road to Long Melford. L on A134 for about ½ mile (800m), then R on uc road to Liston. Turn L then R after about ½ mile (800m) on B1064 through Foxearth to Cavendish (*see 7 below*). From Cavendish w on A1092 for about 2½ miles (4km) to **Clare**.

At junction marked '45' (m above sl) sw of Clare turn L on uc roads to Ashen and Ridgewell. L for about 300yd (250m) on A604, then R on uc roads to Stambourne and Finchingfield (*see 8 below*). Leave on B1057 to Great Bardfield, where turn R on uc road through Little Bardfield and Bardfield End Green to **Thaxted** (*see 9 below*). Leave Thaxted by uc road by church and windmill through Debden Green and Debden to **Saffron Walden**.

• HIGHLIGHTS •

1 The Breckland forests
This forest road gives an attractive glimpse of the man-made plantations which now cover a large

area of Breckland to the north and west of Thetford. (Perhaps, in view of my strictures not to hurry, it is ironic that I was first introduced to this fine route by a 12-hour time-trial race—not the sort of occasion on which one is meant to be looking at the scenery!) Here there is enough mixture in the woodland for the predominant conifers not to be too obtrusive—and in any case pines were indigenous to the acid soils of the Breckland heaths. It is possible to make detours to the other larger forests but they are traversed by few minor roads and have few tracks which are rights of way.

2 Walberswick and Southwold
From Newdelight Walks a fine sandy track, a little soft in places but mostly ridable if you pick your line with care, passes through birch and oak copses and over heathland to join a minor surfaced road to Walberswick. An uncoloured road leads from GR 492 747 to a footpath crossing of the River Blyth, leading down the N bank of the river to a bridleway to Southwold. It is possible to return from Walberswick to Newdelights by the B1387 across Tinker's Walks, then the B1125. It is best to avoid the A12.

3 Westleton Walks
This superb firm-based track leads through delightful woodlands and is easily ridable. From the junction at GR 452 680 it is possible to reach the Royal Society for the Protection of Birds' Minsmere reserve, which is open to the public except on Tuesdays, Sundays and Bank Holidays.

4 Hadleigh
Hadleigh is a superb small town with much of the relief plaster decoration known as 'pargeting' and some fine timbered buildings. Here a great deal of the relief work is coloured, and many of the buildings too are colour-washed. There is a particularly attractive grouping of buildings around the church.

5 Kersey
A much-visited village with a surprisingly steep high street, lined by half-timbered buildings, dropping to a picturesque watersplash. Another place to prosper in wool days, it gave its name to the kersey and kersymere cloths.

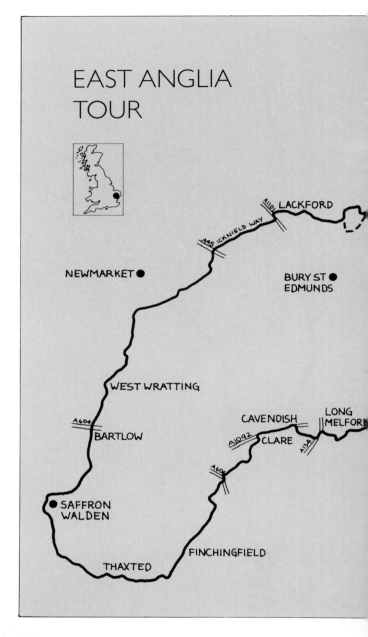

EAST ANGLIA TOUR

6 Lavenham
Lavenham is *the* Suffolk timbered wool town. Despite its popularity with tourists, the narrow streets and overhanging sixteenth-century buildings retain their atmosphere and are here concentrated in a richness unsurpassed in the county. Set a little apart, the great fifteenth-century church, a veritable cathedral to the glory of wool, dominates the town. Be there early or mid-week to beat the crowds.

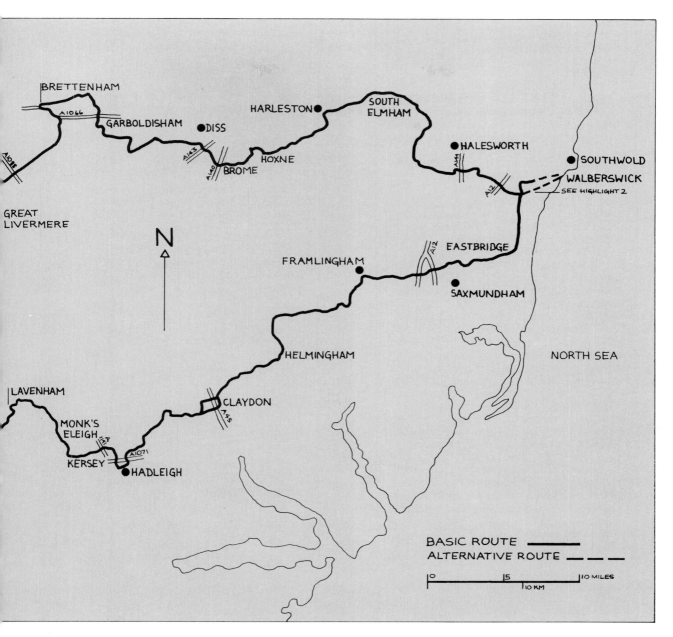

7 Cavendish and Clare

Cavendish always features on picture-postcards of Suffolk, but is none the less attractive for that. The cluster of cottages surrounding the village green and church form a perfect composition. Clare is a small town with superb and elaborate pargeting on many of its buildings.

8 Finchingfield

If Cavendish features in every Suffolk card or calendar, then Finchingfield appears on every Essex one. Once again it's the grouping of houses and church, this time on a rising slope above the village pond.

9 Thaxted

Another Essex classic, with its timbered Guildhall the perfect lead-in to the narrow little lane leading up to the great tall-spired church, internally quite the lightest and airiest I know.

• INFORMATION •

Starting point

As described, the tour starts and finishes at Saffron Walden, Essex. Other possible starting points would be: Newmarket, joining the route at Ashley or Gazeley; Bury St Edmunds, joining at Ingham, Ampton or Great Livermere; Diss, joining at Palgrave or Brome; Saxmundham, joining at Rendon; Ipswich, joining at Little Blakenham; or Colchester, joining at Hadleigh.

Access

Rail routes are: to Audley End for Saffron Walden from London (Liverpool Street) or Cambridge; to Newmarket or Bury St Edmunds from Cambridge or Ipswich; to Colchester or Ipswich from London (Liverpool Street) or Norwich; to Diss from Norwich or Ipswich; to Saxmundham from Ipswich. Some bicycle restrictions. Main access roads are A11/M11 to Saffron Walden and Newmarket, A45 to Bury St Edmunds and Ipswich, A12 to Colchester Ipswich and Saxmundham.

Accommodation

There are B&B possibilities in Bury St Edmunds, Eye (nr Diss), Ixworth (nr Troston), Lavenham, Newmarket, Scole (nr Diss), Saxmundham, Southwold, Stradbroke (nr Hoxne) and Thaxted. There are campsites at: Alpheton (nr Lavenham), Diss, Lonely Farm (nr Rendham), Newmarket, Saxmundham, West Harling Heath (forest), Weybread (nr Shotford Heath) and Wortwell (nr South Elmham and all those churches). The only youth hostel on the route is Saffron Walden; others near(ish) to it are Alpheton (nr Lavenham) and Blaxhall (S of Saxmundham).

Tourist information offices

Saffron Walden, Bury St Edmunds and Southwold.

Cycle shops

There are cycle shops in Saffron Walden, Haverhill, Newmarket, Bury St Edmunds, Diss, Harleston, Wrentham, Framlingham, Stowmarket and Ipswich.

Maps

The route is on OS 1:50 000 sheets 144, 154, 155, 156 and 167. Total tour distance is about 195 miles (315km).

Near Letheringham

WEST SUSSEX, NEW FOREST AND THE ISLE OF WIGHT

• LONGER TOURS •

This tour brings together three distinctly different areas of southern England. It samples first the part-wooded, part-open chalk hills of the South Downs, and some of the clay valleys that border them. Then it crosses to the Isle of Wight, and finally returns to the mainland to visit the woodlands and heaths of the New Forest. All three exemplify in their way the pleasures and problems of cycle-touring in southern England.

Like that of East Anglia, this landscape is very much a man-made one: there are attractive villages, pleasant small towns and an often park-like countryside. However the nearness of London and the generally warmer and sunnier climate of the south bring with them the pressures of popularity and population. At weekends, even in spring and autumn, the well-known spots can become crowded, but there are quiet places and quiet times; late autumn we have found very colourful and tranquil. At least the 'Forest Full' signs which sometimes appear beside the A31 and A35 refer only to the very popular campsites! Many of the tourist traps do retain their fundamental attraction, and such spots as the Needles or Bucklers Hard are well worth seeking out when the crowds are at home.

In following this route I became even more conscious than on any of the others of merely sampling a minute fraction of what the country has to offer. At every Sussex crossroads, two attractive possibilities had to be ruled out; sandy New

Forest tracks beckoned, but had to be left for another day. Obviously you are not restricted to the exact route and there are many possible diversions and alternatives. I have avoided on this route including any of the possible off-road choices, partly because the ease of following them in this part of the world is very dependent on the weather. An upland chalk-based track can be superb in a dry spell and unbelievably sticky and slippery in the wet. If you have a taste for a little adventure, some of the short main-road sections early in the route—pretty well unavoidable if you are to stay on surfaced roads without going miles away from the general direction—can be bypassed by using the waymarked South Downs Way. This designated long-distance path is available to cyclists throughout its length. Similarly on the Isle of Wight parts of the Tennyson Trail follow bridleways; I have seen cyclists on fine June days enraptured by the open down and the call of the larks—and I have seen them on damp spring ones poking at their wheels with bits of stick to unclog the cement-like mud. Use your discretion!

The South Downs are one southern arm of the band of chalk that also underlies the routes in Dorset, East Anglia and the Berkshire Downs. Later sands, gravels and clays fill in the great dip in the chalk that lies either side of Southampton Water, more extensively to the west to form the heaths and woodland of the New Forest. The Isle of Wight is a microcosm of the mainland with a character of its own. The earth movements which hardened the chalk of the Needles tilted the rock strata so that you pass through the succession more rapidly as you cross the island from north to south—and you encounter some quite surprising sharp little hills. Take heart though: Ventnor on the island's cliff-ringed south coast is the sunniest place in Britain.

The New Forest is one of the most intriguing areas in southern England, perhaps because its open heaths and pinewoods seem almost northern in character. Originally designated as a hunting preserve for William the Conqueror, it has never been all 'forest' in the sense of continuous woodland. There is today a picturesque mix of ancient broad-leaved oak, beech and birch forest, some indigenous pine and later coniferous plantation. These are spaced out by great tracts of rolling heather and gorse heath with rough grazing which I find in many ways more impressive than the wooded parts. There are animals in the forest: the ponies are well known (they are not wild) but others are also grazed, including large numbers of free-range pigs. The Forest is crisscrossed with sandy tracks; few are rights of way in the normal sense but there are certain concessions for CTC members.

• THE ROUTE •

There are two possible starting points, Brighton and Chichester; the routes converge at South Harting.

From Brighton to South Harting

Leave **Brighton** by uc road NW to fork at GR 279 086; bear N over shoulder of hill, then past foot of Devil's Dyke to Poynings. L at church through Fulking to junction with A2037, then L on A2037 through Upper Beeding, then join A283 through Bramber and Steyning to junction with B2135 at GR 171 123. R on B2135 to Ashurst, then L on uc road to Dial Post. R on A24 for about ¼ mile (400m), then L on B2224 for just over 1 mile (2km) to GR 147 213. Straight on where B-road goes R, by Whitehall to Broomer's Corner, then R and L to join B2139. L on B2139 for just over 1 mile (2km), then R on uc roads to West Chiltington and Storrington. In Storrington R on A283 for just over ¼ mile (500m), then L on B2139 to Houghton. R at foot of hill to Bury, then R and L across A29 to West Burton and **Bignor** (see

1 below).

From Bignor follow uc roads through Sutton to crossroads at GR 982 177, then L to A285 just S of Heath End. L on A285 for about 300yd (250m), then R on uc road across Lavington Common to Selham. L through South Ambersham and West Lavington to Midhurst. Leave Midhurst SW on uc road to Bepton, then R on minor roads through Didling, Treyford and Elstead to **South Harting**.

From Chichester

Leave **Chichester** NE to roundabout at end of bypass at GR 877 059. L on uc roads to Woodcote crossroads, R through Waterbeach over ridge to East Dean. L through Charlton and Singleton to join A286 to **West Dean** (see *2 below*). At GR 857 124 turn R on uc road to Chilgrove. In Chilgrove turn R on B2141 through North Marden over Harting Downs to South Harting—route from Brighton joins here.

Leave **South Harting** W on B2146 through Nurstead to GR 756 216; turn L on uc road through Buriton to cross A3 onto minor road. Continue W on minor road along foot of downs to GR 685 210. Choice of route: *1* S by Broadhalfpenny Down (see *3 below*) then down to Hambledon (see *4 below*); or *2* by East Meon, Coombe, Teglease Down and Chidden to **Hambledon**. (It is also possible to vary the second variant by detouring from Chidden to Broadhalfpenny Down.)

Leave Hambledon S on B2150, then at GR 642 140 fork R on uc road through World's End, then L (at GR 617 112) and R to cross A333 at Staple Cross. Straight on on uc and minor roads to climb to Nelson Monument (see *5 below*). L at crossroads just past monument along **Port Down** ridge road with tremendous views across Portsmouth Harbour to roundabout at GR 648 066. Take exit from roundabout signposted to Queen Alexandra Hospital and Cosham with a 3 ton limit. At foot of hill under hospital bridge, R on A3 and immediately fork L to cycle bridge over A27/M27 at GR 658 045. Follow A2047 and signs to **Portsmouth Harbour** Stn and Isle of Wight **ferry** (see *6 below*). (There is an alternative 'low-level' route from Chichester via Hayling Island and ferry—see *7 below*.)

From ferry terminal at **Fishbourne** take B-road to A3054, turn R for just over ¼ mile (500m), then L on uc road to Havenstreet. From junction marked '47' (m above sl) just NE of Havenstreet, follow uc

• INFORMATION •

Starting and finishing points

As described the route starts in Brighton or Chichester and finishes at Salisbury. It would also be possible to start at Portsmouth, travelling direct to the Isle of Wight, or from Southampton, travelling by Red Funnel Ferries direct to Cowes, Isle of Wight.

Access

Rail routes are to Brighton from London (Victoria), to Chichester from Southampton, Portsmouth, Havant or Brighton, to Portsmouth and Havant from London (Waterloo), to Lymington via Brockenhurst from London (Waterloo) or Weymouth, Dorchester and Bournemouth, and to Salisbury from London (Waterloo) or Exeter. There are also some through trains from the north and the midlands to Southampton, Portsmouth and Brighton. Main access roads are the M23/A23 to Brighton, the A3/A286 or A29/A27 to Chichester, and the A3 to Portsmouth. Routes from Salisbury are by the A30, then M3 or A34. Sea routes are to Portsmouth from le Havre, St Malo and Cherbourg, France, and Jersey and Guernsey, Channel Islands. There are also ferries from Dieppe, France, to Newhaven.

Accommodation

There are B&B possibilities in Bepton, Bignor, Brighton, Brockenhurst, Chichester, East Dean, Fordingbridge, Fulking, Godshill (the New Forest one), Lymington, Midhurst, South Gorley, South Harting and Steyning on the mainland; and in Bonchurch, Brightstone, Chale Green, Freshwater, Totland Bay and Yarmouth on the Isle of Wight. There are campsites at Boldre, Brockenhurst, Cosham, Fordingbridge, Godshill (New Forest), Goodwood, Hambrook (nr Fulkington), Hooksway (nr Chilgrove), Lymington, Red Shoot and Southbourne (nr Fulkington) on the mainland; and at Brightstone, Chale, Niton, Totland Bay, Wroxall and Yarmouth on the Isle of Wight (the Camping Club recommends booking at Isle of Wight sites—this could well be desirable even for lightweight campers in the summer). There are youth hostels at Portsmouth, Burley (New Forest) and Salisbury on the mainland, and at Wootton Bridge, Sandown, Whitwell and Totland Bay on the Isle of Wight. If you need to consult directories or listings, check under East Sussex (for Brighton area), West Sussex, Hampshire, Isle of Wight, Wiltshire.

The Needles, Isle of Wight

roads s over Mersley Down (extensive views s) to Newchurch, then fork R to cross A3056 at Hale Common. Continue on minor road to cross A3020 at Sandford (*see 8 below*) and on to Wroxall. Turn R on B3327, then R again on uc cliff-top road to St Lawrence, Whitwell and Niton. Join A3085 by Chale to GR 474 782, turn R on uc roads through Pyle, Atherfield Green, Little Atherfield and Yafford to **Brightstone**.

Leave Brightstone on uc road N over Westover Down to Calbourne, cross B3401 to GR 426 877. Turn R through Five Houses, then L to cross A3054 at Hebberdens and on to **Newtown** (*see 9 below*). Leave Newtown s to A3054, then turn L at Shalfleet church along winding roads to Wellow,

Thorley Street and Thorley. At bend in B3401 at GR 367 888 turn L on uc road by Wilmingham to join B3399 to Afton. Cross A3055 to join road out to **Alum Bay** and **The Needles** (*see 10 below*). Return by B3322 to Totland, then A3054 to **Yarmouth** for **ferry** to Lymington.

Leave **Lymington** by uc roads E by South Baddesley, then choice of routes to Bucklers Hard (GR 408 999) (*see 11 below*). The choice of routes to Hatchet Gate (GR 370 017), and B3055 to **Brockenhurst**. Cross A337 and B3055 to follow road to Rhinefield ornamental drive. This crosses the A35 at GR 266 063 and continues to pass under the A31 at GR 235 096 (*see 12 below*). Turn R at GR 221 097 and follow road round past Red Shoot to Rock-

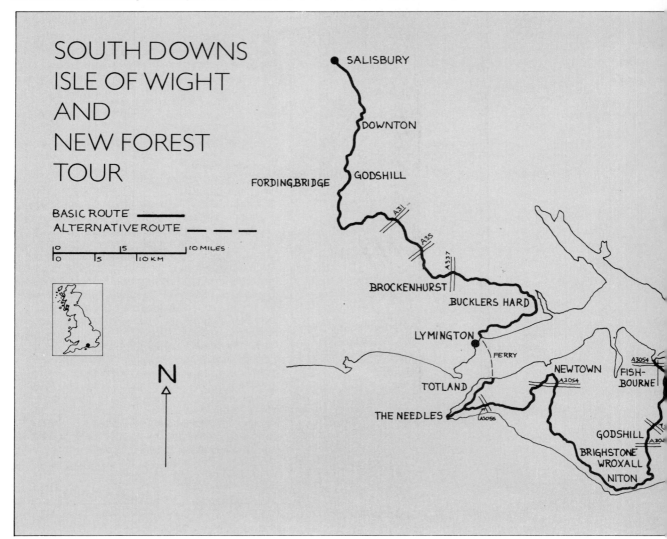

SOUTH DOWNS
ISLE OF WIGHT
AND
NEW FOREST
TOUR

BASIC ROUTE ———
ALTERNATIVE ROUTE — — —

0   5   10 MILES
0   5   10 KM

ford. From Rockford follow uc road N through Stuckton and Godshill. At GR 176 149 at Godshill turn L on uc road to Woodgreen and Downton; loop by Castle Hill (GR 166 161) is well worth following (*see 13 below*). In Downton cross B3080 and continue on uc road to **Salisbury**.

• HIGHLIGHTS •
and a few practical points

1 Bignor Roman villa
The Roman villa at GR 987 147 is open to the public (except in winter) and has some very fine mosaic floors, said to be the best of their kind outside Italy.

2 West Dean and Singleton
There is an interesting open-air museum at West Dean, where typical Sussex buildings from a variety of sites have been re-erected as a collection of vernacular architecture in the form of a composite village street. The collection is continually being augmented. Between Singleton and West Dean there is also the Chilsdown vineyard, at the Old Station House and open to visitors. Apart from the pioneering one noted at Hambledon (*see 4 below*), there are several smaller vineyards along or close to the route. The English Vineyards Association leaflet gives details of all these. It is well worth obtaining a copy (see 'Useful Addresses' section).

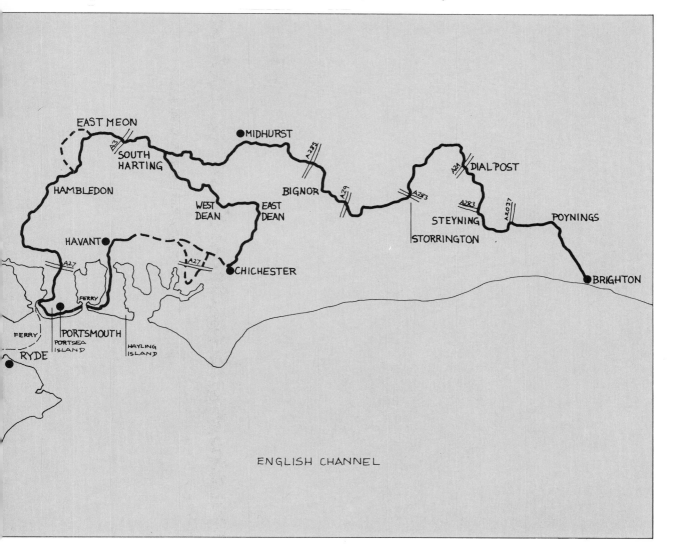

• INFORMATION •

Tourist information offices
Chichester, Southsea, Beaulieu, Lyndhurst and Salisbury on the mainland. Cowes, Ryde, Sandown, Shanklin, Ventnor, Yarmouth and Newport on the Isle of Wight. The Isle of Wight Tourist Office (Quay Store, Town Quay, Newport, PO30 2EF (tel: (0983) 524343)) produces a booklet *Cycling on the Isle of Wight* which gives details of routes, cycle shops and hirers, and cycleways on the island. They also produce an accommodation booklet.

Cycle shops
There are cycle shops in Brighton, Gosport, Portsmouth, Southampton, Lymington and Salisbury on the mainland, and in Cowes, Ryde, Sandown, Freshwater, Ventnor and Newport on the Isle of Wight.

New Forest off-road routes
As already noted many of the unsurfaced tracks are not rights-of-way in the usual sense, although there is permissive access to some of them. On behalf of its members the CTC has obtained from the Conservators of the New Forest general permission for them to use all tracks within the Forest for ordinary non-competitive cycling. Forest wardens may ask users for proof of CTC membership. The CTC's address appears in the 'Useful addresses' section.

Maps
The route is on os 1:50 000 sheets 184, 185 (very briefly), 195, 196, 197, 198 (if starting from Brighton). The 1:63 360 Tourist sheet New Forest can replace 184 and 195. The tour distance from Brighton to Salisbury is about 180 miles (290km). Starting from Chichester reduces the total by some 40 miles (65km).

New Forest ponies at Goshill

3 The birthplace of cricket

The game of cricket was first played on the fine grass of Broadhalfpenny Down: the local Hambledon club was founded in 1760. There is a commemorative monument at GR 676 167 opposite, appropriately enough, the Bat and Ball inn.

4 Hambledon

Another Hambledon down, Windmill Down, is the site of a further pioneering venture: the first postwar English vineyard was established here in 1952.

5 Nelson

The great obelisk of the Nelson monument bears fulsome tributes to the Admiral from those who served under him. The nearby nineteenth-century Fort Nelson, one of a series which rings Portsmouth Harbour, is at times open to the public. Nelson's Trafalgar flagship, *HMS Victory* is close to the station at Portsmouth Harbour (*6 below*) and is also open to the public.

6 Isle of Wight ferries

There are two Isle of Wight ferry services from Portsmouth Harbour station, to Ryde and Fishbourne. The Ryde service is now operated by a limited-capacity high-speed catamaran which does not always have bicycle space; the Fishbourne service is a car ferry and has plenty. Bicycles travel free.

7 From Chichester via Hayling Island

A possible and considerably shorter route from Chichester to the Isle of Wight ferry terminal is to leave Chichester NW by the B2178 to East Ashling, then the B2146 to Funtington. At GR 798 083 continue straight on where the B2146 goes sharp right, along uc road to cross B2147 (L and R, about 100yd (100m) apart) and then by Aldsworth and Southleigh Forest to Havant. Leave Havant S on B2149, cross A27 then follow A3023 across bridge to Stoke on Hayling Island. Follow uc roads to w extremity of island to take ferry to Portsea Island. Follow uc road round coast of island through Old Portsmouth to Portsmouth Harbour station and Isle of Wight ferry. It is also possible to make a detour after leaving Chichester to visit the attractive village of Bosham with its tidal ford. Avoid using the A27: it's an appalling road for cycling.

8 Godshill

From Sandford it is about 1 mile (1½km) w along the A3020 to the attractive (and popular) village of Godshill, probably the most-photographed place on the island.

9 Newtown

This is a fascinating place. Originally intended to be developed as a port, it was defeated by the silting of the Newtown River, now a quiet and almost eerie waste of marsh. Part of it is a nature reserve. The remarkable and picturesque Town Hall stands apart from the rest of the village as a monument to the town which never grew.

10 Alum Bay and the Needles

Alum Bay with its cliffs with vertical bands of differently coloured sands is now rather commercialized—there's even a chair-lift down to the beach—but the coloured cliffs remain impressive seen from below, or from above. There's a good viewpoint on the path out to the Needles. These sharply-pointed rock 'stacks' with their colourful red-banded lighthouse are the western prolongation of the hardened chalk spine of the island. They are best seen either from the end of the Old Battery or from the cliffs above.

11 Bucklers Hard

This is yet another popular spot but well worth a visit if you can get there mid-week or out of season. Bucklers Hard was a shipyard in the days when ships were of oak, of which the New Forest was one source. There is a very picturesque run of former shipwrights' cottages down to the Beaulieu River.

12 Rhinefield

This route follows what is almost a linear arboretum with many exotic trees as well as some fine stretches of native species. Where the road emerges onto the open heath it also gives a taste of the magnificent open spaces of the Forest.

13 Castle Hill

The road from Godshill round by Castle Hill passes through a sample of the real Forest, with its scattered cottages, each with enough of a clearing to support it and sited for the best of shelter and sunshine.

MID-WALES

• LONGER TOURS •

Mid-Wales holds many attractions for the cycle-tourist, partly because it is readily accessible from a large part of England but also because of the extensive network of minor roads and ridable tracks, something which craggier Snowdonia conspicuously lacks. Although beginning at Shrewsbury in the English county of Shropshire, the route spends most of its time in the Welsh county of Powys, which roughly corresponds to the old kingdom of the same name. The county and the route offer quite a variety of landscape: river valleys, forests, man-made lakes and open mountain and moorland. Certainly for me at least, a lot of the pleasure of Powys is in the feeling of being in the high places with their broad horizons and sweeping panoramas. The route takes in several favourites.

Parts of Powys are very sparsely populated, with long distances between anything other than isolated farms, and the route description warns of some quite extensive foodless stretches. Certainly there are parts where you will travel for miles without seeing a soul: it was in Powys that we spent the whole of one August holiday afternoon riding along a network of small lanes and met only a tractor-borne shepherd.

You do not have to be particularly sensitive to perceive that Powys is not in England. One of the successes of those trying to assure a continuing place for the Welsh language has been the provision, as an accepted policy, of road signs in both Welsh and English. Unlike their English counterparts, Welsh place-names have not been subjected to Scandinavian or Saxon influences, and only a little to Roman and Norman ones, so many are directly translatable. It is quite fascinating to roam the map with a modern dictionary and discover the appositeness of some of the names, and then confirm it on the ground. It is always reassuring to discover that the ridge marked *Craig Ddu*

really does look to be the line of black rock that the name suggests, or that *Ty'n yr Cwm* is indeed the house in the valley. Many larger places have become known by quite different English names and these are now being reclaimed, so you will find, for instance, such places as the Victorian English Builth Wells now reverting to Llanfair ym Muallt. Despite its difficult appearance to English eyes, mostly because some letters have quite different values in Welsh, it is basically a phonetic language ('. . . like Polish', explained our teacher, reassuringly). Welsh also shares with the other members of both branches of the Celtic languages a system of 'mutations', whereby some initial consonants change to softer, aspirated or nasal forms in certain circumstances, largely as an aid to flowing speech. The effect on place-names can be that adjectives change among other things according to the gender of what they describe (*du* or *ddu* for black, for example), or that names such as the *Buallt* area in which Builth Wells lies become softened to *Muallt* in the combined name. The Ordnance Survey leaflet on Welsh and Scottish place-names gives examples.

The mid-Wales route is quite a hilly one: this is inescapable in what is, after all, a mountainous area. Most of the steeper hills are short pitches pulling out of a river valley, while many little roads which broadly follow streams do tend rather to climb and plunge, probably originally to bypass difficult or boggy stretches. The mountain climbs are generally steadier, and there are some superb open downhill runs. As in all mountain areas the weather can change very rapidly, and it is always cooler and windier at the tops of passes or on high open ridges.

In view of the unpredictability of the weather in this mountainous region, it is a good idea to give particular thought to what you wear when cycling this beautiful route.

• INFORMATION •

Starting and finishing points

As described the tour starts at Shrewsbury and finishes at Abergavenny. It would also be possible to start at: Welshpool, joining the route just before Bettws Cedewain; or Church Stretton, joining the route at Bridges. A possible alternative finishing point would be Hereford, leaving the route at Hay-on-Wye or Llanfihangel Crucorney.

Access

Rail routes are: to Shrewsbury from London (Euston), Birmingham and Wolverhampton, or from Manchester and Crewe, or from Chester; to Welshpool from Shrewsbury; from Hereford to Shrewsbury, Newport, Worcester, Birmingham, Oxford or London (Paddington); from Abergavenny to Newport, Hereford or Shrewsbury. The route also intercepts the central Wales line from Shrewsbury to Swansea at Cynghordy, Llangammarch Wells and Builth Road (for Builth Wells). Some bicycle restrictions possible, particularly on central Wales line until bridge near Llandovery, undermined by flood waters in autumn 1987, is replaced. Main access roads are the A5 and A49 to Shrewsbury and the A40 to Abergavenny.

Accommodation

There are B&B possibilities at Abergavenny, Boughrood, Builth Wells, Church Stoke, Cusop (nr Hay-on-Wye), Dylife, Erwood, Glasbury, Hay-on-Wye, Llanidloes, Llanthony, Llanveynoe (nr Longtown), Llanwrtyd Wells (near Llangammarch Wells), Longtown, Meole Brace, Montgomery, Pandy (nr Llanfihangel Crucorney), Ratlinghope, Rhayader, Shrewsbury, Staylittle, Stiperstones, Talgarth and Wentnor (nr Bridges). There are campsites at Abergavenny, Boughrood, Bronllys, Cwmyoy, Hay-on-Wye, Llangammarch Wells, Llangurig, Llanidloes, Llanthony, Olchon, Pandy (nr Llanfihangel Crucorney), Pontygelli (nr Agergavenny), Ratlinghope, Rhayader, Talgarth and Wentnor (nr Bridges). There are youth hostels at Shrewsbury, Bridges, Blaencaron (nr Tregaron), Dôlgoch (above Llyn Brianne), Ty'n Cornel (very remote, above Llyn Brianne), Bryn Poeth Uchaf (remote, above Cynghordy), Capel-y-Ffin. If you need to consult directories or listings, check under Shropshire, Herefordshire, Powys and Gwent.

On the old Machynlleth coach road, below Dylife

• THE ROUTE •

Leave **Shrewsbury** sw by uc road to cross A5 and then pass through Nobold, Annscroft and Longden to Pulverbatch (*see 1 below*). Climb over Cothercott Hill (345m) and then through pass to Bridges. At GR 393 966 turn R up hill, forking L at GR 388 971 to pass over end of **Stiperstones** ridge (*see 2 below*) to Pennerley and Shelve. About 1 mile (1½km) beyond Shelve turn L on A488 for just over 1 mile (2km) to GR 319 979. Turn R on uc road through The Marsh (*see 3 below*) to Priestweston, then to outskirts of Old Church Stoke, where turn R to **Church Stoke**. Leave Church Stoke w on A4489, then immediately R on uc road by Rhiston, Gwarthlow and Pen-y-Bryn Hall to B4385. (By this time you will have crossed the England-Wales border five times; you are now definitively in Wales.) Follow B4385 to **Montgomery** (*see 4 below*), and continue on B4385, bearing R under railway where B4386 forks L.

Cross River Severn and at GR 196 985 bear L on uc road past Trwstllewelyn to cross A438 and follow uc road to Betws Cedewain. Cross B4389, then after about 200yd (200m) turn R to follow uc roads (choice) to join B4568 at GR 059 930. Turn R on B4568, then B4569 to Caersws. Cross A470, still on B4569, to Trefeglwys. Fork R opposite church in Trefeglwys on uc road through Llawryglyn, forking right at GR 925 910 for **Staylittle** (*see 5 below*). Turn R on B4518 for rather under ¼ mile (300m) and then L on uc road through forest past Cwmbiga to follow N bank of River Severn—here only about 4 miles (6km) from its source on Pumlumon; interestingly the Wye rises only about 2 miles (3km) away—they do not meet until Chepstow, by which time the Severn has become Britain's longest river. At fork above Mount Severn (GR 944 841) turn sharp R (unless travelling on into Llanidloes, 1 mile (1½km) NE) and then L immediately after bridge, to follow uc roads to **Llangurig**. Unless you plan to visit Rhayader (below) this will be the last chance to shop for nearly 30 miles (50km).

Cross A44 (L and R) and follow uc road down w side of River Wye to junction at GR 959 684. Here there are two alternatives to the basic route—*see 6 below*. Basic route turns right (unless visiting **Rhayader**) on uc road to Cwmystwyth; this is the old Aberystwyth coach road mostly across open moorland and rough grazing to Cwmystwyth—if

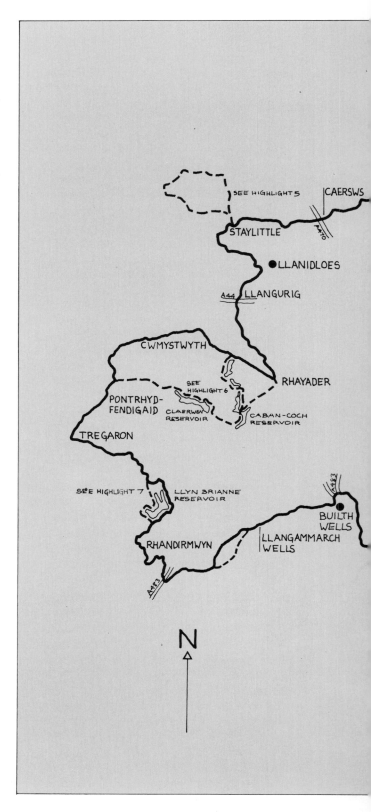

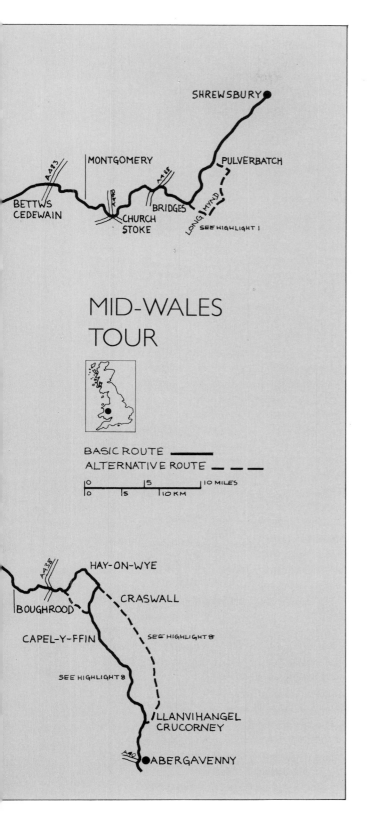

MID-WALES
TOUR

BASIC ROUTE ━━━━━
ALTERNATIVE ROUTE ▬ ▬ ▬

you are not visiting Rhayader there is still no shop for about 18 miles (nearly 30km). After Cwmystwyth at GR 780 742 fork L on B4574, then B4343 to **Pontrhydygroes**. Continue on B4343 through Ysbyty Ystwyth, Ffair Rhos and Pontrhydfendigaid to **Tregaron**.

In Tregaron turn L over river bridge, then L again on very hilly uc road, signposted as mountain road to Abergwesyn. Once again there is no shop or pub for about 22 hilly miles (35km). At junction at GR 762 577—by what is the most isolated telephone box I know—fork R on uc road to **Llyn Brianne** (*see 7 below*). At junction at GR 805 537, turn R on very scenic uc road to follow E side of Llyn Brianne to Rhandirmwyn. About 1½ miles (2km) S of Rhandirmwyn, at GR 781 421, turn L to Cynghordy and A483.

At Cynghordy turn R on A483 for rather over ¼ mile (500m), then left on uc road through Tirabad (choice of routes) to Llangammarch Wells. Continue on S side of River Irfon to **Builth Wells**. From Builth Wells cross river and turn R at roundabout on A483, then A481 to GR 062 517. Turn R on B4567 to follow E bank of River Wye. At GR 090 439, turn R on uc road to follow scenic drive on track of former railway beside River Wye to Boughrood, then on B4350 to **Glasbury**. Turn R on A438 to cross river, R after bridge for about ¼ mile (400m), then L on uc road to join Talgarth to Llanigon road—then choice of routes (*see 8 below*) over **Black Mountains** to Llanfihangel Crucorney. At Stanton (GR 315 210) turn S on uc road past Blaengavenny to **Abergavenny**.

• HIGHLIGHTS •
and diversions

1 The Long Mynd

At Pulverbatch the very prominent ridge ahead and to the left is the Long Mynd, well worth a visit for its extensive views E over the Shropshire hills and Wenlock Edge and W towards Wales. The top is for the most part open heather-covered moorland. From junction at GR 423 020 just S of Pulverbatch turn L to climb by Pease Lane, Picklescott and Betchcott, then R at GR 445 976 to top of ridge by Robin Hood's Butts. From GR 433 965 the easily ridable ridge track leads to the Church Stretton to Ratlinghope road at GR 420 953. The route to Bridges is via Ratlinghope.

• INFORMATION •

Tourist information offices
Shrewsbury, Llanidloes, Rhayader, Tregaron, Builth Wells, Hay-on-Wye, Abergavenny.

Cycle shops
There are cycle shops in Shrewsbury, Church Stretton (across Long Mynd from Bridges), Welshpool, Newtown, Llandrindod Wells, Llanidloes, Llanwrtyd Wells (mountain bikes), Hay-on-Wye, Abergavenny and Brecon.

Maps
The route is on OS 1:50 000 sheets 126, 136, 137, 147, 161. The basic tour distance is about 200 miles (320km).

Llyn Brianne reservoir

2 The Stiperstones

From the long climb up from Bridges the bristly ridge of the Stiperstones is very prominent ahead. The stones themselves are outcrops of the very old and very hard Stiperstones Quartzite. A track leads up from the road to the stones. There are tremendous views in all directions from the top.

3 Corndon Hill

A superb alternative to the road route through Priestweston is to follow the track from GR 302 976 to Old Church Stoke over the shoulder of Corndon Hill. The first, uphill, part is a firm-based stony track, the descent mainly on sheep-cropped turf. Both are readily ridable. Once you are over the top there are broad views s and w—including the scene on the cover of this book, taken one August bank holiday weekend.

4 Montgomery

Montgomery, *Trefaldwyn* or *Y Drefaldwyn*—'the town of Baldwin', the original builder of the stronghold there—is a pleasant little border town with much half-timbering. The local history society has helpfully labelled many of the buildings, detailing their history.

5 The Machynlleth coach road and Bwlch Glynmynydd

From Staylittle there is a magnificent detour which takes in two of my favourite Welsh roads. It is quite strenuous, but the tremendous views across to Cader Idris and Aran Fawddwy are well worth it. The circuit begins at GR 883 938, at the junction marked '309' (m above sl), where you follow a uc road w towards Dylife. Shortly after the junction, on the first climb, the enormous cleft of the valley of the Afon Twymyn opens up to the R; a grassy scramble brings you within sight of the noisy waterfall at Ffrwd Fawr at the head of the valley. Dylife was once a lead-mining village but little now remains. From here the road climbs to its exposed 509m summit, but as you turn the corner there is the whole E face of Cader Idris and the Dyfi valley spread before you. The road falls away in a tremendous and exhilarating—and often very windy—descent. At the junction at GR 804 985 the return route doubles back sharply to the R to follow a very hilly 2½ mile (4km) course

through Melinbyrhedyn to Talywern. (The straight-ahead alternative at GR 804 985 continues into the town of Machynlleth.) At Talywern turn R for the long but relatively gentle climb up the valley to the miniature pass of Bwlch Glynmynydd, 305m. From here a brisk descent returns you to the B4518 at Dolgadfan. The return route to Staylittle on the B4518 is a longish but gentle climb, with a final short downhill run. I would consider the approximately 20 mile (30km) circuit to make a quite full morning or afternoon's ride.

6 The Elan and Claerwen reservoirs

There are two further possibilities from the start of the Aberystwyth coach road at GR 959 684. Both routes drop first into the village of Llansantffraed-Cwmdeuddwr and turn R to follow first the B4518, then its continuation as a uc road to the junction by the Carreg Ddu reservoir at GR 911 640. The first, all-road, alternative then continues along the road past successively the Carreg Ddu, Pen-y-garreg and Craig Goch reservoirs with their solid Victorian dams and works, to join the old coach road to Cwmystwyth at Pont-ar-Elan. The second possibility turns L over the bridge at GR 911 640 to follow the fine open valley of the Afon Claerwen to GR 871 636, beside the Claerwen dam. Here the road becomes a firm-based shale track and the route follows this along its superb and tortuous path round the bare shores of the Claerwen reservoir. At the head of the reservoir the track becomes slightly rougher for a spell and there is an unbridged crossing of the Afon Claerddu, which you can normally manage dry-shod by stepping from boulder to boulder. This part of mid-Wales is one of the few places where the quite rare red kite breeds and several times we have sat and watched these great birds of prey wheel overhead in the sky above the Claerwen. After a further mile (some 1½km) you reach a surfaced road once more with fine views s over the small lakes which are the headwaters of the Afon Teifi. The road rejoins the basic route at Ffair Rhos. The 16-mile (25km) stretch from the Carreg Ddu reservoir to Ffair Rhos can take a full morning or afternoon.

7 Llyn Brianne

There are two possibilities around Llyn Brianne,

the new lake formed by damming the Afon Tywi. The first, the basic route, follows the very attractive and highly scenic road (scenic as in views and scenic as in railway) on its twisting and switchback career to the E of the lake. This road is becoming rather popular at holiday times, though, and there is a quieter alternative on an unsurfaced but readily ridable track which branches off by a minute chapel at GR 785 533, eventually returning to the basic route just after crossing the dam.

8 The Black Mountains

There are many ways of crossing the escarpment of this fine range, including two superb tracks following the valleys of the Grwyne Fawr and Grwyne Fechan streams. The two road crossings possible from Hay-on-Wye are over the 551m Bwlch-yr-Efengyl ('Gospel Pass') or the less spec-tacular but nonetheless very attractive 442m summit leading to the valley of the River Monnow. Both roads leave Hay-on-Wye by the same road, signposted Capel-y-Ffin, at GR 227 420—and both routes involve quite a strenuous climb. At GR 248 395 the Monnow valley route goes straight on to Craswall, while the Bwlch-yr-Efengyl route turns R. After an initial steep pitch it comes out onto a tremendous natural lawn, with broad views of both the escarpment and the Wye valley below. It is possible to reach this 'lawn' directly from the Talgarth to Hay road by several quite tough little roads, all of them good, with the one via Pennant especially fine. The Bwlch-yr-Efengyl and Capel-y-Ffin road is unfortunately another which has become too popular at summer weekends and holidays—sadly the case with so many. Nevertheless, it still holds a special place for me: it was my first-ever mountain pass.

NORTHUMBRIA, THE BORDERS AND THE ROMAN WALL

• LONGER TOURS •

Northumberland, the setting for by far the greater part of this tour, is a largely unspoilt and unvisited county. Yet even here recent developments have changed part of the landscape, with one of the largest tracts of afforestation in Britain, and yet another claimant—Kielder Water—to be the largest man-made lake in Europe. The hills on whose slopes the forests lie are the Cheviot Hills, culminating in the great rounded dome of the Cheviot itself, 815m. The centre of this dome is of granite, the remnant of an intrusion of a mass of molten rock into the surrounding sandstone in a burst of volcanic activity some 380 million years ago. In a further spell some 90 million years later another feature was developed: the Great Whin Sill. Immense pressures forced molten rock actually *between* the more or less horizontal layers of the deposited sedimentary rocks to form a great sheet of the very hard volcanic rock, dolerite. This is more resistant to the wear and tear of erosion than the softer sedimentary rock and so stands proud where it reaches the surface: the north-facing crags which Hadrian's Wall so artistically follows are part of the edge of the Great Whin Sill, as are the coastal crags on which Bamburgh and Dunstanburgh castles are perched.

Streams flow in a radiating pattern from the slopes of the Cheviot, often following geological fault lines and carving steep-sided valleys. To see the best of the hills it is worth taking the time for one or two out-and-home detours up these lonely valleys. Some of the streams are the head waters of salmon rivers, particularly the Coquet and the Breamish. In autumn you can watch the great fish leap in the legendary manner, as they try to make their way back to the pools where they were hatched.

The Scottish part of the route is no more than a token visit to the fine Border country, a region of tranquil river dales and often austere but handsome towns: tall Jedburgh and cobblestoned Kelso we found particularly attractive, and very different.

No visit would be complete without a look at Hadrian's Wall, the remains of that Roman feat of engineering which crossed the country from the Solway to the Tyne. Parts have been restored and there are explanatory exhibits at some of the museums. I suppose that nowadays one tends to forget the original defensive role of the Wall in admiring the perfection of line with which the structure follows natural features, apparently almost flowing along the edges of the crags. As so often when form has to follow function a true art emerges.

The cycling in this part of the world varies. There are sharp climbs and drops where the route crosses the 'grain' of the river valleys, and some long but not particularly steep hauls as the road climbs over the border from Kielder and then over Wauchope Forest shortly after. But

Dunstanburgh Castle

many of the roads along quiet river valleys or on the short excursion out to the Northumbrian coast are quite gentle. The one thing they all share is a general lack of traffic—except perhaps the Military Road, B6318, along the Wall, and the brief meetings with A68 and A1 where you cross them.

As far as accommodation and the replenishment of supplies is concerned, the route is mixed. On the high moor you may well go some way between shops or pubs, and some of the small villages too have no shop: I don't recollect seeing much between Wooler and Bamburgh, for example, nor between Embleton and Glanton. On the Scottish side there are gaps as well, particularly on the first part after Saughtree.

• THE ROUTE •

The route as described is in the form of two circuits from the small Northumberland town of **Bellingham**. The first and much larger—some 170 miles (270km)—circumnavigates the Cheviot, the second, of nearly 50 miles (80km), visits Hadrian's Wall. In place of the second circuit it is possible to follow a linear route from or to **Carlisle** or **Penrith**, also visiting the Wall.

Round the Cheviot
From **Bellingham** either of 2 uc roads (N or S side of the River North Tyne) to Kielder Water (*see 1 below*) and Kielder. Continue through forest over border to Saughtree. R on B6357 (fine open moorland climb, then Wauchope Forest) to GR 590 089, L on uc roads to Bonchester Bridge. L on A6088 for 200yd (200m), then R on B6357; after about ¾ mile (1km) fork L on uc road towards Bedrule and at foot of steep hill just before bridge at GR 597 177 turn L to join A698 to Denholm.

In Denholm turn R on B6405, then R after bridge over River Teviot on uc road to follow north bank of river to Ancrum: this is **Teviotdale**. Join B6400, R and L at A68, still on B6400 to Nisbet, where bear left on uc road to GR 692 281 (from here it is possible to continue through Roxburgh to visit fine border town of **Kelso**, with Abbey, castle and attractive cobbled streets in centre; route to Town Yetholm would then be B6352). Basic route goes R across River Teviot to Kalemouth, R on A698 for about 200yd (200m), then L on B6401 to Morebattle (possible out-and-home detour up

Kale Water through Hownam to Hindhope) and Town Yetholm (further possible out-and-home detour up Bowmont Water to Sourhope or Cocklawfoot).

In Town Yetholm turn R on uc road to **Kirk Yetholm**, village which marks the northern end of the Pennine Way. Continue on road round foot of hills, crossing back into England at Yetholm Mains, to join B6351 through Kirknewton to Akeld, then join A697 and fork R on uc road into **Wooler**. **Wooler** is a pleasant Northumbrian small town with shops and accommodation.

Leave Wooler north-eastwards by B6348 to Chatton (possibility of visit to Chillingham—*see 2 below*—either from here or on return route) and then on to junction at GR 096 295, marked '147' (m above sl). Bear L on uc road through Warenton to cross A1 (L and R) at New Mousen. Continue to join B1342 to Bamburgh (much-restored and lived-in castle), then B1340 to **Seahouses** (*see 3 below*). Continue along B1340 via Beadnell (attractive small harbour), or by minor roads inland, to join B1339 to Embleton. From here it is possible to follow very minor road to Dunston Steads (GR 245 224), then take path past Dunstanburgh Castle superbly sited ruin on coast, to **Craster**, then return by uc roads to Embleton.

Leave Embleton on uc road to GR 220 235, L on B1340 for just over ¼ mile (500m), then follow uc roads past Doxford Hall and Tyneley to cross A1 at North Charlton (L and R). Superb moorland road over to Hepburn. At foot of hill at GR 060 245, turn L (*or see 2 below*) through Old Bewick (tremendous views across to Cheviot) to join B6346 to Eglingham. Turn R on uc road through Beanley to **Powburn** (possible out-and-home detour up valley of River Breamish through Ingram—*see 4 below*).

Leave Powburn S on uc road which bears R where main A697 bends L, to Glanton by Great Ryle to Prendwick. From here follow road which skirts foot of hills through Alnham, Scrainwood, Biddlestone to Low Alwinton (*see 5 below*), then Harbottle and Holystone to join B6341 at GR 974 996. R on B6341 up very attractive valley to Elsdon. Choice of route: *1* by B6341 and A696 to Otterburn, then B6320 to Bellingham; or *2* by uc road S to Raylees, R on A696, L at Monkridge to East and West Woodburn, R and L at A68 on uc road to **Bellingham**.

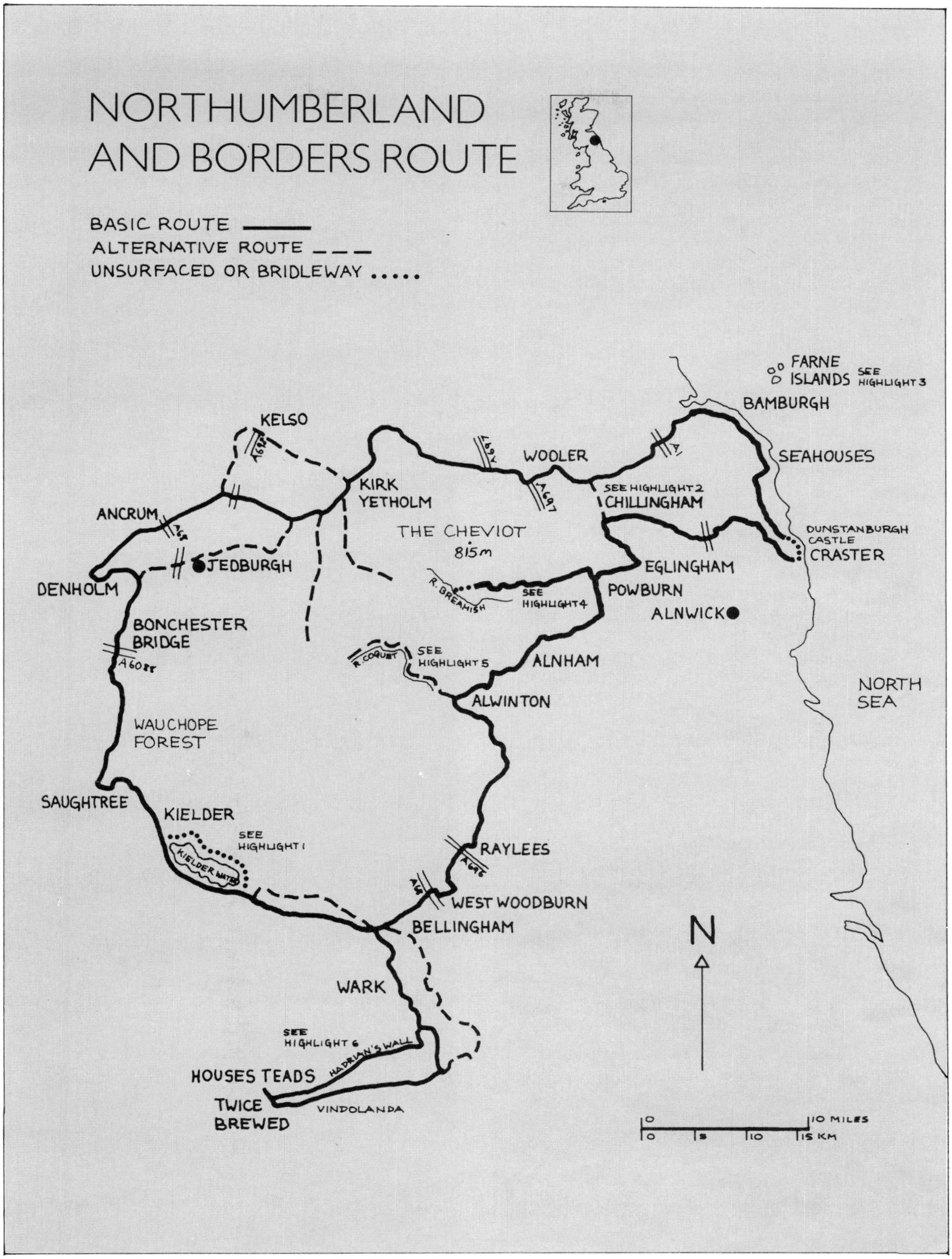

NORTHUMBERLAND AND BORDERS ROUTE

BASIC ROUTE ——————
ALTERNATIVE ROUTE _ _ _
UNSURFACED OR BRIDLEWAY .....

FARNE ISLANDS SEE HIGHLIGHT 3

BAMBURGH

SEAHOUSES

KELSO

WOOLER

A697

KIRK YETHOLM

SEE HIGHLIGHT 2

CHILLINGHAM

DUNSTANBURGH CASTLE

CRASTER

ANCRUM

THE CHEVIOT 815 m

A697

JEDBURGH

R. BREAMISH

SEE HIGHLIGHT 4

EGLINGHAM

POWBURN

ALNWICK

DENHOLM

BONCHESTER BRIDGE

A6088

R. COQUET

SEE HIGHLIGHT 5

ALNHAM

ALWINTON

NORTH SEA

WAUCHOPE FOREST

SAUGHTREE

KIELDER

SEE HIGHLIGHT 1

KIELDER WATER

RAYLEES

A68

WEST WOODBURN

BELLINGHAM

N

WARK

SEE HIGHLIGHT 6

HADRIAN'S WALL

HOUSES TEADS

TWICE BREWED

VINDOLANDA

0   10 MILES
0   5   10   15 KM

• INFORMATION •

Starting and finishing points
As described the tour is an unequal figure-of-eight, with both loops starting and finishing at Bellingham, Northumberland. It is also possible to start or finish at Penrith or Carlisle: itineraries are detailed in the route description. It would also be possible to start from: Morpeth, joining the large loop at Holystone or Bellingham; Alnwick, joining at Glanton; Newcastle upon Tyne, joining at Chollerford or Bellingham; Berwick upon Tweed, joining at Akeld, Wooler or Chatton; or Jedburgh, Kelso or Wooler.

Access
Rail routes are to Newcastle, Morpeth or Berwick upon Tweed. Many bicycle restrictions; Berwick has the advantage that sleeper trains call there—these have no bicycle restriction at present. Main access roads are A1 and then minor roads to Bellingham or Wooler. A1 to Newcastle or Morpeth, M6/A6 to Carlisle or Penrith, A68 to Jedburgh, A68, then A6069 to Kelso.

Accommodation
There are B&B possibilities in Bellingham, Greenhead, Jedburgh, Kelso, Kielder, Kirk Yetholm, Low Alwinton, Saughtree, Seahouses, Town Yetholm, Twice Brewed, Wark and Wooler. There are campsites at Alwinton, Ancrum, Bamburgh, Bardon Mill, Beadnell, Bellingham, Craster, Haltwhistle, Jedburgh, Kelso, Kielder and Wooler. There are youth hostels at Greenhead, Once Brewed, Acomb (4 miles (6km) from Chollerford), Bellingham, Kirk Yetholm, Wooler and Rock (nr Embleton).

Tourist information offices
Haltwhistle, Kielder Water, Jedburgh, Kelso, Wooler, Seahouses, Alnwick.

Cycle shops and hire
There are shops at Kielder Water, Hawick, Kelso, Berwick, Alnwick, Morpeth and Hexham.

Maps
The northern loop of the tour is on OS 1:50 000 sheets 74, 75, 80, and 81; the southern loop to Hadrian's Wall needs in addition 86 and 87. Starting from Carlisle requires sheet 85, and from Penrith sheet 90. Total tour distances are about 170 miles (270km) for the northern loop, and about 50 miles (80km) for the southern loop to Hadrian's Wall.

Hadrian's Wall between Steel Rigg and Housesteads

To Hadrian's Wall

From **Bellingham** s on B6320 through Wark to GR 877 740, where R uc road to Simonburn, L up fine, gated road to join B6318, the Military Road built by General Wade some 1600 years after the Romans built their wall and using some of the materials of it; R to 'Once or Twice Brewed' (signs vary: original pub was 'Twice Brewed', YH and centre is 'Once Brewed'!) (possibility of visiting **Hadrian's Wall**—*see 6 below*). L on uc road for about ½ mile (800m) to GR 754 662, L past Vindolanda fort, then L on uc Roman road by Grindon Hill and Newbrough to B6319 and Fourstones. Then *either* L at GR 893 687 on uc road over hill to rejoin B6320 near Simonburn, *or* round by Walwick Grange and Chollerford to join B6320 there. Return to **Bellingham** by B6320. There is an alternative and *much* hillier route on the E side of the river from Wark, through Birtley and Redesmouth.

To return to **Carlisle**, follow either route as far as 'Twice Brewed' (the B6318, being dead straight, can be dispiriting in large doses, and can be fairly busy in summer), then continue on B6318 to Greenhead (at least the last bit is downhill). R, still on B6318, through Gilsland to GR 615 670, then L on uc road to Banks, Lanercost and Brampton. Then follow B6264, or loops of uc road, to Carlisle. For **Penrith**, follow B6413 s Castle Carrock, then R on uc road, bearing L at GR 532 551 through Armathwaite and Staffield to join Eden Valley 'weekend' tour route at Kirkoswald.

• HIGHLIGHTS •

1 Kielder Water

The Kielder Water reservoir and parts of the surrounding forest area have been developed as a tourist attraction, with facilities for a number of water-based activities. Bicycles may be hired at Hawkhope Car Park, at the N end of the dam which impounds Kielder Water, at GR 713 881. The public road runs to the south of the Water; it appears possible to follow a track on the north side, along which there are a couple of camping areas (but without special facilities). Food is available at the visitor centres at Tower Knowe (GR 700 868) and at Kielder Castle (GR 631 935). There is also a small but convenient campsite at Kielder village (GR 628 938).

2 Chillingham Wild Cattle

Chillingham Park has a unique herd of wild white cattle which can be visited. Although they are contained within the extensive park, these cattle have never been domesticated nor interbred, certainly for at least 800 years. Indeed the park was originally built (somewhere around 1220) around the herd, rather than their being driven into the park! To visit them, enquire at the cottage at the end of Chillingham village, GR 062 261. Since the cattle are wild, visits are in small groups led by an experienced guide who can judge the safest close approach—and who is able actually to find the herd, since its precise position is unpredictable.

3 Seahouses

Seahouses is a small and attractive fishing port which now also depends on visitor traffic for its livelihood, following the decline of the herring fisheries. Boat trips are available to the rocky Farne Islands some 2 to 5 miles (3 to 8km) off shore. The cliffs of the islands—yet another manifestation of the Great Whin Sill—are thick with seabirds, including a large colony of puffins. There are also many seals. Even on a bright and fairly calm day there can be quite a bit of spray: we found cycling capes very useful in the open boat! Also visible is the red tower of the Longstone lighthouse on one of the outer islands. It was from here that the keeper's daughter, Grace Darling, rowed out in 1838 to rescue the crew of the doomed *Forfarshire*. There is an RNLI Grace Darling museum in Bamburgh. Both Bamburgh and Seahouses have a number of eating places.

4 The Breamish valley

The lovely Breamish valley is a well worth-while out-and-home detour from Powburn. The road to the hamlet of Ingram may be reached either *1* from the centre of Powburn by following the uc road to Branton and then turning R on the uncoloured road at GR 044 163 to cross the Breamish by the footbridge at the ford, or *2* by following the A697 N for about 1 mile (1½km) and then turning L on uc road by a line of low cottages to Brandon. About 1½ miles (2½km) W of Ingram the hitherto flat road becomes quite hilly (and later very hilly). A private road which shortly becomes a public path turns L at GR 976 162, and after crossing the

River Breamish again climbs spectacularly over the shoulder of the hill giving exquisite views down the valley. On the November days when we climbed the valley, the woods and fells were a rich pattern of mixed colour, dappled with the shadows of passing clouds.

5 Salmon on the Coquet

Both the Breamish (above) and the Coquet are salmon rivers. Although on our autumn travels we have seen a few fish leaping on the Breamish, by far the most prolific display we found was at a succession of small falls on the River Coquet just below the bridge where the uc road from Alwinton up Coquetdale to Barrowburn crosses (GR 892 064). Here we sat into the deepening dusk of the early November afternoon, utterly fascinated, as the great fish made their way upstream.

6 Hadrian's Wall

Undoubtedly the most spectacular part of the Wall is the 2- to 3-mile (3 to 5km) stretch from the excavated fort at Housesteads (GR 790 687, reached from the road at about GR 796 686) to the point where the Twice/Once Brewed road crosses it at Steel Rigg (GR 751 677). This is also the best preserved and excavated part: the museum at Housesteads gives invaluable background detail. The actual wall can only properly be followed on foot and it is well worth following some of it to admire the way it outlines the rise and fall of the crags. It is not fast walking. Although at its best on a fine day, we found it very impressive in an autumn drizzle. As the billows of mist swirled up from the unseen Crag Lough below, we certainly wondered how popular a posting it must have been for legions presumably more used to Mediterranean sun and the warmth of central Europe.

Other Roman items in this once very important military area include a small Mithraic temple beside the Military Road at about GR 855 713 and the reconstructed fort at Vindolanda (GR 770 663) on the return route.

NORTH-WEST COAST OF SCOTLAND

• LONGER TOURS •

In the north and west of Scotland we at last reach a part of Britain which is on a dramatic scale comparable with that of continental Europe. Population is sparse, a combination of the difficulty of making a living from the often inhospitable soil as well as some unsavoury episodes from England's colonial past. Distances between settlements can be quite considerable: there are some stretches of up to 40 miles (65km) without a shop or even a bar, while gaps of 20 to 30 miles (30 to 50km) are common. This means that you will have to be quite self-contained for food at times—stock up when you have the chance. Spare parts are also quite remote. Cape Wrath, the north-westernmost point of the mainland, is as far from London as Biarritz or Leipzig. Even Glasgow and Edinburgh are over 200 miles (320km) away from Cape Wrath in a straight line, and a lot further by any practicable route.

Both the north and west coasts are marked by sea inlets—miniature fjords—stretching some miles inland, sometimes known as sea-lochs and at other times as 'kyles', an anglicized form of the Gaelic word *caol*—a strait. At one time several of these could only be crossed by ferry. With the completion of a fine new EEC-aided bridge across the narrows between Kylestrome and Unapool in 1985 the main coast road ring is complete—although a little of the sense of adventure has gone. The intricate nature of the coastline extends road distances and this tour is longer and more ambitious than the other ones. It is possible to divide it into sectors—Inverness to Ullapool or Kyle of Lochalsh to Oban, say. The information panel gives distances for the various sectors, but a look at the map will show that it is possible to head back to Inverness or points on one of the railway lines from several places on the west coast.

The scenery of the far north-west is grandly stern and almost treeless. The impressive barrenness is surprisingly colourful, with bracken and bents running from light green, through dark green, gold and an almost orange-brown as the seasons pass. In places, too, heather adds its purple while seaweed often gleams yellow along the tide line. Look closer at some of the apparently neutral tints and you will find yet another intricate and impossibly subtle generation of colour: in the multicoloured grains that make the soft grey shore sand, in the variety of minerals in the rocks and in the almost invisible flowerlets of the hardy sessile plants.

The geology is quite complex—indeed, there are sections which are not even completely mapped. Most of the coastal rocks are very old limestones, sandstones and slates, with some igneous areas, notably on Skye. But the main inland rock types, and coastal ones in the extreme north-west, are what is known as metamorphic: their structure and mineral make-up have been changed by pressure and heat over the 500 and more million years since their first deposition. The most noticeable of these rocks are the schists with their laminations and layers of glinting mica crystallites. This area, too, was the last to be covered in ice during the most recent ice age and the glaciers have left their mark in scooped-out valleys and hummocky areas dotted with innumerable small lakes.

Cycling on the Bealach na Bà

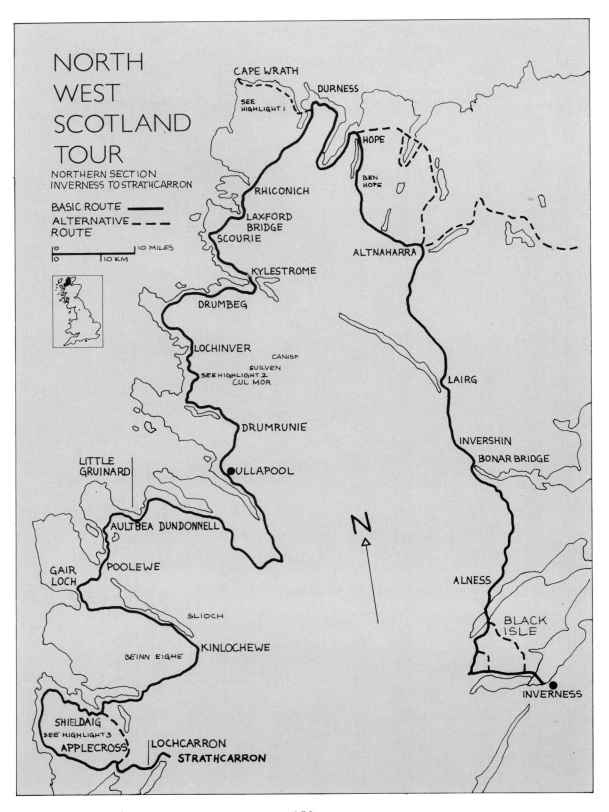

NORTH
WEST
SCOTLAND
TOUR
NORTHERN SECTION
INVERNESS TO STRATHCARRON

BASIC ROUTE ———
ALTERNATIVE
ROUTE - - -

0   10 MILES
0   10 KM

CAPE WRATH
SEE HIGHLIGHT 1
DURNESS
HOPE
BEN HOPE
RHICONICH
LAXFORD
BRIDGE
SCOURIE
ALTNAHARRA
KYLESTROME
DRUMBEG
LOCHINVER
CANISP
SUILVEN
SEE HIGHLIGHT 2
CUL MOR
LAIRG
DRUMRUNIE
INVERSHIN
BONAR BRIDGE
ULLAPOOL
LITTLE
GRUINARD
AULTBEA DUNDONNELL
POOLEWE
GAIR
LOCH
ALNESS
SLIOCH
BLACK
ISLE
KINLOCHEWE
BEINN EIGHE
INVERNESS
SHIELDAIG
SEE HIGHLIGHT 3
APPLECROSS
LOCHCARRON
STRATHCARRON

N

But although the terrain is rugged and mountainous, the roads—with a few noticeable exceptions—do not climb to tremendous heights nor are the gradients necessarily steep. It's almost as though the bravado which leads road-builders up hill and down dale with abandon in sissier parts is replaced by a bit of common sense when confronted by this sort of landscape. Unless you go out of your way to take in the splendid 626-metre summit of the Bealach na Bà, the basic route goes no higher than 338m, between Ullapool and Aultbea. You will note that this route involves considerable distances on classified B- and even A-roads. This is because they are often the *only* roads, but even the most main do not carry heavy traffic for most of the year. Also, in this part of the world an A rating does not mean a multi-lane highway, while some B-roads even have grass growing down the middle. Many of the A-roads have quite recently been widened and straightened; in some cases lengths of old road are left which you can use as alternatives.

The weather is often changeable and very much under the Atlantic influence. Rain can be expected, but then so can rapid clearances. Like Scandinavia, the north of Scotland quite often experiences in the middle of summer some prolonged warm dry spells, frequently when England is wet and cloudy. At midsummer, too, the northerly latitude means longer days—up to an hour and a half more daylight than in southern England—and short nights of no more than deep twilight. Later in the summer the insect life awakens and that Scottish speciality, the minute midge, can make camping and outdoor picnicking rather vexing. Autumn, given a reasonable break with the weather, is superb. Even in winter we have spent some fine weeks in this spectacular part of Britain, admittedly based on a cosy centre rather than moving on every day.

• THE ROUTE •

Start **Inverness**, or train to Lairg or Kinbrace. From Inverness N over Kessock Bridge, minor roads on Black Isle, then A9 across Cromarty Firth. A836 to Bonar Bridge, Invershin. A836 or B864 to **Lairg**. A836 to Altnaharra, then choice of routes (all good) to N coast: *1* B873, then A836 to Tongue; *2* A836 direct to Tongue; or *3* uc road by Loch Meadie and Loch Hope to Hope. If starting from Kinbrace, then B871 to join B873; L to Altnaharra and Hope, or R to **Tongue**. (Fine open moorland roads with large and small lochs but no sustenance between Lairg and Altnaharra, nor between Altnaharra and Tongue.)

From Tongue A838 across Kyle (or hilly uc road round Kyle to rejoin A838) via Hope and Loch Eriboll to **Durness** (fairly hilly coast road with sea loch and cliff scenery); possibility of Cape Wrath detour (*see 1 below*). SW on A838 to Rhiconich and Laxford Bridge, then A894 to Scourie (fine steady climb, wide views at top, then striking chaos of white stone and black pools). A894 to Kylestrome Bridge and Unapool (shop). R at junction '72' (m above sl), GR 232 314, on B869 to Drumbeg (shop), Stoer, Clachtoll and **Lochinver**. (This fine scenic road would be my candidate for the hilliest road in Britain: don't be impatient and you'll find it worth it. Alternative easier route via A894 to Skiag Bridge, then R on A837 to Lochinver.) Lochinver is small fishing port with several food shops.

From Lochinver S on winding uc road—the 'Mad Little Road of Ross' (*see 2 below*)—to join further uc road at GR 062 112, L past Lochs Bad a' Ghaill and Lurgainn to A835. R on A835 to **Ullapool**—fishing port and largest town on route. Continue on A835 to junction at bridge, GR 209 777 (fine climb above loch and then through woodland). R on A832 over moorland of Dundonnell Forest (highest point on basic route) to Little Loch Broom, Gruinard, Laide, Aultbea, Poolewe and **Gairloch**. (Up and down road—sharp descent and climb to Gruinard Bay—playing hide-and-seek with superb coast; tropical garden at Inverewe—mild climate attributed to Gulf Stream.)

From Gairloch continue on A832 through Talladale to Kinlochewe. (Fine part-forested road by inland Loch Maree; extensive views of Slioch mountain and Beinn Eighe, site of Britain's first nature reserve.) R on A896 to Torridon and **Shieldaig** (fine loch and Torridon mountain views). From Shieldaig choice of routes: *1* strenuous detour round uc coast road to Applecross then over 626m pass of Bealach na Bà to Kishorn (*see 3 below*); or *2* direct by A896 to Kishorn. From Kishorn A896 to Lochcarron and junction at GR 932 432.

• INFORMATION •

Starting and finishing points

As described the route starts from Inverness and finishes at Oban. It would be possible to start from: Kinbrace station, joining the route between Altnaharra and Bettyhill; Thurso, but this involves a hilly 42 miles (nearly 70km) along the north coast to Tongue. Alternative possible finishing points are: Ullapool, returning by road (62 miles (100km)) to Inverness; Kyle of Lochalsh; Mallaig; or Fort William.

Access

Rail routes are: to Inverness from Perth, Glasgow, Edinburgh or London (Euston); to Lairg, Kinbrace or Thurso from Inverness; to or from Kyle of Lochalsh to Inverness; from Mallaig to Fort William; from Fort William to Glasgow or London (Euston); from Oban to Glasgow and London (Euston). No bicycle restrictions at time of writing but introduction threatened; overnight trains with seating/sleepers (no restriction) from London (Euston) to Inverness and Fort William. Main access roads are the A9 to Inverness and the A82 to Fort William. There are air services to Inverness airport (Dalcross) from Glasgow, Edinburgh and London (Heathrow).

Accommodation

There are quite long distances between accommodation possibilities in places. However, there are once again quite a lot of small informal B&B addresses which don't appear in the major listings. We spotted B&B possibilities at Alness, Applecross, Aultbea, Ballachulish, Bonar Bridge, Durness, Fort William, Gairloch, Isleornsay, Kinlochewe, Kyeakin, Kylesku, Lairg, Lochcarron, Mallaig, Plockton (nr Kyle of Lochalsh), Shieldaig, Tarbet, Tarskavaig, Tongue, Torridon and Ullapool. There is no direct equivalent of the English pub in this part of the world but many hotels have bars which fulfil the same function, including sometimes light meals. The liberalization of the licensing laws means that many are open in the afternoons. However, although fewer than in the past, many villages and hotels in the far west tend to close down completely on Sundays.

There are campsites at Achmelvich, Achnachaird, Applecross, Arisaig, Armadale, Aultbea, Benderloch, Bettyhill, Bunchrew, Calmine, Connel, Durness, Gairloch, Glen Nevis (nr Fort William), Lairg, North Kessock, Oban, Oldshoremore, Plockton, Poolewe, Scourie, Stoer, Taynuilt, Tongue and Ullapool. In the wilder parts 'wild' camping is generally tolerated, pro-

• INFORMATION •

vided the land is not obviously cultivated or attached to a property, and provided also that you are not likely to pollute water supplies. It will almost certainly be necessary for you to have picnic meals at some time on this trip, so plan ahead and stock up when you can.

There are youth hostels at Inverness, Carbisdale Castle (nr Invershin), Tongue, Durness, Achmelvich (nr Lochinver), Ullapool, Aultbea, Carn Dearg (nr Gairloch), Torridon, Kyle of Lochalsh, Broadford (Skye), Armadale (Skye), Garramore (nr Arisaig), Glen Nevis (nr Fort William), Glencoe (nr Ballachulish) and Oban. If you need to consult directories or listings, check under Highland Region, and Strathclyde for the area from Ballachulish southwards. If the listing uses the old Scottish counties, see under Inverness-shire, Sutherland, Ross and Cromarty, and Argyll.

Tourist information offices
Inverness, North Kessock, Bonar Bridge, Lairg, Bettyhill, Durness, Lochinver, Ullapool, Gairloch, Kyle of Lochalsh, Broadford, Mallaig, Fort William, Ballachulish, Oban.

Cycle shops
After Inverness there aren't any, although there is a small repair business in Spean Bridge (8 miles (13km) NE of Fort William). There are two shops rather off the route in Muir of Ord and Thurso. A few garages carry some very basic cycle spares.

Maps
The route is on OS 1:50 000 sheets 9, 10, 15, 16, 19, 20, 21, 24, 25, 33, 40, 41, 49. The tour may also be followed without difficulty as far as Fort William on OS 1:250 000 Routemaster sheet 2; the last part is on a corner of sheet 4. The total basic distance from Inverness to Oban is about 475 miles (750km)! This is made up of: Inverness-Ullapool—230 miles (370km); Ullapool-Kyle of Lochalsh—130 miles (210km); Kyle of Lochalsh-Camusnagaul (for ferry to Fort William)—65 miles (105km); and Camusnagaul-Oban—50 miles (80km).

Mallaig harbour

R on A890 to Strathcarron, over railway lc and R beside loch (one or two quite steep pitches) to junction at GR 861 341. R on uc road to Duirinish, Drumbuie and **Kyle of Lochalsh** (variety of food shops). Ferry to Kyleakin on island of **Skye**. Follow A850 to junction with A851, then A851 through Isleornsay to Armadale; hilly detour over peninsula to Tokavaig and Tarskavaig gives superb views of Cuillins to NW. From Armadale ferry (Mon-Sat only) to **Mallaig** on mainland. (This is only a lightning visit to Skye; there is obviously much more to see on the island, given time.)

From Mallaig A830 to Arisaig and Lochailort. Choice of route: *1* continue on A830 through Glenfinnan to Kinlocheil, where R on A861 along S shore of Loch Eil (possibility of small ferry, about 3 services/day, to **Fort William** from Camusnagaul) to Corran (*see 4 below*); or *2* R on A861 beside Loch Ailort and Loch Moidart to Salen on Loch Sunart, then A861 through Strontian and Glen Tarbert to Corran. Ferry from Corran across Loch Linnhe to A82, R on A82 to new Ballachulish bridge over Loch Leven, L at roundabout on A828 via Appin to Connel Bridge (possibility of avoiding detour round head of Loch Creran by taking footpath over former railway bridge at Creagan, GR 977 447). On S side of Connel Bridge take uc road at GR 910 342, then first R after about 3 miles (5km) to **Oban** (*see 5 below*).

• HIGHLIGHTS •
and detours

I am tempted to write that, once you have reached Lairg, this route is *all* highlights, but the following favourites should not be missed if at all possible.

1 Cape Wrath from Durness
Cape Wrath is the north-westernmost point of the British mainland; it is also often assumed (by those who are aware that John o'Groats isn't) to be the most northerly but that distinction belongs to Dunnet Head, some 55 miles (90km) to the east. A single narrow and hilly road leads out to the lighthouse on the Cape, so the trip is an out-and-home one—the total return distance from Durness is about 24 miles (38km) and in practice requires a whole day. The road is from time to time closed for military exercises, and the only access to it is by ferry across the Kyle of Durness.

The ferry, a small semi-open vessel which was completely filled by the four of us and our bicycles when we crossed, leaves from a small slipway near the Keoldale Hotel, about 2 miles (3km) by road south-west of Durness. There is a basic timetable (details are available in Durness) but in practice the boat runs on demand during the summer months. The boatman will tell you on the outward trip the time of the last chance of return. Ease of boarding and landing is very much affected by the tide and may involve some paddling: try to keep the bicycle out of the salt water.

Once on the other side, the road climbs very steeply from the landing up the bracken-covered hillside, soon coming out into the open high above the Kyle. On the day we crossed there were hundreds of seals basking on the great sandbanks towards the entrance of the Kyle, far below us. After about 1½ miles (2km) the road drops sharply again to cross the Daill River, climbing away steeply up to the plateau once more. The road surface varies: in places it is really quite good, but in others calls for care where weather has undone it again.

The landscape is one of rather dour rolling hills, with the intense black peat exposed from time to time. Here you will find wetland plants— the ubiquitous white puffs of bog cotton and, when we passed in June, a number of small orchid-like plants. The mood of the place varies enormously with the weather: the colour of a sparkling day can be transformed by a sea mist to a looming white emptiness.

The road climbs steadily to its 174-metre summit, then drops to cross the Kearvaig River. The last 3 miles (5km) or so is quite up-and-down until the last steady pull up to the rather sombre lighthouse perched on its impressive 100m cliffs. From this gaunt headland at a latitude of 58 deg 40 min N, there is no land directly to the north between Cape Wrath and the polar ice, nor any to the west until you reach the northern tip of Labrador, nearly 3000 miles (5000km) away.

2 'The Mad Little Road of Ross'
I'm not sure who coined this name for the winding 14 miles (about 22km) from the southern end of Lochinver village (GR 094 221) to the junction by Badnagyle (GR 062 112), but it was obviously somebody highly impressed by its hundreds of

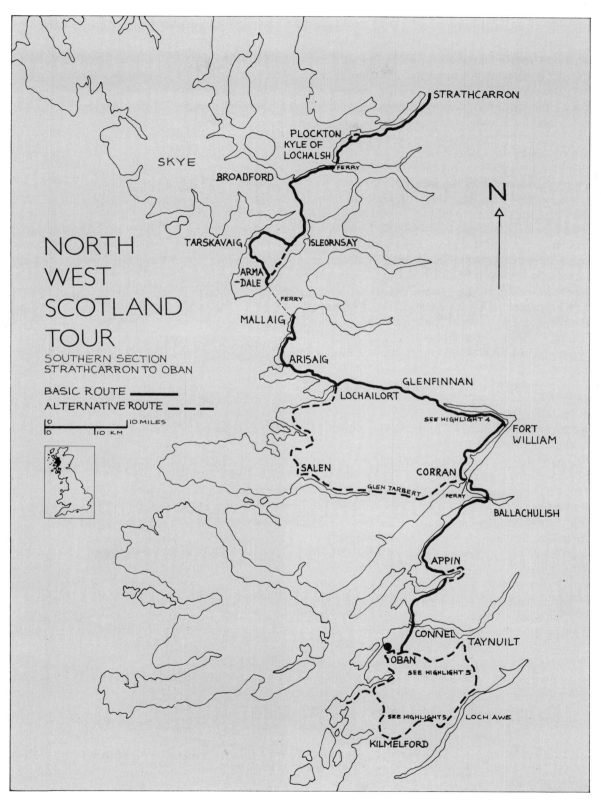

NORTH
WEST
SCOTLAND
TOUR

SOUTHERN SECTION
STRATHCARRON TO OBAN

BASIC ROUTE ———
ALTERNATIVE ROUTE – – –

0 ————— 10 MILES
0 ————— 10 KM

changes of direction and gradient. It goes without saying that it is not a road for high-speed cycling: expect it to take at least a whole morning or afternoon. Nowadays the whole of it is well surfaced.

The first half of the route stays relatively close to the sea, with some excursions inland, with a magnificent backdrop of the great peaks of Canisp (846m) and Suilven (731m). Seen end-on, as it is from near Lochinver, Suilven appears an almost perfect cone. The road drops to the shore in a couple of places, Loch Kirkaig and Loch an Eisg-brachaidh, and at both of them we have seen seals and an immense range of seabirds.

At least part of the charm of the Mad Little Road, though, comes from the little oak woods and rushing streams by which the road makes its way inland. The second half of the route, away from the sea, is through a wild tumbled landscape of hills and lochs, dominated by the peaks of Cùl Mór (849m), Cùl Beag and Stac Pollaidh. Eventually the road drops through the last of the oaks to the broad valley of the River Polly, followed by a long open climb to the junction at Badnagyle.

From here it's a fine lochside 8 miles (13km) to the main Ullapool road at Drumrunie (GR 166 053), passing close under the impressive cone of Stac Pollaidh.

3 Applecross and the Bealach na Bà from Shieldaig

This tough but extremely rewarding detour is about 36 miles (58km) in total, from about ¾ mile (1km) south of Shieldaig village (GR 819 526) until it rejoins the A896 at Tornapress (GR 837 422). It is at least a day's ride, possibly more if you are laden. The first 12 miles (20km) are very hilly with short steep ups and downs. The middle 13 miles (22km or so) down the west coast to Applecross are relatively gently rolling, while from sea level at Applecross you are faced by the magnificent 6-mile (10km) climb to the 626m top of the Bealach. From there it's all downhill to Tornapress.

At one time, Applecross could be reached only by sea, over the Bealach na Bà or by a winding coast path from Shieldaig. This last has now been made up to a well-surfaced road and now forms

Glencoe and Loch Leven from Ballachulish Bridge

the all-season route to Applecross. The first part, while hilly, has magnificent views across to the Torridon hills. There are also some fine, wooded stretches, with mixed pines, oaks and birches—quite a blaze of brown and golden colour when we passed in November. The plantation above Arinacrinachd, though, marks the last trees before Applecross, for the west coast is bare and rocky with heather, some bracken and very rough pasture. The views are superb, though, across the island of Raasay to the mountains of Skye. Applecross is a tree-fringed haven with a wide sandy bay.

From here, the climb of the Bealach na Bà averages about 7%, 1-in-14, with successions of easier and steeper pitches. By about halfway up you are out onto a bare rocky landscape, dotted with a myriad of small lochans, a landscape almost as the retreating glaciers left it. There is a top section which is relatively flat—frustratingly the actual top is not marked—before you enter the startling cleft of the Bealach itself with its plunging view to Loch Kishorn.

4 Beside Loch Eil and Loch Linnhe

This, for a change, is an easy and quiet road and one which stays within sight of its two sea lochs for virtually its whole distance. At GR 959 794, just west of the head of Loch Eil, the A861 turns south off the main A830, the Mallaig to Fort William road. The whole route is an alternation of wooded groves—some mixed, some planted conifers—with open grazing which offers broad views of the Lochaber hills, culminating in Ben Nevis (1344m).

Whenever we have been along this road we have been struck by the number of herons we have seen: each minor promontory on the shore seems to have its thin grey figure peering seawards. The islet of Rubha Dearg at GR 098 758 seems to be home to a great many of them. About ½ mile (800m) further down the shore is the little slipway from which the Fort William ferry leaves. The ferry is intended mainly to take schoolchildren and shoppers across to Fort William, saving

a 20-mile (30-odd km) road journey, so the hours of operation are arranged to suit. If you are intending to take the train from Fort William it makes a fine end to the trip. The bicycles have an interesting journey, lashed to the cabin rails.

Once you turn the corner opposite Fort William where Loch Eil becomes Loch Linnhe, the road begins to become a little more up and down, with more variety in the woodland. Look back from time to time as there are some very fine views of Ben Nevis. The curved inlet of Inverscaddle Bay is again a contrast, with its very green saltmarsh grazing and birdlife. We have also seen seals down this stretch, although there seem to be more on Black Rock (GR 048 671) near the opposite shore. The regular ferry at Corran returns you to the eastern side of Loch Linnhe; it runs about half-hourly in daylight hours, more frequently at busy times.

5 Loch Awe from Oban

Oban is quite a good centre and this circuit from there is one of our favourites; if you are intending to take the train back towards Glasgow you can board it at Taynuilt at the end of this route. Like most of the other detours which one can take it is rather hilly; the total distance is about 35 miles (55km) to Taynuilt, with a further 10 miles or so (16km) back to Oban.

Leave Oban southwards on the A816 as far as Kilmelford (GR 849 130). (The B844 which turns off at the bypassed village of Kilninver, about halfway, allows an interesting detour to Clachan and its 'Bridge over the Atlantic'—a graceful arch which crosses the sound between Seil island and the mainland.) At Kilmelford a narrow unclassified road to the left climbs steeply away and then winds superbly in and out of the contours past a series of attractive lochs before dropping through Inverinan Forest to the shores of Loch Awe. Just before Kilchrenan you join the B845, which brings you to Taynuilt. The most attractive route back to Oban is by the unclassified road which follows Glen Lonan.

SOME PRACTICAL CYCLING ADVICE

• BICYCLES AND CYCLING •

This book is not intended to be a technical and mechanical textbook on bicycles but the sections which follow are intended to give an outline of what is accepted as good practice.*

* A much fuller treatment of these topics, and many others as well including maintenance, appears in some of the books in the bibliography, particularly my own *Cycle Tourer's Handbook* (Batsford, 1987) and Richard Ballantine's *Richard's New Bicycle Book* (Pan, 1987)

Bicycles for easy cycling

There are only three fundamental factors which really make the major difference between bicycles which are easy to propel and those which are not. These are: your *riding position* which depends on choosing one of the right size and then adjusting it to fit; the *gearing* which determines how easily you'll go up hills; and the overall *weight* of the bicycle and its load. The first two are rather more important than weight *per se*, and all other factors—except the fitness of the rider—are secondary.

Riding position and size of bicycle

A comfortable and effective riding position depends on achieving the right equilibrium between your points of contact with the bicycle—hands, feet and seat. For the sort of riding envisaged in this book, a position in which the back and arms, seen from the side, form the two equal sides of an isosceles triangle, each at an angle of between 45 and 60 degrees of the horizontal, is likely to be the most comfortable. The precise degree of lean is accomplished by adjusting the handlebar to saddle distance—the base of the triangle—but first the more critical saddle to pedal distance has to be fixed. It is also essential for cycle-touring that you should be able to stand astride the bicycle's top tube ('crossbar') without difficulty. Various other built-in dimensions, such as the distance above the ground of the 'bottom bracket' (the axle onto which the cranks are fixed), also affect practical frame size. A rule of thumb which allows for all these is that the bicycle *frame size* should be two-thirds the rider's full inside leg measurement, from crutch to ground, measured without shoes. Thus, somebody with an inside leg measurement of 33in (84cm) would need a 22-in (56cm) frame. This frame size is measured from the centre of the bottom bracket axle (see above) up the line of the 'seat tube'—the frame tube leading up from the bottom bracket towards the saddle—to the top of the actual frame where the 'seat [or saddle] pillar'—the (usually) aluminium tube onto the top of which the saddle is fixed—goes in. It seems quite common for bicycles to be sold which are too big for their potential riders; this can cause particular problems for small ones, those with inside leg measurements below about 30 in (76 cm). Not only are they likely to find it uncomfortable or even impossible to stand astride a loaded bicycle but also, since many of the other frame dimensions are in proportion to the basic size, that their forward reach will be too stretched. A good specialist cycle dealer will make sure that you buy the right size of frame or bicycle.

For comfortable and effective pedalling the saddle has to be adjusted, by moving the seat pillar up or down, to such a height that your leg is not uncomfortably stretched at the lowest point, nor too flexed at the highest. It has been found that you can get a fair approximation to this by raising the saddle until the top is about 90% of your inside leg measurement above the bottom bracket, still measured along the angle of the seat tube. The top of the saddle should be horizontal. You can test the height by sitting on the saddle and pedalling slowly backwards with your heels on the pedals, using footwear with at the most thin heels. Your leg should be just about straight, but not stretched, at the longest reach. Make the necessary small adjustments to the saddle height until this is right. The saddle should be adjusted forwards or backwards until, with the ball of your foot on the pedal in the correct pedalling position, the hinge of the knee is directly over or a shade, up to perhaps an inch (25mm), behind the centre of the pedal when the cranks are in a horizontal quarter-to-three position. You may need to make another very slight adjustment to the saddle height after this. The whole treatment is rather easier to carry out than to describe! Once again, a good specialist cycle dealer will anyhow want to adjust a new bicycle to fit you before you leave the premises. It is, even so, useful to know how to find your position should you ever want to borrow or hire a bicycle. (When I used to travel around on business with the chance of getting hold of a bicycle for a day or an afternoon, I used to carry a length of string with two knots showing my saddle height so that I could make a quick adjustment; with experience you can judge the fore-and-aft setting by eye.)

Achieving the right forward reach cannot be arrived at by simple adjustment—it depends on the length of the top tube of the frame, which is utterly fixed, the shape of the handlebar and the length of the handlebar 'stem'—the forward-pointing part with the clamp holding the handle-bar bend. Both these last two can be changed by a dealer or competent user; one of the advantages of having a bicycle built to measure (see below) is that the length of these items will be appropriate from the start, while the top tube length can be decided appropriately, within limits. In other cases the simplest solution is to sit on the bicycle and see whether it is comfortable or whether you need a longer or shorter stem. The choice is entirely your own, but comfort is of paramount importance.

For this type of riding the actual shape of handlebar doesn't really matter—as long as you

Opposite: *Cycling past Canisp*

find it comfortable. The dropped pattern gives more choice of position for differing conditions, but in practice most leisure riders spend most of their time 'on the tops'—with hands either side by side and a few inches apart, or on or near the brake levers. The possibility of varying the hand position between transverse and parallel to the length of the bicycle is useful to avoid aches through being too long in one position, but this can also be achieved with some types of flat bar. It also pays to cultivate keeping elbows slightly bent to avoid transmitting road vibration to the shoulders and neck. As a starting point the top or flat part of the handlebar should be about level with the saddle. You may want to adjust it a little either way with experience.

Gearing

There are two points to be considered here: the ratio and range of the gears, and how the variation is achieved. The size or ratio of the gear is a measure of how far you travel along the ground for each turn of the pedals. A 'high' gear ratio is one which enables you to travel quite a long distance for each pedal revolution and a 'low' one entails a short distance. At a given speed you will have to impart a higher force to the pedals, but at

Below: *A standard* dérailleur *gearing mechanism*

a slower rate, with a high gear; a very low gear may be easier to turn but might involve pedalling uncomfortably fast. Although comfortable pedalling rates ('cadence' is the trendy term) vary, they lie in a fairly narrow range, probably about 45 to 80 rpm for the sort of riding we're considering. Thus, in practice, a given gear is appropriate to a particular speed of travel. Speed is in turn governed by your inclinations and the terrain, and since you have been enjoined not to hurry unduly, low gears are going to be very useful.

You should be warned if you mix with cyclists that there are about as many differing opinions on gears as there are people ready to give advice. You should also be warned that there is a bizarre way of expressing gear ratios in Britain and the USA. They are quoted in inches, which seems logical enough, until you discover that they do not refer to the distance travelled per pedal revolution (which is properly known as the 'gear development'), but as the diameter of wheel on a direct-drive bicycle that would have the same effect. (The last direct-drive bicycles were the old High Ordinaries of about a century ago; it is by the way an unforgivable solecism to call them by the music-hall term 'Penny-farthing'.) Measured by this convention the gears you will find most useful will be in the range from about 25 to 60in, with ones up to perhaps 75 for those heady days when the wind is behind. This is a range of 3:1; coupled with the lower pedalling rates naturally used at low road speed and the brisker ones at higher, these should cope with road speeds from about 4mph (about 6½km/h), walking pace, to 20 or so (32km/h). Faster than that and you can freewheel.

The variable gear ratios are usually achieved by shifting the chain between different-sized rear sprockets on the freewheel (up to 7, though 5 or 6 are more practical for touring) and different-sized chainwheels fixed to the cranks (2 or 3). Small chainwheels and big sprockets give low gears, large chainwheels and small sprockets give high gears. Lever-controlled gear mechanisms do the shifting. Too-large differences between the gears are rather jerky to cope with— going up suddenly feels much too hard, going down as though you're pedalling on nothing. I would recommend 44, 36 and 26-tooth chainrings at the front and an evenly proportioned range

from 15 or 16 to 26 or 28 teeth on the rear freewheel, combined with one of the new definite-position 'indexed' gear mechanisms. This is only one way of achieving the range of gears that you need, but one that I have found to work especially well with beginners. Most off-the-peg bicycles have larger chainrings, a lot of gears that are too high and not enough low ones. You may have to insist; this does seem to be something of a blind spot with dealers who normally deal with racing bicycles. One easy way of getting a bicycle with low gears is to acquire one of the increasingly-popular 'mountain' or 'all-terrain bikes'. For many of the routes in this book a mountain bike would be quite suitable, though you might find the lack of variation in hand position a disadvantage on longer road stretches. Mountain bikes are not particularly light—perhaps a third to a half more than a conventional lightweight—but that may not matter too much as you will see in the section below.

It is also possible to obtain 3- or 5-speed hub gears. These have fixed ratios which are rather too widely spaced while the overall range from top to bottom is relatively restricted. They are, however, largely maintenance-free and easy to operate.

Lightweight bicycles

It is obviously easier to propel a light bicycle than a heavy one, especially uphill. It is also easy to become obsessed with lightness. For enjoyable cycle-touring you need a reasonable compromise between lightness and reliability.

Most of the appropriate components these days are made from intrinsically light aluminium alloys: chainwheels and cranks, handlebar assemblies, seat pillars, hubs, wheel rims, brakes, pedals. Except for exotic carbon-fibre, cast magnesium and epoxy-glued aluminium versions, frames are made of special steels of varying quality and sophistication. They are made lighter by using thinner-gauge tubes of stronger steel compositions, some of the lightest only applicable to specialized racing use. In point of fact, the difference in weight between the lightest steel frame and quite an ordinary one amounts to a very small proportion of the total weight of the bicycle. The much larger difference in 'feel' between one with a hand-built high-quality frame

and the other is likely to arise at least as much from other desirable engineering properties of the better material, and from the fact that more care will have been put into the design and construction of the better frame. If you *do* want to take up cycle-touring seriously (with keen interest, not lack of mirth, that is), then there is nothing to beat having a frame and the rest of the bicycle built up to your measure by one of the many specialist artisan builders whose names appear in the cycling periodicals. If you want to share the arcane secrets of 531, SIS, 700C and SFQR, these are the people to guide you. It will not be cheap—although the extra over an off-the-peg and possibly not-quite-right model may not be as much as all that—but you'll have a friend for life.

Light wheels and tyres *do* make a considerable difference to the ease of riding, but once more don't overdo it. There is something of a vogue for very narrow rims and tyres and these are unlikely to be the best for minor-road riding. For these routes a moderately light tyre but with a nominal section around 32mm, fitted to the appropriate width light rim, is likely to be best. At least the mountain bike has shown that narrow wheels and high gears are not necessarily the best for adventurous travel. Tyres should be pumped up to the pressure marked on the tyre wall. A properly inflated tyre calls for a great deal less effort than one that is too soft. Once again you are referred to the textbooks cited for more detail on wheels, frames and the rest of the components.

Comfort

The two considerations which most affect your comfort on a bicycle, once your riding position has been established, are riding within your natural personal limits and being suitably clad for the exercise and the weather.

Taking it steady

I don't know if it is because to the untutored eye a light touring bicycle looks to some extent like a racing one, or it may be that on a bicycle going faster doesn't involve a complete change of action, but there seems to be a tacit assumption that once on a bicycle you should go as fast as you can. (Yet nobody out on a ramble expects to break into a trot.) There's nothing wrong with the tough and thrilling sport of bicycle racing—but there's everything wrong with confusing it with enjoying the routes in this book.

Every cyclist has a natural rhythm and effort of riding, which is likely to change with experience and fitness. It becomes most apparent when the going is uphill, when most people find it irksome to go much slower and uncomfortable or impossible to go faster. You have to accept this: if you are with companions, each should climb at the appropriate personal pace and rendezvous at the top, or at intervals. Don't try to hang back or, worse, struggle to 'keep up'.

In the same way everyone has a natural length of time for which this natural effort can be sustained. If you are new to cycling this may be no more than an hour or two at a time, followed by a longish rest. At least to begin with be prepared to underestimate your abilities—you can always explore that interesting detour at the end of the day if you're still full of beans. You may well surprise yourself at the distance you can cover. After all, four hours' riding, spread over a day, at only 7 or 8mph (11 to 13km/h) will still take you 30-odd miles (about 50km).

Clothing and the weather

Even though you are going to be riding steadily and within your means, cycling is an athletic exercise. You need clothing that will allow you freedom of movement, protect you from heat and cold and not chafe where you sit on it. Special cycling clothing is mostly derived from racing practice and you may find the more extreme manifestations rather bizarre. You can wear virtually what you choose for the sort of cycling the weekend routes involve (preferably not overcoats and wellingtons, though) but they should still follow the same precepts. Shirts, pullovers and jackets need to be quite long at the back because of the leaning-forward position, and shorts or trousers must be soft enough to allow full movement. Jeans usually don't. 'Proper' cycling shorts may look strange or excessively revealing but they are extremely comfortable to wear. They also have no hard seams across the saddle area, which conventional trousers and underwear often have. These often lead to discomfort for which the saddle is blamed. (Saddles, by the way, are very personal; you may have to try several before you find a really comfortable one. The softest and

Above: *Taking a break...*

Opposite: *The weather on mountainous routes can be unpredictable*

springiest are not necessarily the most comfortable after a few miles. There is much fuller guidance in my *Cycle Tourer's Handbook*.)

Because of the effort you put in uphill and the cooling effect of the air going down, cycling in effect exaggerates climatic differences. Sweating is the body's natural cooling mechanism and uphill clothing has to be porous enough for it to evaporate. Conversely downhill clothing has to be windproof enough to prevent chilling; a road speed of 30mph (50km/h) into a slight headwind amounts to facing a full gale! You will probably find on some of the longer hills on, certainly, the Dorset, Peak District and Cotswold routes, and on the three more mountainous longer tours, that you will need to take some clothing off for the uphills, and put some more on for the downhills. You may find going down that you need to wear gloves and a windproof cagoule at much higher ambient temperatures than you would have expected. Even on the flat your airspeed is a good deal greater than when walking.

If you're travelling in the colder seasons you will certainly find gloves necessary. I find two or three pairs of woollen gloves or nylon fleece, rather than heavier gloves or gauntlets, offer the best compromise between windproofing and steaming up. Cold feet are a problem for many people: some swear by overshoes, others by an extra woollen pair of socks and looser-fitting shoes. A walk up a hill soon warms your feet. In cold weather one of the spun polypropylene undervests (and, possibly, tights) such as the Helly Hansen Lifa, can be very cosy. Some of the other 'thermal' underwear tends to retain moisture. Windproof cagoules are fine for downhills or when you're exploring—but you will probably find them far too clammy for prolonged riding or uphill.

A brief word on footwear. Most lightweight cycle pedals are designed to be used with cycling shoes. These are usually externally narrower than ordinary shoes as they have no outside welt. The best incorporate sole stiffeners to spread the pedalling load and are very comfortable in use. They are not so comfortable for walking. You can cycle in any reasonable lightweight shoe but a fairly stiff sole is desirable and you may have to have pedals changed if the shoe is too wide. Mountain bikes have what the makers term 'bear-trap' pedals—presumably an order heftier than conventional 'rat-traps'—which are designed to be used with anything up to walking boots. You may find it easier to carry a pair of light soft shoes for walking round places of interest, rather than make the cycling shoes serve for everything. I should avoid the very specialized racing shoes with built-in deep slotted plates on the sole or those with a ski-binding-style lock. They are virtually impossible to walk in.

Rain, I'm afraid, is a necessary feature of a green and pleasant land. There is no way of keeping *completely* dry on a bicycle. All that you can hope for is keep out the worst and to keep warm—but not so hot that you get wetter by sweating. It is cold from chilling that is the main discomfort of being damp. If you can stay warm until you can get a change of clothing you will have won the battle. Probably the traditional cycling cape, which gives some cover to hands and legs as well as the body, is the most effective. It's not perfect and a nuisance in a strong wind but except for very short distances, much more effective than closer-fitting cagoules and waterproof jackets.

All these items, and anything else you want to take with you, have to be carried. In general all loads should be carried on the bicycle, in suitable saddlebags or panniers securely fixed to appropriate carriers, not on your back. Some mountain bike users prefer a small securely held backpack as better suiting their particular technique, but for on-road use bicycle-mounted loads are more comfortable.

Safety

Cycling safety is largely a matter of common sense. In that it depends on being balanced on a couple of inches of tyre, a bicycle is inherently unstable. This means taking care on wet or slippery surfaces and not making sharp manoeuvres. A bicycle should be ridden in straight lines or long smooth curves, not little weaves and cusps.

The parts of the machine that concern control, particularly brakes, tyres and steering, should be kept in first-class condition at all times. There are quite steep downhill stretches on some of the routes. On an open moderate descent, such as the one down from Chrishall Grange on the Cambridgeshire route, you can let the bicycle have its head if the road is clear. But on the sharp, narrow, winding sort of hill you find in the Weald you must keep the pace down to one from which you can stop quickly and in full control. Don't apply brakes sharply, and particularly not on loose gravel, mud or wet leaves.

These routes deliberately avoid trafficked roads as far as possible, but coping with other traffic, too, is a matter of common sense. You must behave completely predictably, indicating your intentions clearly and in good time, checking behind first that the road is clear enough for you to carry them out safely. You must make yourself obvious to other traffic by being in the right position and not creeping up in blind spots. If you are being passed by heavy vehicles, remember that there is a lot of air turbulence round them and be ready for it.

• BICYCLES BY RAIL AND ROAD •

Few of us are fortunate enough to live where we can go out of the front door and be immediately in delectable cycling country. In suggesting starting points for these routes and tours I have presupposed some other means of getting there. In Britain that generally means travel by rail or road.

Rail

Ever since 1977, after a six-month experiment, bicycles have theoretically travelled free on British Rail; before that they travelled at the same fare as dogs or children. And ever since 1977 the privilege has been steadily eroded. There are now basically three ways in which you can take your bicycle by train. On nearly all routes which have locomotive-hauled trains or the older diesel or electric multiple units with separate guards' vans there are few restrictions and carriage is free. Any restrictions generally cover rush-hour travel in urban areas. So far overnight sleeper trains all fall into the unrestricted category. On routes with new lightweight multiple units or sliding-door stock there are varying restrictions according to route and area, ranging from complete bans to rush-hour limitations. Most of those units which do carry bicycles have 'convertible' accommodation for bulky luggage and bicycles, where tiltable seats have to be folded away. This can be unpopular if the train is full. At the time of

writing carriage is free on these routes when it is possible, although paid-for booking schemes are envisaged on some. The third category comprises the Inter-City 125 trains which now cover the majority of fast daytime main-line journeys. Again restrictions vary from area to area, but on most lines some trains do carry bicycles provided space is reserved and paid for in advance. 125s and the new lightweight multiple units have limited space and can normally carry only 2 to 5 bicycles at a time.

On trains with separate luggage space you place the bicycle, labelled with your name and destination, in the guard's compartment yourself. Don't leave it obstructing doors or control equipment. If you secure the bicycle to anything, which is desirable on long journeys or if you leave bags on, don't lock it to any fitment but instead use an elastic strap. Guards may have to rearrange luggage at subsequent stops. It's always worth removing valuables and detachable items such as pumps and bottles, and—on longer journeys—bags. On sliding-door and convertible-space trains, you stay with your bike.

Note that most railway engineering work takes place on Saturday nights and Sundays. The substitute bus services sometimes provided do *not* undertake to carry bicycles, even if trains on that route normally do. It is wise to check before relying on a particular service for Sunday travel. While it is possible to learn the day-to-day cycle-carriage rules for one's own often-used lines, the system is byzantine in its complexity and far from satisfactory. British Rail periodically produce explanatory leaflets.

Road

Small wonder, then, that many cyclists have taken to carrying their bicycles by car—despite misgivings about adding to the level of motor traffic. It is possible to buy roof racks with special fittings for carrying bicycles, either right-way-up, with or without front wheels, or upside-down. There are arguments in favour of both. Upside-down racks carry the machines ready to ride, but if bicycles belonging to different people are to be carried regularly there may be quite a lot of readjustment of position of the fittings each time. The reason is that these racks secure the bicycles by their saddles and handlebars and, as we have seen,

the distance between these varies widely according to the size of the rider. The wheelbase varies far less, and so if a wide variety of bicyles is to be carried right-way-up racks are easier. The front wheels usually have to be carried separately, either in special fork fittings or inside the car. Many estate cars can quite easily carry a couple of bicycles inside with no dismantling and even more with the front wheel removed. When fitting bicycles to roof racks make sure that they are firmly fixed to the rack, and the rack to the car. Observe the car manufacturer's roof load limitations; it is also desirable to restrict maximum speed somewhat, since the extra load affects handling to some extent. It also increases wind resistance and puts up fuel consumption, sometimes quite spectacularly.

As far as I am aware at the time of writing no scheduled coach company accepts fully assembled bicycles as standard passenger's luggage but this may well change.

Air

Most airline companies will accept bicycles as passengers' accompanied luggage on scheduled flights. On domestic British routes a charge is usually made, depending on the distance travelled. However, both the bicycle and any other checked hold luggage must be within the normal free baggage allowance, usually 15kg (about 33lb), otherwise a quite hefty excess baggage charge is payable. Since a lightweight touring bicycle weighs somewhere around 12kg on its own, this can be a limitation. (On international flights a higher allowance applies.) The degree to which the bicycle needs to be dismantled depends on the aircraft used (and to some degree on the whim of the handler who loads it). It is always worthwhile removing pedals, and you may in addition be asked to turn handlebars sideways to make the bicycle more compact, and occasionally to remove the front wheel as well, strapping it to the frame. All loose items such as pump, bottles, lights and of course bags should be removed. We have also found it an advantage to shield the chain and gear mechanism with a large piece of heavy card or something similar. Some airlines supply large plastic bags into

Where to next...?

which the bicycle fits, probably the most satisfactory solution. When air travel with a bicycle goes smoothly it is a marvellous way of reaching a touring area with the least delay; when you are called on to start taking your bicycle to pieces just as they are calling your flight it can seem less so. It's certainly desirable to allow yourself an extra half an hour over the normal check-in time. Things seem to be more relaxed at smaller airports than at large ones, and similarly more relaxed at London-Gatwick than London-Heathrow (and the rail link from London (Victoria) to Gatwick has plenty of bicycle space).

• BICYCLE HIRE •

There are now quite a number of centres hiring out bicycles, either for a few hours or longer term. Many are located close to or at particular tourist spots—such as on the former railway trails in the Peak District, or on Rutland Water in the southeast Midlands. Details where available are given in the information panel for each route. Lists of hire centres are also obtainable from the English

Tourist Board and—to members—from the CTC. Most local tourist offices also have information. In addition quite a few cycle shops will hire out machines, often from any secondhand stock they have.

As we have already seen, having a bicycle that is adjusted to fit you is quite important if you are to ride any distance in comfort. Because of the wide range of size of hirers, most of the bicycles at many of the hire centres are the easily-adjustable small-wheel ones. These are all right for fairly small distances on more or less level roads or tracks—which, to be fair, is usually what they're hired out for. Don't expect them to be suited to longer or hillier routes, though. Insist as far as possible in having the bicycle adjusted to *your* idea of the correct saddle height, rather than necessarily the hirer's. For a longer-term hire you can reasonably be more insistent on having a bicycle rather nearer to your requirements.

Bicycle hire is not on the whole cheap: daily charges, particularly for a single day, can work out between a half and a quarter of the cost of hiring a small car for the same period.

BIBLIOGRAPHY AND USEFUL ADDRESSES

· FURTHER READING—BOOKS ·

The Cycle Tourer's Handbook by Tim Hughes (Batsford, 1987; ISBN 0 7134 5136 X)

Textbook offering discussion and technical advice on comfort, safety, types of bicycle, equipment, clothing, maintenance and repairs, riding techniques and cycle camping.

Richard's Bicycle Book by Richard Ballantine (Pan, ISBN 0 330 26766 3)

A racy and enthusiastic paperback introduction to cycling by a convert to mountain bikes.

The Highway Code (HMSO, 1987, ISBN 0 11 550785 X) and *Know your Traffic Signs* (HMSO, ISBN 0 11 550550 4)

Two explanatory booklets.

Ordnance Survey Maps: A descriptive manual by J. B. Harley (Ordnance Survey, 1975; ISBN 0 319 00000 1)

The definitive manual on os maps.

Follow the Map: the Ordnance Survey guide by John G. Wilson (A&C Black, 1985, ISBN 0 7136 2459 0)

A colourful fully illustrated explanation of how to interpret and use os maps—including using the National Grid—with some side delvings into natural and man-made features of the landscape.

Cycling Off-road and the Law by Neil Horton (published by the CTC and *Bicycle Action* magazine, 1987)

A guide to access and the use of public rights of way in England, Scotland and Wales.

The Ridgeway Path by Seán Jennet and *The Dorset Coast Path* by Brian Jackman (both HMSO, ISBN 0 11 700743 9 and 0 11 700847 8 respectively)

Northumberland National Park by Tony Hopkins and *Peak National Park* by Roland Smith (both Webb & Bower, 1987, ISBN 0 86350 132 X and 0 86530 135 4 respectively)

The official guides prepared for the Countryside Commission.

The Making of the English Landscape by W. G. Hoskins (Hodder, 1977, ISBN 0 340 21916 5)

The effect of its inhabitants on the historical evolution of the English landscape.

Lost Villages of England by Richard Muir (Michael Joseph, 1982, ISBN 0 7181 2036 1)

A lively study of the way in which changes of settlement have helped to shape the English countryside.

The Concise Oxford Dictionary of English Place-names by Eilert Ekwall (Oxford University Press, 1960, ISBN 0 19 869103 3)

The definitive scholarly (and utterly fascinating) work explaining the much-overwritten palimpsest that is the gazeteer of English place names. The list includes town and village names, along with major rivers, hills and so on. Dip into it at your peril: it will be hours before you can put it down!

Place Names on Maps of Scotland and Wales (OS)

A glossary of Gaelic, Welsh and Scandinavian words which appear on os maps.

· FURTHER READING—MAGAZINES ·

Cycling Weekly

The cyclist's Thursday news magazine. Generally more coverage of racing than leisure cycling but has useful technical items and listings of frame and bicycle builders and suppliers. Also good for secondhand sales and wants.

Cycling World

Touring and leisure-based monthly, but orientated rather towards the conventional cycling-club world.

Bicycle Action and *Bicycle Magazine*

Glossy and colourful monthlies having a go at most topics. Equipment and hi-tech orientated, also strong on mountain bikes.

Cycletouring

The CTC's magazine which appears every two months and is free to members. Some official CTC business but also has accounts of rides and tours, authoritative independent technical reviews, countryside and travel news. Good for specialized sales and wants and accommodation update.

SHOTOKAN KARATE

*Traditional Karate
for a Richer Life*

*Traditional Karate
for a Richer Life*

SHOTOKAN KARATE

SHOJIRO KOYAMA

TRANSLATED BY JOE MCKEOWN

W H ALLEN
PLANET

Copyright © 1988 Shojiro Koyama
Translation copyright © 1988 Joe McKeown

Set in Candida and Optima by
Phoenix Photosetting, Chatham, Kent
Printed and bound in Great Britain by
Adlard & Son Ltd
for the Publishers W.H. Allen & Co. Plc
44 Hill Street, London W1X 8LB

Design Cecil Smith

Jacket photo by Zao Grimberg, courtesy of
The Image Bank

ISBN 1–85227–001–2

TABLE OF CONTENTS

INTRODUCTION	**7**
1 KARATE AND MODERN LIFE	**8**
2 BENEFITS OF KARATE	**11**
Benefits for Children	**12**
Benefits for Young Adults	**14**
Benefits for People Over 40	**14**
3 SHOTOKAN KARATE	**17**
Teaching Philosophy	**18**
Basics	**21**
Flexibility	**28**
Stances	**38**
Techniques	**46**
Kata	**50**
Importance of Kata	**51**
Kata becomes Kumite	**52**
Correct Kata	**54**
Kumite	**60**
4 MENTAL ATTITUDE AND KARATE TRAINING	**62**
5 SELF TRAINING IN THE DEVELOPMENT OF BASIC PHYSICAL STRENGTH	**64**
Weight Belts	**65**
Muscles for Karate	**71**
Rubber Tubing	**71**
Practical Goals in Self Training	**106**
CONCLUSION	**107**
BIOGRAPHIES	**108**
REFERENCES	**109**
GLOSSARY	**109**

INTRODUCTION

M ost people today think of karate as a competitive sport, and many karate students mistakenly believe that the goal of their training is to defeat opponents and win tournaments. However, experiencing failure is an important part of a beginner's training. Because they place too much emphasis on winning, many enthusiastic beginners end up quitting in frustration before they have a chance to realize the true essence of karate.

In Japan, karate is practised as a traditional martial art, and it is still considered a process by which a karateka (karate performer) acquires wisdom for daily living. This wisdom was gained over centuries of war-ravaged history by warriors faced with the physical and mental extremities of front-line combat. Karate is more than just the mastering of certain physical techniques; the training is mental as well, and should teach what these warriors knew: discipline, confidence and control.

The purpose of this book is to demonstrate the value of traditional karate for modern men and women, not as a sport for their diversion, but as a life-long endeavour for their physical and mental well-being. Section 1 is a general discussion of karate's place in the modern world. In Section 2, the benefits of karate are examined with reference to three different age groups. Section 3 includes a discussion of the traditional martial arts teaching philosophy and looks at the kihon (basics), kata (forms) and kumite (sparring) of Shotokan Karate, a traditional Japanese karate style. The book ends with a discussion of the proper mental attitude of a successful karateka and some valuable advice on self training to improve physical strength and karate techniques.

KARATE AND MODERN LIFE

 I n many ways modern technology has made today's world more exciting than the world of our ancestors. Our great-grandparents probably did not travel far from their homes very often. Our ancestors without television were deprived of pictures and news reports from all over the globe. Yet despite our numerous entertainment, information and travel possibilities, it would be difficult to prove that our lives are any happier than the lives of people in more simple times. The easy diversion offered by technology can distract a person from what is really important in life.

Someone once said that there are just two rules for living a happy life: read the Bible and keep your bowels open. What is meant is that people need to be more concerned with what is happening inside their minds and bodies than with the whirl of external events vying for their attention. First, one should have a common-sense life philosophy. Next, one should refrain from overeating or overdrinking, and avoid getting too excited or too depressed. The anxiety caused by severe mood changes, as surely as the overindulgence of our appetites, can cause physical dysfunction.

The oldest known Chinese book on food, written in 1330 by a physician at the Mongol court, extols moderation in eating and drinking as well as in living.

*He who would take good care of his health should be sparing in his
tastes, banish his worries, temper his desires, restrain his emotions, take
good care of his vital force, spare his words, regard lightly success and
failure, ignore sorrows and difficulties, drive away foolish ambitions,
avoid great likes and dislikes, calm his vision and his hearing, and be
faithful in his internal regimen. How can one have sickness if he does
not tire his spirits and worry his soul? Therefore he who would nourish
his nature should eat only when he is hungry and not fill himself with
food, and he should drink only when he is thirsty and not fill himself
with too much drink . . . Being well-filled hurts the lungs and being
hungry hurts the flow of vital energy.*

It is noteworthy that people 600 years ago made no distinction between
the physical and spiritual well-being of an individual. They understood
that spiritual turmoil causes poor health just as surely as do intemperate
eating and drinking.

For our day, the injunctions to 'temper our desires' and 'drive
away foolish ambitions' are particularly appropriate. It does not take a
sociologist to discover that our society is obsessed with winning. One
need only look at the programmes on television. The good guys always
win, so that in people's minds winning is somehow associated with
being a good person. Many people today lack a common-sense
approach to life because they have adopted unrealistic expectations of
winning. They are inflamed with the desire for success; their egos are
too big.

In karate such people either quit after a short period, or they
begin to change their attitudes. Typically, the overambitious karate
student becomes obsessed with the excitement of sports competition
and trains only to be tournament champion. However, since just one
person can be champion in any tournament, all the other participants
must learn to cope with losing. Either they learn to cope, or they give up
karate in frustration.

While karate students should try to win, defeating opponents and
winning tournaments are not the chief goals of karate. Rather, students
in our style are encouraged to choose tournaments carefully,

participating in only those that are well run and that promise to provide good learning experiences. In everyday training and in life, the goals are the same: to improve and to strive to realize one's own potential.

Our grandparents may indeed have been happier in their simpler times, not having to deal with the distractions and negative influences of modern life. For us to restore a proper perspective to our lives, we must be attentive to our health, and we must endeavour to follow a common-sense life philosophy. Quite simply, practising karate helps to counteract the distractions and obsessions of modern life by reminding us of our priorities in living. As Master Funakoshi Gichin, the founder of Shotokan Karate, has stated, 'The ultimate aim of the art of karate lies not in victory or defeat, but in the perfection of character of its participants.'

BENEFITS OF KARATE

F| or all participants, karate provides a rigorous, regular exercise
programme in the setting of a formal class. In this respect, karate
is similar to aerobic dancing. In addition, however, karate training gives
people the structured setting necessary for learning valuable life skills.
Students learn how to defend themselves, and they improve their spatial
perception, sensitivity and control. Self-confidence also comes with
continued training.

One prominent Phoenix physician, Dr Thomas L. Embry MD, has
noted the following medical benefits of karate:

- Promotes health of musculoskeletal systems through activities
  such as preparation exercises which stretch muscles and
  muscle groups, and which put all joints through a full range of
  motion.

- Promotes optimum development of most organ systems of
  youngsters through vigorous activity.

- Indirectly and possibly directly lessens the morbidity and/or
  prevents the development of chronic diseases such as the
  following: coronary heart disease, obesity, hypertension,
  diabetes mellitus and arthritis.

Other benefits of karate vary, depending on the age of the participant.
Here, benefits for three groups will be discussed: children 17 and under,
adults 18 to 40, and people over 40.

Benefits for Children

arate provides children with an excellent form of regular exercise. Training engages all of a child's muscle groups and helps him or her to develop grace, coordination, balance and timing. Moreover, this kind of physical training has benefited hyperactive children by providing a constructive way to burn off energy, and it has succeeded in raising the energy levels of lethargic youngsters.

Along with karate's physical rewards, youngsters also receive mental or spiritual benefits. Children learn discipline, courtesy and sensitivity through training in a traditional Japanese style of karate. Because our style is drawn from the real-life experience of front-line combatants, training is particularly effective as a preparation for life.

Many adults in our complicated, competitive society find it difficult to cope with adversity. Hospitals are filled with people suffering from stress-related ailments, and nervous breakdowns are becoming commonplace. Why do some people seem to handle life's difficulties better than others? The ability to cope with adversity is not a gift from God; it is learned behaviour, and it is best learned when we are young. Training in traditional karate ensures that a youngster will make miniature mistakes, and that he or she will be exposed to miniature disappointments. This experience will enable him or her to deal better with life's larger problems at a later stage.

The competition a student experiences in our style of karate is consistent with the combat origins of this martial art. Whereas some karate organizations divide competitors into weight classes and have six-point matches, we have no weight system for competitors, and matches are won by the first person to score a single point. We do not sponsor double elimination tournaments like those of some karate organizations. Warriors in battle understood that they would receive no second chance, that the first 'point' would decide the battle. Very often in life's most important contests, we are also afforded only one chance.

Because our system of competition is so rigid, young people meet failure often. Typically, a child's reaction to failure will take one of three forms. The first form is negative: the child makes excuses, perhaps by claiming that the judging of his match was unfair. The second reaction is also negative: here, an individual will become very angry at himself for losing, and think 'I'm bad.' This reaction puts tremendous pressure on the person to succeed the next time. The third reaction is a positive one: after losing several times in matches, the competitor begins to analyse why he or she has failed. The frontal associative area of the brain begins to discover new methods for achieving results. If a student continues karate for more than just the first few months, this exploratory behaviour after a mistake becomes a habitual response to adversity. Now, if an error is made it is seen as a challenge for creating new ideas. The individual no longer fears mistakes; rather, he or she begins to enjoy the risk of competition.

While some students who initially react to failure in a negative way will give up karate in frustration, many others learn in this rigid system that failure is necessary for success – that failure is, in fact, an opportunity for improvement. Because our karate remains true to the harsh realities of the combat situation, children following this system develop strong spirits for facing the harsh realities of life.

Benefits for Young Adults

F or young people in the age group 18 to 40, karate provides many of the benefits that it does for children, but it also serves as an important constant during times that for most people are filled with change. The years from 18 to 40 represent a period of time during which careers are developed, family units are formed, and lifestyles are established. During this period, proper physical and mental health are of the utmost importance, not only to deal with current realities, but also to set the stage for a healthier later life. Regular training in karate promotes the good health and sound mental attitude necessary for a long and pleasant life.

Benefits for People Over 40

F or people over 40, karate has special relevance. It is at this time that the body starts its campaign to deteriorate. Deterioration is, of course, inevitable, but it can be slowed greatly. Karate exercises and training methods serve to improve and maintain good circulation, clear complexion, and proper functioning of the autonomic nervous system.

The body is purged and purified by the sweat of training.

Certainly, the benefits to be gained from karate come only from hard work. Unfortunately, some people begin karate only to discover that it is harder than they expected, and they give up. This is unfortunate, because the sweat of training is just what so many discontented people in today's world need.

With good transport and instant long-distance communication available to virtually everyone in our society, and with the modern conveniences that technology has put into our homes, people have more leisure time at their disposal than ever before. Some seek relaxation by meditating or doing yoga; others listen to music; still others drink alcohol or take drugs. Ironically, some wealthy people in our society have very little work or suffering in their lives, yet they find it difficult to enjoy their leisure. The news is filled with stories about fabulously rich celebrities who injure or kill themselves with drink or drugs. Because these people overindulge themselves looking for ever greater pleasures, or perhaps simply because they have too much ease, their lives are often filled with anxiety and discontent. One wonders whether, with all their wealth, they could ever enjoy anything as much as as hot, tired labourer enjoys a drink of cold water at the end of a day's work.

Without some degree of suffering, there can be no real pleasure to be found in life. Blue skies every day cease to be beautiful; only after experiencing cloudy, dreary days can we appreciate a blue sky. So it is with our bodies. To find real pleasure in life, to be really relaxed, we must experience some discomfort. When karate students understand this, their training becomes easier. Training is not torture, but good, healthy work.

Moreover, evidence suggests that karate's health benefits go beyond those of similarly strenuous sports such as running, swimming and aerobic dancing. To understand, consider for a moment the life of man before he became civilized. When men wore no clothes, and fighting – against man and beast alike – was a natural part of life, they naturally suffered more bruises, wounds and broken bones than men today are used to. Nevertheless, primitive men recovered from their calamities more quickly than modern men can; they had stronger resistance to disease and superior recuperative powers.

Consider also some stories about how people respond to the hardships of war. At the end of World War II, the people of Tokyo, Japan were subjected to terrifying daily air raids. Bombs were falling everywhere, food was very scarce, and people feared for their lives. Despite these hardships, or more probably because of them, no one at this time caught a cold. Compare this with life in present-day Western society, with nearly everyone catching one or two colds, or more, every year. When people's concerns are about imminent, real dangers, they seem to grow stronger, with less susceptibility to disease and greater powers of recovery.

It is wonderful what medical science and modern technology have done to protect us from disease and to keep us comfortable in our homes. Nevertheless, compared with those who are thrown into life-and-death situations, the concerns of most men seem trivial, and we are weaker beings for this.

In order to develop more robust and durable constitutions, men and women today need the stimulation that comes from experiencing a small element of danger and from receiving minor injuries. Karate training provides this stimulation on a regular basis and in a controlled form. One cannot avoid bumps and bruises during training, even with careful participants. In sparring there is always danger, and students of karate need a seriousness, an intensity, that aerobic dancing and other sports do not require.

SHOTOKAN KARATE

S hotokan Karate is a Japanese martial art. It differs from many Westernized versions of karate largely because it remains firmly rooted in a strong martial arts tradition. The Japanese have always viewed karate as a means of survival on the battlefield: every punch or kick of an opponent is considered a potential death blow.

Western versions of karate, on the other hand, are often practised more as sports — and spectator sports at that — than as martial arts. Soft to full contact is allowed, and participants tend to use flashier, less stable techniques. The use of pads in full-contact karate removes the art even further from the realities of a combat situation. With big gloves on his hands, a defender no longer has to make an efficient, complete block to ward off an attacker's blow. Of course, the heavily padded hands and feet make focusing one's power at the point of impact impossible. Scoring with one focused, decisive technique is no longer the goal, and the match degenerates into a contest dependent largely on the strength of the participants. In this case, the number of muted blows delivered versus the number received is what matters.

In contrast, Japanese karate allows no contact and no grabbing. Rather, students are taught to focus punches and kicks just short of their targets. This type of practice teaches students to judge distance between themselves and their opponents better than if they spent time simply pounding into bags or opponents. Moreover, our conditioning may well be of significant spiritual benefit. Whereas one who practises hitting something or someone every day may be conditioning himself to hit as a response to conflicts in daily life, our kind of practice teaches students sensitivity and control.

Emphasis in this style is on low, stable stances, and participants tend to use more conservative techniques than do participants in a more sports-oriented karate. All this is in keeping with the tradition that a failed attack could mean death for that attacker, rather than simply the loss of a point.

People who train in the traditional karate styles often think in terms of gaining mastery in three different areas: kihon (basics), kata (forms) and kumite (sparring). Though the distinction between the three areas blurs as students advance, Shotokan Karate will be examined with reference to all three. First, however, something should be said about our teaching philosophy, for it is very different from those with which many Westerners are familiar.

Teaching Philosophy

T hose who have seen the film *Karate Kid* have seen an accurate portrayal of the traditional student–teacher karate relationship. The relationship and the philosophy behind it differ in two important ways from the teaching methods popular in our society. From a Western point of view, the relationship seems to be one of total subservience of student to teacher, but it is also a relationship that breeds an important kinship between the student and his sensei.

In our society, there are many experienced coaches and teachers who are clever and knowledgeable, but too ofen they spend little time with their students. Teachers and students interact only on a technical level. For example, suppose a secondary school mathematics teacher discovers that a student is taking drugs outside of school. Many teachers in such a position will think that their job is simply teaching mathematics; they will not see it as their business to become involved. Of course, this attitude is self-perpetuating: students then do not expect their teachers to take a personal interest in them. In athletics, many students want only the technical training and not the philosophy or discipline that go along with the teaching. Even in karate, some students feel that they have paid for technical instruction only, as though they could learn karate in the same way that they learn important dates in history. Many of these students show a lack of respect and a lack of courtesy, both of which are the instructor's due in the traditional martial arts system.

In the film *Karate Kid*, the student shows respect by saying 'Yes, Sensei' many times. It may seem like a slave's response to his master, or a private's to a sergeant in the army. Some people regard this behaviour as undemocratic. They don't like to be a slave to the instructor; they are independent decision-makers. Yet karate training is very similar to training for the front line in the army; it is also like driving a car or swinging a golf club or tennis racquet. In all of these endeavours, if one thinks and then acts, it is already too late.

Many of our skills depend on our learned ability to react reflexively. When tennis star John McEnroe hits two volleys at the net in the span of a second, he is obviously not thinking of the mechanics of each shot. He acts on instinct, with no conscious deliberation. Brain physiologists tell us that such conditioned reflexes are under the control of the right hemisphere of the brain and that this hemisphere's unique ability is spatial perception. In karate tournaments, understanding the orientation of yourself in relation to your opponent and your surroundings comes from a sort of intuition rather than from conscious thought, and this intuition comes only when the brain's right hemisphere has been conditioned. As with playing tennis or golf, effective fighting requires an ability to act without referring to the analytical left side of the brain.

How do we develop our brain's right hemisphere? That is exactly what the film *Karate Kid* is about. The old man commands his student to wash cars and paint fences with a certain motion of his arms. When the boy complains about the work, the old man insists that he do it without question. At first, the sensei does not specifically teach karate techniques through verbal communication. However, an unspoken communication takes place that leads to the development of the student's right hemisphere. Through his 'mindless' repetition of certain movements, the boy learns to execute techniques reflexively, without conscious thought.

Also significant in the film is that the boy is invited to enter into the karate master's personal life. Some may think that the boy is treated like a slave, but the youngster is allowed to work at gardening with the old man; the two eat and drink together. The boy learns about the old man's past and gains a respect for the character of his sensei. In such a situation, the student begins to trust his instructor as he never could otherwise. Consider a father who tells his son throughout the boy's childhood, 'I love you', but without ever being home to have dinner with the family, or being around to spend time with the boy. The father says 'I love you', or gives the boy advice to follow, but the boy does not trust the father completely; he questions the statement or the advice. Consider, on the other hand, a father who communicates non-verbally the same message of 'I love you' by spending time with the child and making the boy an important part of his own life. This boy trusts his father's advice and is less likely to be suspicious of what his father tells him.

The feeling of respect, or love, or kinship between a son and his father or between a student and his teacher is not rational; it is intuitive and it shows development of the right hemisphere of the brain. Conversely, when no kinship exists between a teacher and a student, the student will tend to use his left hemisphere too much. It is this left hemisphere that analyses, judges, and questions the value of instructions, especially when those instructions promise no quick, evident results.

The feeling of kinship that exists in a traditional student–teacher martial arts relationship enables the instructor to teach in a style that discourages the student from depending on his left (analytical) hemisphere. In a traditional karate class, students are shown a

movement or a series of movements, and they then do their best to
reproduce what they have seen. They repeat movements on command
from their instructor. There is little explaining of theory or application,
and questions from students are not encouraged. The knowledge that a
karate student seeks is, after all, not a verbal kind of knowledge that
can reside in the intellect. By the time we think in words – 'block',
'punch' – it is already too late. What a person seeks in karate is to
condition himself to act or react, in the most efficient way possible,
without thinking. It therefore makes sense to emphasize doing and
reacting rather than thinking and analysing.

     The point is not that students should be totally submissive to all
their instructors, never questioning anything an instructor says. It is just
that karate, like driving a car or hitting a good tennis shot, requires
conditioned reflexes rather than conscious understanding. One learns
by doing, not by thinking, and this learning is clearly facilitated by the
traditional martial arts relationship between student and teacher.

Basics

*T*he basic movements that a student learns when training in this
style of karate are natural movements for the human body. This
is in contrast to many styles of karate which require students to emulate
the movements of a monkey or some other animal. While a human
being may succeed in programming his body to reproduce the actions of
some animal, mastery of the monkey technique, for example, will
undoubtedly take many years. In the end, what is achieved is still a
copy of movements natural to another species.

Our style of karate is based on the assumption that the action and reaction of arm and leg movements in walking constitute the natural and most efficient way for a human being to cover distance. Because of the way the human body structure differs from the monkey's, it is natural for a human to walk more erectly than a monkey does. Of course, most men also have limitations in strength and flexibility that monkeys and other animals do not have.

It is true that certain elaborate spinning techniques, which for most people would not be natural movements, can be effective. The fact that these techniques are out of the ordinary gives them an element of surprise. However, after these techniques have been seen five or six times, they are no longer different and they lose their effectiveness. A straight front kick or reverse punch is quicker and more efficient for the body structure of most people.

Also efficient for *Homo sapiens* are the four basic blocks in our karate. As Figure 1a illustrates, a person's arm leverage is maximized when his elbow is kept close to his body; no one carries an umbrella with his elbow out to the side or very far in front of his body. Figures 1b, 1c, 1d and 1e show the proper application of this leverage, with the elbow kept close to the body, in the inner block, the knife-hand block, the downward block, and the upper block.

Though this style of karate tends to strengthen and focus movements that are natural for the human body, the method is not easily mastered. Muscles as well as reflexes must be conditioned, and most people in our society need to work at increasing their flexibility. All of this takes time.

1a

A person's arm leverage is maximized when his elbow is kept close to his body. Figures 1b, 1c, 1d and 1e show the proper application of this leverage, with the elbow kept close to the body.

THE INNER BLOCK (Chudan-uke)

1c

THE KNIFE-HAND BLOCK (Shuto-uke)

THE DOWNWARD BLOCK (Gedan-barai)

THE UPPER BLOCK (Age-uke)

■ *Flexibility*

Flexibility is important because it protects an individual from injury and will increase the range and speed of techniques. While all joints should be loosened and all muscles stretched or 'warmed' before any workout, especially important in karate is the development of the hip area. The kinds of exercises pictured in Figures 2 to 6 will develop this area, and students should do these every day.

Notice that in Figures 2 to 4 the person holds on to a rubber tube or his belt and uses it to pull himself down. He is stretching to his capacity and then holding at this point for several counts. This method of stretching is superior to the bouncing up and down that many students do (sometimes with a partner pushing from behind). Too

Above and opposite page: Flexibility exercises for development of the hip area, which students should do every day. Using a rubber tube or his belt, the student pulls himself down and stretches to capacity, holding at this point for several counts.

5

Another hip flexibility exercise in which a partner helps the person to arch backwards as far as possible, and holds him there for several counts.

violent bouncing tears capillaries and can easily cause painful muscle pulls. In Figure 5, a partner helps the person to arch his back backwards as far as possible, and the partner holds him there for several counts. Finally, to develop the inner thigh muscles as well as loosen the hip joints, a person lies face down with his knees out to the sides at right angles (Figure 6); the partner pushes the hips down slowly and then releases the pressure. As flexibility increases, students should stretch themselves further and increase the number of times they hold the stretched position. The length of time that each maximum stretch is held can also be increased.

To develop the inner thigh muscles as well as loosen the hip joints, a person lies face down with his knees out to the sides at right angles; the partner pushes the hips down slowly and then releases the pressure.

Using a partner to help stretch legs and hips for front kicks. The person being stretched has both arms extended to the sides to prevent his body from leaning to either side.

Using a wall and a partner to stretch legs and hips for side kicks. It is important to keep the torso erect, so the person being stretched reaches high up on the wall.

Above and opposite: The correct way to stretch for a roundhouse kick with the help of a partner, using a wall to keep the body as erect as possible over the supporting leg.

Once students have been training for several months, they should begin using a wall and a partner to help stretch legs and hips. Figures 7 and 8 illustrate stretching for the front and side kicks, respectively. Once again, a partner stretches the person to that persons's capacity and holds him there for several counts. Note that in Figure 7, the person being stretched has both arms extended to the sides. He does this to prevent his body from leaning to either side. In Figure 8, the person being stretched reaches high up on the wall to stop himself from leaning too much into the wall. Finally, Figures 9 and 10 illustrate the proper way to stretch for a roundhouse kick. Once again, the person being stretched uses the wall to keep his body as erect as possible over his supporting leg. For the kind of flexibility training that employs a wall and a partner, keeping one's torso erect is important.

Whatever the type of stretching being done, students should never forget that increased flexibility takes time. Those who insist on trying to become limber quickly only end up slowing the process. They may pull muscles. Impatient people also tend to be too intense during stretching, and this causes muscles to tighten.

The negative effect of an inappropriate mental attitude towards stretching is most easily seen in youngsters. Children are naturally limber, and with daily stretching they should have no trouble retaining and increasing their flexibility. However, children are often impatient to see the results of their efforts, or it may be that they feel a pressure from

STRADDLE STANCE (Kiba-dachi)

This is an extremely stable stance, in which the weight is distributed equally over four points, the heel and ball of each foot, much as weight is distributed in the legs of a chair.

To perform the kiba-dachi correctly, the outer edges of one's feet should be perfectly straight, or parallel, with the knees pointed outwards, so that the bottoms of the feet seem to grip the floor, and the back should be straight, with the buttocks tucked under.

parents who are keen to see their children progress in karate. Whatever the cause, children with too tense or serious an attitude will not benefit from stretching; they actually lose some of their natural flexibility. A mind unburdened by the problems of daily life – a relaxed mental attitude – is as important in flexibility training as it is in training for karate stances.

◼ *Stances*

Stances and movements across the floor in this style of karate are derived from the motions of the human body in walking. As is natural in walking, a person's torso should be perpendicular to the floor in all of the stances. However, karate stances are lower and more stable than people are used to, and it takes time and training for these stances to feel comfortable.

The stance that is likely to feel most uncomfortable in the beginning is called kiba-dachi. This stance, illustrated in Figure 11a, is excellent training for all of the other stances, so students should strive to do it correctly. One important point to remember about kiba-dachi is that the outer edges of one's feet should be perfectly straight, or parallel. Knees should be pointed outwards so that the bottoms of the feet seem to grip the floor, and the back should be straight, with the buttocks tucked under. At first, this stance is uncomfortable because our muscles and joints are not used to it, but this is an extremely stable stance. As Figures 11a and 11b illustrate, weight is distributed equally over four points, the heel and the ball of each foot, much as weight is distributed in the legs of a chair.

When we stand in a good kiba-dachi stance, our leg muscles are somewhat tensed and our body weight is being supported by muscles rather than bones. If we allowed our feet to angle more comfortably outwards and our weight to go back on our heels, our skeletal structure would be supporting our body weight. In this poor stance, it takes an extra instant to move any limb. The brain must first send an impulse down the spinal column and through the motor neurons in our peripheral nervous system in order to stimulate a particular muscle. Only then can the limb respond.

With our weight distributed 50–50 between the heels and the front of the feet, and with the outer edges of the feet straight, we are able to react much more quickly. Now the feet are gripping the floor, and this means that leg muscles are already stimulated. One of our three types of sensory receptors (nerves that receive rather than send information), the proprioceptors, are stimulated. Because these nerves give our bodies skeletal awareness, the brain no longer has to send a signal to activate a muscle before a particular limb can respond. The limb is prepared to move in a flash, reflexively.

Of course, a student of karate must condition himself to have strong stances, and once again the kind of training required is both mental and physical. Consider for a moment an exercise such as jogging. Physically, jogging is very good exercise, but during the exercise one's centre of gravity is raised. The bouncing up and down in jogging requires no mental discipline, and though being relaxed may make jogging easier, the exercise hardly promotes or requires relaxation.

Standing in a good kiba-dachi, on the other hand, provides both physical and mental training. For one thing, a beginner student – even one with very strong legs – can usually not remain in the stance for more than five or ten minutes. His centre of gravity is too high, and he is too excited because he is trying too hard. Nevertheless, the student must practise standing in his stances for increasing periods of time. He might close his eyes and think to himself, 'I'm strong', in order to keep going. The student should relax his muscles as much as possible; his jaw and face muscles, his back muscles, the muscles in his arms – all his muscles except those needed to support him in the stance should be completely relaxed. The student will begin to feel his centre of gravity drop, and the stance will feel strong.

Soon the student will understand that relaxing is the key to being able to hold a solid stance. When a person is tense, angry or excited, the pain of trying to hold the stance for more than ten minutes is too much to bear. As the student learns composure, this mental attitude allows him to hold a good kiba-dachi for an hour or more.

In addition to simply standing in a stance, students might use a rubber tube or a partner to help them train for good stances. In Figure

Above: A partner and the wall are used to exaggerate the need to keep the back straight in the stance. If the body is not erect and directly over the stance, the legs will tire quickly.

Opposite: A rubber tube may also be used to help develop the feeling of gripping the floor with one's feet; the student must struggle to keep the knees pointed outwards.

13

12, a partner and the wall are used to exaggerate the need to keep the back straight in the stance. If the body is not erect and directly over the stance, the legs will tire quickly. Figure 13 illustrates the use of a rubber tube to help develop the feeling of gripping the floor with one's feet; the student must struggle to keep the knees pointed outwards.

Another difficult stance for most students is the back stance shown in Figure 14d. As the sequence of pictures illustrates, the position of the back leg in this stance is the same as in kiba-dachi. The outside edge of the back foot is straight and the back knee is angled outwards. While the torso does shift back over the back leg slightly (so that 70 per cent of the weight is on the back leg), the upper body does not lean back or to either side; the torso must be erect, with the buttocks tucked under.

Figures 14a to 14d illustrate the use of rubber tubing to train for the proper back stance. Note that in Figures b and c the movement should be as though the centre of the foot were pivoting on a nail. The front foot pivots at the same time that the knife-hand block (prepared for in 14a) is executed. The shoulders are low rather than high and tense, and though the hips end up at a 45° angle, orienting the body away from the opponent, the navel is aimed forward in the same direction as the eyes.

For stepping in the back stance, an exercise like the one shown in Figure 15 is useful. The weight of a partner on his shoulders forces the student underneath to keep his back straight while going from one back stance to the next.

Using rubber tubing to train for the proper back stance, with the knife-hand block prepared.

BACK STANCE (Kokutsu-dachi)

Top right and bottom right: When moving into the back stance, the front foot moves as though pivoting on a nail, at the same time that the knife-hand block is executed.

Above left: The position of the back leg in the back stance is the same as in kiba-dachi. The outside edge of the back foot is straight and the back knee is angled outwards. The torso shifts so that 70 per cent of the weight is on the back leg, but the upper body does not lean back or to either side. The torso must be erect, with the buttocks tucked under and though the hips end up at a 45° angle, orientating the body away from the opponent, the navel is aimed forward in the same direction as the eyes.

Opposite: For stepping in the back stance, the weight of a partner on the shoulders is useful. It forces the student underneath to keep his back straight while going from one back stance to the next.

15

■ *Techniques*

No one will learn to deliver strong karate techniques by reading words on a page, any more than one can become a great pianist by reading about how to play the piano. One's mind and body must be conditioned first. Stances must be strong, and a student must learn how to relax for his technique to be sharp. Every block and strike should be fast and focused, like a whip. The feeling of limbs becoming whips can happen only if the student is completely relaxed before – and during – the technique. Relaxation is the key. Not until the very end of the technique do the student's centre (the abdomen, about two inches below the navel) and his foot or hand tighten. The kiai (loud shout from the diaphragm), must happen with the focus of the block, kick or punch.

The feeling of going from total relaxation to a total focus of power may be compared to sneezing. Before sneezing we usually experience a tightness in the chest; this is during the 'ah, ah' stage when our torsos raise up and our heads tilt back. Immediately before the sneeze, our bodies relax. Then, 'atchoo!' The relaxation prior to the spasm of sneezing, and then the spasm – this is what good karate feels like.

When tightness occurs only at the end of a technique and all movement stops at once, energy jumps from the karateka's body. When there is tightness in the body before or during a karate technique, energy is expended internally rather than at the point of contact with an opponent; energy is wasted.

A karate student must aspire to achieve that whip-like feeling in his techniques. This means relaxing as completely as possible before and during blocks and strikes, and it also means focusing power 100 per cent in an instant.

To focus the power of the entire body at the point of impact, one should practise punching before a wall. Figures 16a to 16c show the focusing of a half punch, a three-quarters punch, and then a full punch. This exercise requires concentration and control. If techniques are to be powerful, the punching must not be with the arm only; the entire body must go from relaxed to tense in an instant, in order to stop the fist a centimetre from the wall.

A HALF PUNCH

16b

A THREE-QUARTERS PUNCH

A FULL PUNCH

Kata

K atas are ancient exercises conceived as defences against multiple opponents. The five basic katas in Shotokan Karate comprise between 19 and 27 separate movements, and students are expected to memorize and master each kata much as a gymnast masters a particular routine. However, kata differs from gymnastics in at least two important ways.

First, a kata is not a flexible routine that may be easily changed or modified. Katas were developed by successful warriors from their battlefield experiences. These men were geniuses at surviving in combat, so a student who practises kata has no basis for changing either the movements or the intent of the kata.

The second way a kata differs from a gymnast's routine is that the katas are not practised merely for aesthetic enjoyment (although a kata can be beautiful when performed correctly). Katas are first of all training for self-defence. Throughout a student's early training, he is told to focus his techniques on imaginary opponents; this is to help the student to understand the purpose of each movement. Then, after much practice, the student may evolve away from the combat roots of kata and begin to realize the aesthetic possibilities of these exercises. In fact, doing a kata can be like playing a musical instrument. After years of practice, the instrument is more a part of the musician than a separate entity, and so it is with the karateka and his kata. When the student has made a kata a part of himself, he is ready to begin expressing that kata artistically.

Importance of Kata

Currently being debated in Japan is the question of how to teach English to university students. The old way of doing it was to provide students with the basics first. Students began by learning the eight parts of speech: noun, pronoun, verb, adjective, adverb, conjunction, article and preposition. The problem perceived with this method was that even though students would learn the fundamentals of how the foreign language works, they would graduate unable to speak or understand spoken English. There is now a group that favours de-emphasizing the basics of English grammar, preferring the teaching of spoken, or conversational English.

The controversy over how English should be taught in Japanese universities is instructive for understanding the place of kata in a karate system. Learning kata, like training in stances and fundamental karate techniques, is similar to learning English grammar. Neither activity gratifies the student with immediate successes (here we refer to the kind of success in karate most beginner students look for: success in fighting); but both activities provide a basis for later excellence.

Conversely, a slight ability to communicate ideas in a foreign language (as with a Japanese person speaking broken English), or a meagre proficiency at free-style sparring, can be gained without much work on basics, simply by doing the activity one is trying to learn. One learns to converse and to spar relatively quickly by conditioning oneself until aspects of the activity become reflexive. A middle-aged Japanese man, uneducated in English, may know enough conversation to get by in the USA after just three years. However, after ten years of living there, his conversation will not have improved, because he knows no grammar. The same can be said of people in karate who practise only sparring. These people, no matter how much they spar, will always be limited as to how far they can progress. In fact, as they get older and lose their strength and the flexibility that had come naturally to them, such people will also lose their sparring ability.

Of course, mastering either a foreign language or karate requires more than just learning the basics. The Japanese student who is well versed in English grammar but who has never lived among English-speaking people will need time and practice before he is fluent in the language. He still needs the conditioning that makes conversation reflexive, and this can come only from speaking English. Nevertheless, with everyday use it will not take many years before the person speaks the new language as though it were his own; soon, even his dreams will be in English.

The case of the karate student who has trained only in basic techniques is similar. Free-style sparring is a reflexive activity that requires conditioning. To excel at sparring, therefore, one must spar. However, it is the training in basics and kata that enables a karate student to reach his potential as a fighter. By practising kata and basics as well as sparring, a karate student will not only excel at kumite, but he will be able to train to the age of 80 and beyond.

Kata becomes Kumite

While sparring is a reflexive activity that requires conditioning, one must not think that this conditioning is somehow different from the rest of karate training. All karate training involves the conditioning of the body and spirit, and kata, in its ultimate expression, actually becomes sparring.

An explanation of the Japanese philosophy of shu-ha-ri may help. Shu means learning from tradition; ha means breaking the chains of tradition; and ri means transcendence. As applied to kata training, the shu stage is similar to what one would be put through at certain dance studios when told to step on footprints that create a pattern on the floor. Usually at this stage students are encouraged to move slowly through katas until all the correct movements and postures have been memorized. Speed will come later when the body has been programmed.

The ha stage is where this programming takes place. The student must do katas over and over, gradually increasing his speed, but also discovering the fine points of timing between moves. Through many repetitions of katas, and by following the instructions of his sensei, the student conditions himself. What is important at this stage is that the student do katas often and to the best of his ability, without worrying too much about mistakes.

What was accomplished in the shu stage, an understanding with the intellect, and what one strives for in the ha stage, an 'understanding' with the body, are vastly different. To illustrate, one can learn the theory of the step-and-punch karate technique in just a few minutes. When one attempts to execute the move, however, it is immediately clear that the body has not yet learned. The body leans too far forward and the front knee is not bent enough. Of course, movements are not yet synchronized, so the timing is off. Eventually, after much practice and instruction, one learns to keep the back straight and the hips low throughout the movement. Little details are gradually worked out, and the technique approaches the point where all movement stops with the focus of the punch. Now, when the technique is executed, the student moves without conscious thought, much as a person places one leg in front of the other to walk.

The conditioning required to master an entire kata is more complex, but putting the body through the movements to be mastered is still the key. The ha stage is when students make karate techniques feel like natural movements, and it is at this stage that most karate students spend the longest part of their training. The most patient and dedicated of these students will transcend the shu and ha stages.

The point of transcendence in any endeavour is difficult to describe. This is true for the ri stage of shu-ha-ri. One does not simply enter the ri stage as the final step in a process through shu and ha. In fact, there is shu; then there is ha; and then there is forgetting. Then comes transcendence at the ri stage. The intellect is so far removed at the ri stage that all techniques are completely automatic, and kata and kumite merge. This feeling may be compared to the transcendence experienced by a concert pianist. Certainly, each of his performances is the culmination of countless hours of practice, sometimes consisting of the most tedious exercises. However, during a concert all the exercises are forgotten and, though his eyes may move across the page of music, the artist's mind is a blank. Memory and thinking with the intellect are transcended, and the performer feels with an astounding sensitivity.

This sensitivity of the great pianist, like that of the karate master, allows the artist to be aware of minute imperfections in a performance. A kata that seemed perfect to a casual observer may not have satisfied the man or woman who performed it. The artist may feel that it was somehow not quite right today, though it might, in fact, have been technically perfect.

Correct Kata

To perform kata well, students must execute the basic stances, blocks and strikes correctly. For the majority of karate students, those labouring at the ha stage of training, this means paying special attention to certain common, subtle weaknesses in kata performance.

First, losing contact between the foot, or part of the foot, and the floor is a mistake that will ruin timing and dissipate the power of a technique. In front stance, the back leg should be firmly anchored, with the big toe, the ball of the foot and the heel all in contact with the floor. When a student executes a step and punch, the toes of the front foot should grip the floor and pull as the back foot pushes off. The legs will scissor closed and then open again. When the student begins in a left-foot-forward stance, the left foot should remain firmly in contact with the ground at all three points (toe, ball and heel) throughout the movement until this foot is anchored as the back foot in a right-foot-forward stance. Meanwhile, it is important that the right foot that is stepping forward slide forward on the ball and toe. Whether the student is moving in front stance, back stance or kiba-dachi, he should avoid stamping his feet.

Another concern for students practising kata has to do with the orientation of the upper body. First of all, during kata the eyes should always be focused in the direction of an imaginary opponent. When stepping forward with the left foot and executing a left-handed downward block, the eyes should look in the direction of the attack while the shoulders and hips are at a 45° angle to the opponent (see Figure 17b). The navel, however, should be pointing as much as possible in the same direction as the eyes – straight at the opponent. One might think of the navel, then, as the barrel of a gun being aimed where the eyes are focused. This creates a tension, an orientation, inside the body towards the opponent, even though the outside of the body is angled defensively, at a 45° angle away from the attacker.

Poor timing of basic movements within a kata is another mistake for which tournament judges often deduct points. After the execution of a technique in one direction, a down block, knife defence or upper block being executed in a different direction should occur at the moment of direction change, not before or after. With the torso kept perpendicular to the floor throughout the movement (and the feet remaining in contact with the floor), a block executed simultaneously with the shifting of the hips allows the student to keep his balance and make the block powerful.

The key to blocking and shifting direction all at once is proper preparation. Figures 17a and b and 18a and b show the downward block and upper block, respectively. To prepare for the downward block, the student should bring the elbow of the blocking arm across and on top of his other elbow. When blocking at right angles to one's left after a left-handed stepping punch, for instance, the right arm extends downwards directly in front of the body and the left arm is brought as far as it can be to the right, but before the hips have changed direction. Now, one is ready to execute the block (Figure 17b) at the moment of direction change.

The preparation for the upper block is slightly different. Again, assuming one has just executed a left-handed stepping punch and will now block at right angles to the left, the right arm will reach up over the head while the left fist is brought to the hip as if in readiness for a punch (Figure 18a). As before, the left foot will be moving back to the other foot but has not yet moved to its final left-foot-forward position, nor have the hips shifted into place during preparation for this block. The block itself consists of the left elbow being driven upwards as the left hip pushes forward and the left foot slides into position (18b). All the movements in a good block stop at once.

In addition to executing individual blocks and strikes so that the power is maximized at the point of focus, one must have proper timing between techniques. The best way to learn this is by following the sensei's count for katas. Soon, a student will be able to differentiate between a complete move, a partial move, and a series of techniques to be executed as one move.

THE DOWNWARD BLOCK (Gedan-bari)

To prepare for the downward block, the student should bring the elbow of the blocking arm across and on top of his other elbow. When blocking at right angles to one's left after a left-handed stepping punch, for instance, the right arm extends downwards directly in front of the body and the left arm is brought as far as it can be to the right, but before the hips have changed direction.

Executing the downward block at the moment of direction change.

THE UPPER BLOCK (Age-uke)

To prepare for the upper block, when blocking at right angles to the left after a left-handed stepping punch, the right arm reaches up over the head while the left fist is brought to the hip as if in readiness for a punch. The left foot will be moving back to the other foot but has not yet moved to its final left-foot-forward position, nor have the hips shifted into place during preparation for this block.

The upper block itself consists of the left elbow being driven upwards, as the left hip pushes forward and the left foot slides into position. All the movements in a good block stop at once.

Finally, Master Funakoshi Gichin, the founder of Shotokan Karate, has specified three musts for kata performance:

1 the proper application (strong versus mild) of strength;

2 the most efficient expansion and contraction of muscles; and

3 proper speed.

Of course, these tenets can be followed only after much training, and they can never be consciously achieved. Under the pressure of an exam or tournament, and given the speed at which kata techniques are executed, the mind is incapable of controlling what happens in a kata. Students can hope to achieve the three musts only if they practise katas enough to make movements reflexive.

Kumite

R ecently, many books about karate have been published by karate masters, and nearly all of these are very basic. Rarely does one see any discussion of free sparring strategy. Why? By now the reason should be clear. Skill at sparring is not something that can be taught verbally. Effective fighting is all conditioned reflex.

The best advice for beginner students, then, is to forget about sparring and practise the basics. Learn the stances, kicks and punches.

In our style, practise heian 1–5, the basic katas; and practise five-step, three-step, and one-step sparring. (This basic sparring is controlled and deliberate, with an attacker announcing his attack so that the defender can execute a particular block.) Some instruction in these basics, like instruction in English grammar, can be found in books, or it can be received from a teacher. Even at this stage of a student's development, however, progress is entirely dependent on continued daily practice.

The time for a student to begin free-style sparring, if he wants to avoid injury, is around the time he receives his brown belt. By this time the student should be pretty well conditioned in the basic stances, blocks and strikes. Now he can begin to condition his reflexes for sparring by doing some free-style kumite. As a novice, the student should expect to make mistakes, for conditioning takes time. Eventually, he will learn.

MENTAL ATTITUDE AND KARATE TRAINING

*I*n order to excel at karate one must make regular training a part of one's life, and one must develop an attitude towards learning that allows for success. Perhaps the best way to describe the attitude of a successful karate student is to compare the temperaments of three different types of students. These three attitudes are found not only in karate dojo, but in classrooms and on practice fields all over the world.

One attitude is commonly seen in students who have little trouble learning the basics of a given subject. In skiing, for example, this type of student manages to go down the small hills with little difficulty on his very first tries. After a few minor successes, such a person concludes that 'this is easy', and he decides that he doesn't need any formal instruction to be a good skier. Unfortunately, natural ability and self training result in a meagre level of proficiency in activities such as skiing and karate. This type of student's complacent attitude will prevent him from realizing his full potential as a skier.

A second attitude towards karate training is frequently seen in the student who does not easily learn the basics. This student is like the beginner skier who tries very hard to improve, but falls down a lot. Each time he falls he curses bitterly, and with each failure his anger at himself builds. He is very determined, but he lacks patience. Though he is not smug about his abilities, even with the help of a good instructor this student will soon become frustrated and give up the sport.

The successful karate student, like the successful skier, must listen modestly to his instructor and imitate the instructor's actions as closely as possible. In skiing, when this type of student falls, he merely gets up and tries again without becoming too discouraged. He understands that through perseverance, and with the continued instruction of a competent teacher, he will eventually learn to excel in the discipline, whether this be skiing, mathematics, piano or karate.

Modesty, patience and dedication, then, are important attributes of a successful karate student. Unfortunately, experienced karate teachers know that many such 'good' students do not get beyond their third or fourth year in karate, and the same is true of promising students training in all kinds of artistic and athletic fields. To achieve excellence, a student must also be goal-oriented.

In golf, there are many players who play often but never seem to improve. Many of these people will say that they don't care much about their scores; they just want to get out in the sunshine and walk the beautiful courses. They play to socialize or to exercise. In karate, some students have no interest in improving their rank. They like karate for the aerobic exercise, and for the good workouts that classes provide.

Of course, these reasons for participation are good ones. It is good to socialize and get outdoors, and it is important for people to sweat through rigorous exercise. The problem is that for most people these attitudes are difficult to maintain. It is human nature to want to see – and have others see – the fruits of our labour. Consider the feelings of the golfer who, after admitting to his 32 handicap, must answer the question 'How long have you been playing?' with 'Ten years'. Such exchanges are embarrassing, despite claims that good scores are not the reason for golfing. The karate student who stays at green belt through several examinations and says he does not care about reaching the rank of brown belt may be reaping many of the benefits of karate training today, but it is unlikely that he will still be training in four years. People like to see improvements, and when they don't, it gets harder and harder to continue in a given endeavour.

The successful karate student, then, is modest and patient, but he is not unmindful of success. The student consistently accepts challenges to reach realistic goals. If he is undaunted by periodic failures, it is because he recognizes that failure is necessary for improvement.

5 SELF TRAINING IN THE DEVELOPMENT OF BASIC PHYSICAL STRENGTH

B eyond their work in a formal karate class, all karate students need to spend time practising on their own. Students should practise kata at home as well as in class, and they should find time every day to stretch and practise basic techniques. Two useful tools for karate training are a weight belt (approximately 15 lb for adults) and the kind of rubber tubing commonly found in the medical profession (see Figure 19).

Rubber latex tubing, which can be obtained from medical suppliers.

19

Weight Belts

W eight belts are good for stretching and strengthening hips, legs and ankles. One exercise for strengthening legs and hips is pictured in Figures 20a to 20c. With feet pointed outwards, as close to directly sideways as possible, the person squats and stretches out his hands as widely as he can (Figure 20a). In Figures 20b and 20c the person describes a wide circle with his hands and then reverses the motion until he returns to the position of Figure 20a. To improve ankle flexibility, one can go from the position pictured in Figure 20c and drop elbows to the floor as demonstrated in Figure 20d. Moving up and down between the positions in Figures 20d and 20c is a good exercise for both ankle and hip flexibility.

Other exercises using the weight belt are pictured in Figures 21a and b and 22a and b. These emphasize the twisting of the hips, and the exercises also strengthen leg muscles for improved stances. In Figure 21a the model, wearing two weight belts, begins kiba-dachi stance with his fists drawn back to his ribs. He then executes a right-handed reverse punch at a 45° angle to the floor, twisting his hips sharply (Figure 21b). The drill is then repeated with the opposite hand.

The next exercise also emphasizes hip twisting, but since the hips also shift forward from Figure 22a to Figure 22b, and because they stay low to the ground throughout the movement, this drill puts tremendous pressure on the thigh muscles. The exercise is especially good for strengthening legs for karate stances.

An exercise for strengthening legs and hips using a weight belt.
Top: With feet pointed outwards, as close to directly sideways as possible, the person squats and stretches out his hands as widely as he can.
Bottom: Moving the hands on the floor in a wide circle, starting from the side.
Opposite top: The hands stretched out on the floor in front of the body.
Opposite bottom: Improving ankle flexibility by dropping elbows to the floor.

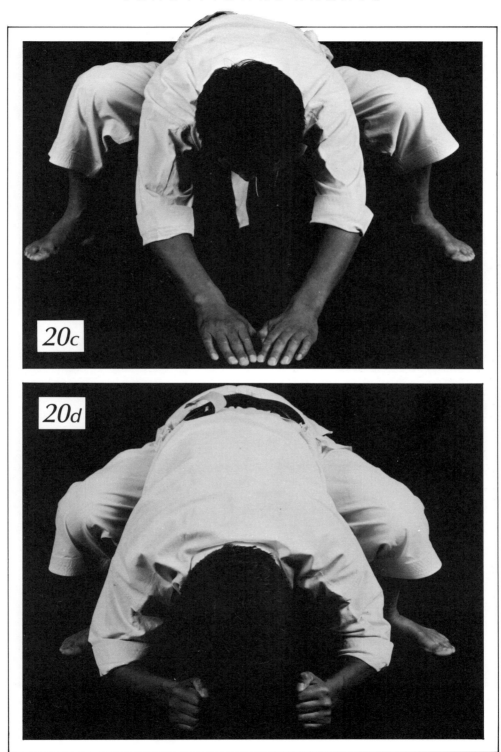

20c

20d

21a

An exercise to emphasize the twisting of the hips and strengthen leg muscles for improved stances, using two weight belts. It begins in kiba-dachi with the fists drawn back to the ribs.

The exercise continues with a right-handed reverse punch at a 45° angle to the floor, twisting the hips sharply. The drill is then repeated with the other hand.

22a

22b

Muscles for Karate

W hile weight belts can be used to improve stances, the kind of weight training used in many Western sports is not recommended for the karate student. Repetitive lifting of heavy weights increases muscle bulk but does not provide the kind of strength required for karate. The karate student needs flexible muscles that can expand and contract very quickly. A karate student's muscles should be such that he is able to focus the power of a swift punch or kick in an instant, just short of its target. To develop this strength, students should train with rubber tubing.

Rubber Tubing

R ubber tubes can be used for developing strength, improving flexibility, and improving the focus of basic blocks, strikes, kicks and sweeps. One exercise used to strengthen legs and hips begins with a person in the sitting position pictured in Figure 23a. The tubing should be taut to begin with, but not stretched out. In one quick movement, the

Opposite top and bottom: Another exercise which emphasizes hip twisting, but since the hips shift forward and stay low to the ground throughout the movement, the drill puts tremendous pressure on the thigh muscles. It is especially good for strengthening legs for karate stances.

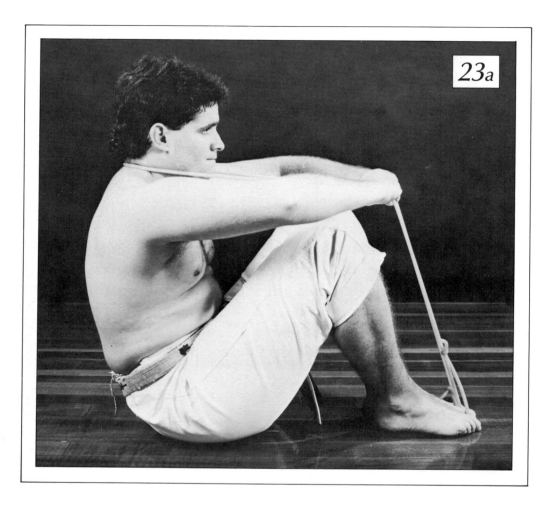

person drives himself upwards through the Figure 23b position into the standing position in Figure 23c. For strengthening arms, legs and hips, the student can, with the same length of tubing, move quickly from the squatting position in Figure 24a to the arms extended position in 24b.

Rubber tubing can be used to increase flexibility in a wide array of simple exercises. One good drill for the shoulders and arms begins with the student kneeling with two or three lengths of tubing stretched behind his head, along his extended arms. As pictured in Figure 25a, a partner places a foot in the middle of the person's back and slowly pulls up and back on the tubing. The partner should hold the person at the maximum point of stretch for a few seconds, gradually release the pressure, and then repeat the exercise. A similar stretching can be

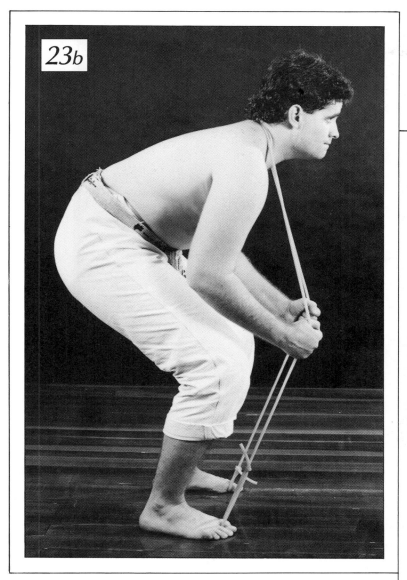

Opposite, above and right: Using rubber tubing to strengthen legs and hips by moving from a sitting to standing position, with the rubber stretching across the shoulders.

achieved without a helper if the person lies face down with tubes running from across his chest to his ankles, as pictured in Figure 25b. The student pulls his own chest and arms up, holds himself there and relaxes.

For strengthening and stretching back muscles, the following exercises are effective. In Figure 26, the middle of the tube has been secured to some fixture such as a doorknob, but it could be held by a partner. The person pulls sideways over the top, slowly stretching the muscles along the side and the small of the back. In another exercise, the person holds a double length of tubing behind his back with his arms extended (Figure 27a). He slowly brings his arms up over his head (Figure 27b) and then back to their original position.

Opposite and above: Strengthening arms, legs and hips by moving quickly from the squatting position to the arms extended position.

Opposite: A good drill to increase flexibility of the shoulders and arms, with the student kneeling with two or three lengths of tubing stretched behind his head, along his extended arms. A partner places a foot in the middle of the person's back and slowly pulls up and back on the tubing. The partner should hold the person at the maximum point of stretch for a few seconds, gradually release the pressure, and then repeat the exercise.

Above: Stretching can also be achieved without a helper if the person lies face down with tubes running from across his chest to his ankles. The student pulls his own chest and arms up, holds himself there, and relaxes.

An exercise for strengthening and stretching back muscles, with the rubber tube secured to a fixture, such as a doorknob, or held by a partner. The person pulls sideways over the top, slowly stretching the muscles along the side and the small of the back.

Another exercise for strengthening and stretching back muscles. The person holds a double length of tubing behind his back with his arms extended. He slowly brings his arms up over his head and then back to their original position.

28a

Preparation for outside middle block (Chudan-soto-uke).

OUTSIDE MIDDLE BLOCK (Chudan-soto-uke)

28c

KNIFE-HAND BLOCK (Shuto-uke)

REVERSE PUNCH (Gyaku-zuki)

FRONT KICK (Mae-geri)

By anchoring the tube behind him- or herself, a person can learn to focus basic blocks, strikes and kicks. Figure 28a shows the preparation for chudan-soto-uke (outer block). Figure 28b shows the completed block. Figures 28c to 28e picture shuto-uke (knife-hand block), gyaku-zuki (reverse punch) and mae-geri (front kick), respectively. All of these techniques, when practised with the rubber tubing, are best executed in a sudden, quick movement: hips twist, abdomen and fists tighten, but shoulders stay low and relaxed throughout the movement. The completed block or strike should be held for several seconds.

Mawashi-geri (roundhouse kick) can be practised with or without rubber tubing and a partner. When using the training aids, the kicker and partner stand in mirror-image forward stances. The kicker runs tubing from his rear shoulder to his rear foot (Figure 29a). Holding his partner's arm for balance, the kicker's first move is to raise the knee of his kicking foot to the side (Figure 29b). The roundhouse is then executed to the partner's face as the kicker pulls the tube with one hand to bring his body as much as possible over the supporting leg (Figure 29c). To practise mawashi-geri without a partner or tubing, one can use the kind of suction cup found in any glass shop (Figure 30a). By gripping this secured handle with the hand opposite the kicking leg, one can keep the torso erect over the supporting leg (Figure 30b).

With rubber tubing attached to the base of a table (Figure 31a), one can begin slowly to condition one's body for the proper execution of yoko-geri-kekomi (side thrust kick) and mae-geri (front kick). For kekomi, the tubing runs around the kicker's hip and is then attached to the kicking foot (Figure 31b). When executing the kick in Figure 31c, it is important to bend the support leg slightly, twist the hips into the target, and straighten the knee of the kicking leg completely.

For mae-geri, the kicker stands with hips square to the table and the kicking foot flat on the table top (Figure 32a). With support leg bent slightly, the ball of the kicking foot is thrust forward slowly (Figure 32b). On both these drills, the kicker should hold the extended kicks for several seconds before repeating the procedure.

Without the table, exercises can be repeated more quickly using a chair for balance and a rubber tube. Figures 33a to 33c show yoko-geri-

Above: With the kicker and partner in mirror-image forward stances, the kicker runs tubing from his rear shoulder to his rear foot. Right: Holding his partner's arm for balance, the kicker's first move is to raise the knee of his kicking foot to the side.

The roundhouse is executed to the partner's face, as the kicker pulls the tube with one hand to bring his body as much as possible over the supporting leg.

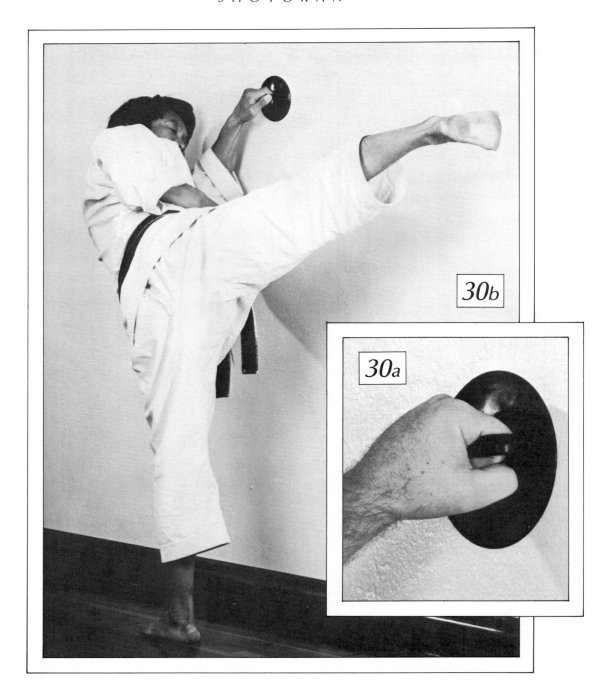

30b

30a

To practise the roundhouse without a partner or tubing, one can use a suction cup. By gripping this secured handle with the hand opposite the kicking leg, one can keep the torso erect over the supporting leg.

keage (side snap kick), yoko-geri-kekomi (side thrust kick) and mae-geri (front kick) all held out against the resistance of the tube.

Some techniques, such as age-uke (upper block), kizami-zuki (jab) and gyaku-zuki (reverse punch), can be practised without anchoring the tube and without any other training aid. For age-uki, the student should stand in a kiba-dachi stance holding the ends of the tube in his fists and with a centre length of the tubing stretched between his feet (Figure 34). The block should be executed sharply and then held for several seconds against the resistance of the tube. The student repeats the process, alternating blocking hand and draw hand each time. A similar alternating of hands takes place between Figures 35a and 35b

With rubber tubing attached to the base of a table, one can begin slowly to condition one's body for the proper execution of side thrust kick (yoko-geri-kekomi) and front kick (mae-geri).

When conditioning for the side thrust kick, the tubing runs around the kicker's hip and is then attached to the kicking foot.

31c

When executing the side thrust kick, it is important to bend the support leg slightly, twist the hips into the target, and straighten the knee of the kicking leg completely. The extended kick should be held for several seconds before repeating.

When conditioning for the front kick, the kicker stands with hips square to the table and the kicking foot flat on the table top.

To execute the drill, the support leg is bent slightly and the ball of the kicking foot is thrust forward slowly. The extended kick should be held for several seconds before repeating.

Conditioning for a side snap kick (yoko-geri-keage), using a chair for balance and a rubber tube.

**Conditioning for a side thrust kick (yoko-geri-kekomi) using a chair for
balance and a rubber tube.**

Conditioning for a front kick (mae-geri), sitting on a chair and stretching against the resistance of the tube.

RISING BLOCK (Age-uke)

The student should stand in a kiba-dachi, holding the ends of the tube in his fists with the centre length of the tubing stretched between his feet. The block should be executed sharply and then held for several seconds against the resistance of the tube. The student repeats the process, alternating blocking hand and draw hand each time.

Above and opposite: The student alternates blocking hand and draw hand when executing kizami-zuki and gyaku-zuki. For the tube to supply the necessary resistance, it must be looped at least once around the person's waist. Each punch should be executed quickly and held out for several seconds.

when executing kizami-zuki and gyaki-zuki. Note that for the tube to supply the necessary resistance, it must be looped at least once around the person's waist. With each technique, the punch should be executed quickly and then held out for several seconds.

Rubber tubing can also be useful for practising leg sweeps. To begin, a student and his partner face each other in their natural fighting stances with the same leg forward and the tube stretching between their front legs (Figure 36a). Keeping his hips the same height, one person pulls back and up very quickly through the position in Figure 36b to

Rubber tubing can also be used for practising leg sweeps.
Above: To begin, a student and his partner face each other in their natural fighting stances, with the same leg forward and the tube stretching between their front legs.
Opposite page: Keeping his hips the same height, one person pulls back and up very quickly through the position in Figure 36b to that in 36c. When the foot returns to its original position, the other person practises the sweeping motion with his front leg. They alternate sweeps to a rapid count as often as necessary.

that in Figure 36c. When the foot returns to its original position, the other person practises the sweeping motion with his front leg. The two alternate sweeps to a rapid count as often as necessary.

Finally, to acquire flexibility and spring in hips, ankles and knees, one should do the exercises pictured in Figures 37 and 38a and b. For increased speed moving forward, the student should assume a runner's starting position with the tube securely anchored behind him (Figure 37). This exercise consists of the student pushing suddenly off and up as if to run.

Above: An exercise to increase speed when moving forward consists of the student assuming a runner's starting position, with the tube securely anchored behind him, and then pushing suddenly off and up as if to run. Opposite page: Another exercise to increase flexibility, where the person stands with his right leg bent and his left knee raised and pointing forward. The stretched tube pulls backwards. From this position, the person makes a front jump step on to the left leg, pulling the right leg up behind the left. The change in hand positions in this drill is good training for covering distance on kizami-zuki.

For the next exercise, the person stands with his right leg bent and his left knee raised and pointing forward. The stretched tube pulls backwards. From this position (Figure 38a), the person makes a front jump step on to the left leg, pulling the right leg up behind the left (Figure 38b). As indicated by the change in hand positions from Figure 38a to Figure 38b, this drill is good training for covering distance on kizami-zuki (jab).

Pictured in Figures 39a to 39c is a series of movements made by a baseball pitcher. For a karate student, what is instructive about the action is the motion of the pitcher's hips. No one throws a ball with just his arm. When a karate student trains with a weight belt or with rubber tubes, he should strive to engage muscles properly in all parts of the body, but he should try especially hard to generate power from the hips.

Above, right and opposite:
A series of movements
made by a baseball pitcher,
generating power from the hips.

Practical Goals in Self Training

W hatever the activity for which one is strengthening muscles, one should not look for quick results. Impatient people design exercise programmes that are too strenuous, and they end up quitting soon after they begin. Moreover, research in applied kinesiology has shown that when one stops a muscle-development programme, the acquired strength starts to diminish within five to ten days. Muscles developed over a long period of time in a gradual process retain their strength for much longer. Such findings suggest that the best exercise programme is not one that seeks to build strength overnight, but one that a person is likely to maintain – permanently.

Research shows that if a muscle or muscle group is exercised at 30 per cent of its capacity, strength will not increase. If 40 per cent is used, the muscle will get stronger. For example, if a man who can do a maximum of 100 push-ups wants to increase his strength, doing 30 push-ups every day will not help. However, if he adopts an exercise programme of 40 push-ups a day, he will eventually, in two or three weeks perhaps, be able to increase his maximum number of push-ups to 110. Of course, to continue to get stronger, this man must now increase his daily push-ups; to work out at 40 per cent of his new capacity, he must now do 44 push-ups a day.

To maintain strong bodies, we need regular exercise programmes that we can stay with throughout our lives. However, those who attempt to exercise muscles to 50 or 70 per cent of capacity every day will usually stop exercising before long, and their acquired strength will decrease relatively quickly. Exercising muscles at 40 per cent of their capacity on a daily basis would be more beneficial in the long run. For karate students, exercise should serve to build flexible rather than bulky muscles, and muscle-strengthening programmes should be in addition to training in basics, kata and kumite.

CONCLUSION

T he Chinese tell a story of a man who admired dragons so much that he became a toy dragon collector. One day he heard a loud knock at his door, and when he opened it, he was facing a real dragon. The dragon said, 'I heard you loved dragons, so I came personally to see you. Perhaps we can be friends.' The man was so frightened by the fierce appearance of the real dragon that he fainted.

The man in this story is like many people who profess an interest in karate. What they don't understand is that true karate-do is not the showy demonstrations seen at tournaments. True karate is the repetition of daily exercises to strengthen and condition the body and the mind. When people see the time and work necessary to excel in karate, many of them lose their enthusiasm. This is unfortunate, because in our world so many people need the physical and mental strength that real karate-do provides.

Karate is an excellent source of the daily exercise necessary for healthy bodies, and the physical trials of karate are a good preparation for life. As a student seeks better ways to score or defend, and as he cultivates stronger, sharper techniques, he enhances his creative problem-solving abilities. Karate will improve a person's power of concentration, his discipline and his confidence – all important attributes for overcoming the trials of daily living.

The Author

S hojiro Koyama was born in Tokyo, Japan in 1935 and began training karate at the age of 15 under the renowned Master Ito. In 1958, he graduated from the Hosei University and received a BS degree in science. Since the age of 15, Mr Koyama has been training continuously. In 1964 he went to the USA and settled in Phoenix, Arizona.

Mr Koyama is presently a seventh dan black belt and is a member of the Japan Karate Association and the International Shotokan Karate Federation, and he is the Karate Collegiate Union Chairman. He now teaches at Arizona State University where he is a physical education faculty member. Mr Koyama is the chief instructor of the Arizona Karate Association.

Translator

J oe McKeown was born in 1957 in Chicago, Illinois. He has a BA in English from Marquette University and a master's degree in English literature from Arizona State. Joe has been training in karate since 1980 and holds the rank of first dan black belt.

REFERENCES

1 Yutang, Lin, *The Importance of Living*. A John Day Book. New York: Reynal & Hitchcock, 1937.

2 Clayner, Benson, Gorden and Schultz, *Applied Kinesiology*. McGraw Hill Book Co., 1970.

GLOSSARY

A

age-uke:
see upper block

autonomic nervous system:
that part of the vertebrate nervous system that regulates involuntary actions

B

back stance (kokutsu-dachi):
similar to kiba-dachi stance, only with 70 per cent of the body's weight on the back leg and with the front foot pointed straight towards the opponent

C

chudan-soto-uke:
see outer block

D

dojo:
training school

downward block (gedan-barai):
a block for low punches and kicks in which the fist of the blocking hand travels from the opposite shoulder down and across the body, stopping above and inside of the front knee

draw hand:
the hand that is pulled back to the hip during a block or strike executed with the other hand

five-step sparring (gohan kumite):
the same as one-step sparring except that the attacker repeats the attack five times

front kick (mae-geri):
a short kick executed to the front with either foot; contact is made with the ball of the foot

front stance (zenkutsu-dachi):
the stance has one leg forward approximately twice as far as a normal step. Legs are shoulders' width wide, and the front knee is bent so that the front toes are not visible. The torso is erect; the buttocks are tucked under

gedan-barai:
see downward block

gohon kumite:
see five-step sparring

gyaku-zuki:
see reverse punch

heian:
Japanese for 'calm' or 'stability'. It is the name given to the first five katas in Shotokan Karate

inner block (chudan-uke):
a block that begins with the fist of the blocking arm next to the ear on its same side, as in a salute. The fist and forearm travel downwards and across the body, stopping at the centre of the body with the elbow at a 90° angle

ippon kumite:
see one-step sparring

karateka:
karate performer

kata:
a series of predetermined blocks and strikes executed against imaginary opponents

kiai:
a loud shout from the diaphragm that occurs with the focus of a technique

kiba-dachi:
a stance in which the feet are spread twice shoulders' width, the outsides of the feet are parallel, and the knees are turned out as far as possible so that the person resembles someone on horseback

kihon:
basics

kinesiology:
the science that deals with the dynamics of body movement

kizami-zuki:
a straight punch with the forward hand from the front stance

knife-hand block:
a block prepared for by reaching one open hand across the body on top of the other arm. The block then travels back along the same line, stopping in front of the body's centre with the elbow at 90°

kokutsu-dachi:
see back stance

kumite:
sparring

mae-geri:
see front kick

mawashi-geri:
see roundhouse kick

one-step sparring (ippon kumite):
controlled sparring in which a designated attacker steps forward with one preannounced attack at a time

outer block (chudan-soto-uke):
a block prepared for when the blocking arm reaches across the body underneath the other arm. In the block the forearm of the blocking arm swings, hinging on the elbow back to the centre of the body. The elbow stops in front of the solar plexus and is bent at 90°

proprioceptor:
a sensory receptor nerve. It receives rather than sends information

reverse punch:
a punch with the rear hand from the front stance

roundhouse kick (mawashi-geri):
a kick in which the kicking foot is snapped outward in a motion from the knee, thereby acting as a pivot like that of a gate, to strike the intended target

sanbon kumite:
see three-step sparring

sensei:
teacher

shu-ha-ri:
shu is learning from tradition; ha is breaking the chains of tradition; ri is transcendence

shuto-uke:
see knife-hand block

side snap kick (yoko-geri-keage):
a short kick to the side in which the knee acts as a hinge. Contact is made with the outer edge of the foot

side thrust kick (yoko-geri-kekomi):
a kick to the side which gains its

SHOTOKAN

power from a pushing of the hip out towards the target. Contact and then penetration are made with the outer edge of the foot

stepping punch:
a technique that involves stepping forwards from one forward stance to another, while simultaneously punching with the rear hand (to begin with) until that hand becomes the forward punching hand. The punch should stop at the exact moment that the front foot settles

three-step sparring (sanbon kumite):
the same as one-step sparring except that the attacker repeats the same attack three times

upper block (age-uke):
a block for the face that ends with

the elbow bent at 90°, and the forearm in front of and slightly higher than the forehead

weight belt:
a training aid strapped around the waist, usually weighing about 15 lb for adults

yoko-geri-keage:
see side snap kick

yoko-geri-kekomi:
see side thrust kick

zenkutsu-dachi:
see front stance